PELE AND HIIAKA

N. B. Emerson

PELE AND HIIAKA

A Myth from Hawaii

by
NATHANIEL B. EMERSON, A.M., M.D.
author of *The Long Voyages of the Ancient Hawaiians*,
and of *Unwritten Literature of Hawaii*
translator of David Malo's *Hawaiian Antiquities*

with an introduction to the new edition
by TERENCE BARROW, PH.D.

CHARLES E. TUTTLE COMPANY
Rutland, Vermont & Tokyo, Japan

Representatives
Continental Europe: BOXERBOOKS, INC., *Zurich*
British Isles: PRENTICE-HALL INTERNATIONAL, INC., *London*
Australasia: BOOK WISE (AUSTRALIA) PTY. LTD.
104–108 Sussex Street, Sydney 2000

Published by the Charles E. Tuttle Company, Inc.
of Rutland, Vermont & Tokyo, Japan
with editorial offices at
Suido 1-chome, 2–6, Bunkyo-ku, Tokyo, Japan

Copyright in Japan, 1978, by Charles E. Tuttle Co., Inc.

Library of Congress Catalog No. 77-83040

International Standard Book No. 0-8048-1251-9

First edition, 1915
First Tuttle edition, 1978
Second printing, 1982

PRINTED IN JAPAN

TO
HER MAJESTY LILIUOKALANI
AND
HER BELOVED HAWAIIAN
PEOPLE

TABLE OF CONTENTS

LIST OF ILLUSTRATIONS

INTRODUCTION TO THE NEW EDITION

HAWAIIAN tradition, through song-chants and the dance of hula, intimately relates the legendary sisters Pele and Hiʻiaka to Hawaiʻi's volcanic landscape and other phenomena of nature. This book's mythological epic, perhaps more than any other, brings primal elements together, and its lyric power and drama are unsurpassed in traditional Hawaiian lore. Here are captured the poetry of Hawaiian places, the feel of the Hawaiian landscape—whose volcanic features are the handiwork of Pele herself—and the unique mood of old Hawaiʻi.

Pele, Hawaiʻi's volcano or fire goddess, is also popularly called Madame Pele. But she has earned another name, that of The Sacred Hewer of the Land. When so inclined, she sends streams of molten lava flowing down the slopes of the island of Hawaiʻi, destroying all in their path. Hawaiʻi is the name both for the island group formerly named the Sandwich Islands and for the island called the Big Island, said to have the most active volcano in the world.

Pele personifies fire and volcanic activity. According to Hawaiian myths of creation, she was born as a flame from the mouth of her mother, Haumea. Haumea is the primary Earth Mother who, with her husband Wakea, the Sky Father, brought forth all living creatures, including men and gods. Pele's home is in the caldera of Kilauea; her chosen place is the firepit of Halemaʻumaʻu and the subterranean caverns of pulsating lava spread below. She outshines all women of heaven and earth in physical beauty.

Pele's younger sister, Hiʻiaka, is almost as beautiful. She was, we are told, born of an egg that Pele carried between her breasts or in an armpit. She is Pele's favorite sister and is especially gifted in the art of healing and in combat against the dreaded *moʻo*, the fabulous reptilian monsters of Hawaiʻi. But where Pele is quick-tempered and suddenly violent, Hiʻiaka is calm and benevolent, forever ready to help mankind. She likes to wander in her groves of scarlet-blossomed *ʻohiʻa* trees, away from the barren lava fields and firepits. Lei-making, chants, and dance preoccupy her. A superb poet, Hiʻiaka is the composer of most of the chants in the legend contained in this book. As a patron of hula, she is venerated by dancers, and her name is often heard at hula performances.

The main theme of Pele and Hiʻiaka's story is found in the love of goddesses for an earthly man. Like the gods of ancient Greece, the Hawaiian gods, who belong to the general Polynesian family of gods, experience the same emotions as mortal men and women. Pele and Hiʻiaka can feel anger, impatience, hate, jealousy, love, and longing, and their susceptibility to these emotions makes possible in the story of their love for the mortal chief Lohiʻau all the depth and conflict that are so essential to drama.

According to Hawaiian belief, spirit *(wailua)* can leave the body of a sleeping person to wander afar. The dream world we regard today as the product of the subconscious was a real world to the Hawaiians. The gods and goddesses also have second selves that venture away from their immortal bodies. In the story, Pele falls into a trance-like sleep. Her spirit travels westward, lured by hula drums. Eventually it reaches Haʻena on distant Kauaʻi, where it sees the chief Lohiʻau as he presides over his court with its hula dancers; he is so overwhelmingly handsome that Pele's spirit is captivated and filled with desire.

Pele's spirit assumes a beautiful physical form and remains with Lohiʻau in erotic dalliance for some days. Then it returns to Pele's body in Kilauea crater. Those who have watched over the sleeping goddess are relieved to see her wake.

Pele asks her assembled sisters if any would go on the long and dangerous journey to Kauaʻi to fetch her dream lover, Lohiʻau, whom she wishes to marry. All demur except Hiʻiaka, who, after receiving special magical powers, sets off on the journey with the assurance from Pele that her beloved forest birds and groves of trees will be protected in her absence.

The journey to Kauaʻi and back is arduous, and the saga of its adventures occupies most of this book. Pele admonished Hiʻiaka not to embrace Lohiʻau. Hiʻiaka is faithful, but when she returns she finds Pele has failed her by destroying some of her birds and forests and her friend, the poet Hopoe. The shock is too great to endure. In her distress at her sister's willful ways, Hiʻiaka makes love to Lohiʻau on the rim of Kilauea, in full view of Pele and those with her. It is then that the sequence of terrible events begins. There is a battle of magic. The bewildered and long-suffering Lohiʻau dies in the flames but is restored in time for a happy ending.

This story rivals Shakespeare's *Macbeth* in its stark settings, violence, evil magic, and psychic conflicts. Instead of witches on a misty moor, however, we have the noble chief Paʻoa meeting the desolate spirit of his friend Lohiʻau on the rugged lava fields. Like a Norse myth, the action unfolds in a series of dramatic scenes with heroic exploits.

Pele is not the original volcano deity of Hawaiʻi. She, with Hiʻiaka, came to Hawaiʻi long ago from the distant land of Kahiki, a name meaning any foreign place but in this instance probably the ancestral homeland of Tahiti. Both goddesses are described as having pale skins and red, or even blonde, hair. The aboriginal fire god, hearing Pele was coming his way, fled, never to be seen again. One can only suppose this earlier fire deity had prior knowledge of Pele's unrelenting character.

Pele and Hiʻiaka are therefore *malihini* or newcomer goddesses. They are so recognized by the Hawaiians. It seems that Pele was the maker of secondary volcanic landscape features, not the base mountains that form the Hawaiian Islands. Many volcanic craters made late in formation of the islands are her creation. On Oʻahu, for example, we have the well-known landmarks of Diamond Head, Punchbowl, Koko Head, and Salt Lake. The magnificent Haleakala crater on Maui is also said to be the work of Pele.

Despite her foreign origin, Pele is distinctively Hawaiian. No goddess of Hawaiʻi is better known. She is said to be responsible for the volcanic eruptions that occur every decade or so and threaten land and inhabitants of the region. Fearful of her devastating lava, some respectful islanders continue to *hoʻokupu* (give gifts) to appease her. Fortunately, she is not a deity that has ever expected human sacrifice, as did Ku, the god of war. Pele seems content with certain traditional offerings such as a red fern frond, some pork, a small fish, bananas, *lehua* flowers, or the red *ʻohelo* berries that grow near her mountain domain. (It should be mentioned that the plucking of *lehua* blossoms is illegal in Hawaiʻi's Volcanoes National Park.) One sacrificial item favored in modern times is a bottle of gin cast into the crater of Kilauea.

If Pele is met, it is said, she should be treated with kindness, for her anger is devastating. Her occasional appearance in the form of a beautiful woman or a wrinkled old lady asking some small favor to test people is reported from time to time. Visitors might bear in mind that she is reportedly as likely to approach non-Hawaiians and resident strangers as she is native Hawaiians. One report was made in 1962 by a motorist who, while driving in the Kalapana region, was stopped by an old woman who asked him for a cigarette, which he gingerly gave her through the slightly opened car window. This strange old lady, he said, then lit the cigarette with a flame produced by the snap of her fingers. On another occasion, in 1964, two visitors—a man and his wife—were walking on a path near Halema'uma'u and passed a handsome blonde woman. The man quickly looked back, but within seconds the woman had vanished.

Pele's appearances are ominous and are usually associated with volcanic eruptions. She often appears in several places within only a short interval. True or false? Who knows! There are strange incidents in Hawai'i, and ghosts of a special kind. There are night marchers, wandering lights, poltergeists, drummers, and eerie appearances which are sometimes threatening. The psychic world is a world of the unknown, especially on Pacific islands. It is best to keep an open mind on the subject and enjoy the tales of Pele and other ghostly beings.

We must now consider the second major aspect of *Pele and Hiiaka: A Myth from Hawaii*. This is the subject of hula, the unique dance of Hawai'i that originated thousands of years ago on the island worlds of the South Pacific. The Hawaiian ancestors, it is believed, came from the South Pacific in two waves: the first from the Marquesan Islands about the 6th century A.D., and a second from the Society Islands around the 14th century. No doubt both Polynesian peoples possessed well-developed dance styles that would, in the isolation of Hawai'i over a thousand years, evolve into hula's most sophisticated, complex, and beautiful form.

Hula is basically religious and expressive of deep, poetic concepts of life. Yet it has many levels, from the purely erotic and comic to that which has the highest philosophical meaning. In traditional culture, hula seems to have had three distinct functions: first, that of influencing the gods to gain their favor in securing the fertility of the land, sea, and the people; second, that of a healing and beautification art; and third, that of celebrating life itself. Chants in the form of dance-songs, mime providing actions to accompany words and meaning, and the rhythm of bodily movement revealed the essential harmony of mankind and nature.

As to the origins of hula, they are obscure. The tutelary deity of hula is Laka, who belongs to the Pele family of fire gods. Laka assumes both male and female forms; as a female she is sister and wife of Lono, the god of fertility and peace who is, incidentally, the god the Hawaiians took Captain James Cook to be when the British maritime explorer reached Hawai'i in 1778. Kapo, a sister of Pele and daughter of Haumea, the Earth Mother, is a benevolent hula goddess identifiable with Laka, and a sorceress of immense power. One of her forms as a hula goddess is the *hala-pepe* tree, branches of which are placed on the hula altars.

The originator of hula is said to have been the poet Hopoe, Hi'iaka's friend mentioned earlier. Indeed, the first extant mention of hula is by Hopoe. Here are two lines from her beautiful chant:

> Ke ha'a ala Puna i ka makani;
> Ha'a ka ulu hala i Kea'au.

> Look, Puna is dancing in the wind;
> Trembling are the *hala* groves of Kea'au.

It seems that Hi'iaka acquired hula from Hopoe and in turn passed the art on to Pele, but some say that Pele learned hula herself by watching Hopoe dance. The precise origins of hula are not known.

In pre-European times the higher forms of hula were esoteric, private, and mysterious. High-ranking practitioners sometimes retired to solitary places to perform austerities and to meditate in a kind of yoga while they awaited possession by a spirit. By the grace of a sought deity or spirit, the meditator entered an ecstatic trance. Any dance resulting from this technique was regarded as private and sacred; no others could perform it unless they were members trained in the school or hula *halau* that owned the dance-chant. The repertoire of a particular *halau* thus became a jealously guarded property. Many of the chants in this book were formerly the priceless possession of specialists. They were not for every ear to hear.

The hula scene of today is much changed. Even the most sacred hula arts have, to some extent, become a common property and a common heritage. Sometimes this privilege is well used and sometimes it is abused. Scholars who have attempted to do in-depth research concerning the "meaning" of hula in its various aspects have encountered confusion in the historical accounts. Some of this can be attributed to the bias of the missionaries of New England who first arrived in 1820. These dour teachers regarded stories like that of Pele and Hi'iaka as being childish and pagan, and they condemned hula as immoral.

The Reverend Hiram Bingham, leader of the pioneer company of missionaries, laid a heavy hand on any one of his converts that he found indulging in hula or traditional chants. The Hawaiians themselves first denied their own traditions and religious system in 1819 by edict of King Kamehameha II. The immediate follow-up by missionaries, however well intentioned, truly became a scourge to traditional Hawaiian culture. King Kalakaua, Hawai'i's monarch from 1874 to 1891, did much to revive hula and many old Hawaiian arts, but the impact of Western culture had come with such fury that hula as well as other great arts suffered considerably.

Hula is at present a reviving art of singular vitality. Contemporary hula has its roots in the past, yet its forms and aims are of necessity different. They reflect Hawai'i's modern, heterogeneous society. We must remember that traditional Hawaiian life is no more, and that a traditional art like hula cannot remain unchanged when divorced from the religious ideals of the society that gave it life. Hawaiian society today is composed of people from differing racial and ethnic backgrounds, and modern practitioners of hula are likewise diverse. Contemporary hula schools, centered largely in Honolulu, vary in seriousness and purpose. Some schools uphold the traditions of ancient hula and in a few instances are associated with Hawaiian families that have been specialists in chant and dance for generations. Other schools teach not only Hawaiian hula but the dances of Tahiti, New Zealand, and other South Pacific islands.

One indication of how things have changed is the way most hula teaching is now directed at young girls. They study the dance more as a social pastime, for the same reason flower arrangement and the tea ceremony are studied by girls in Japan—as a means of acquiring grace and femininity.

In ancient times, sacred dance, chant, and lofty priestly knowledge were the province of highborn men. Hawaiians believed that women were *noa*, that is, secular and ordinary. Participation in the highest ceremonies, such as those conducted in the temples, was denied them. Today men are reestablishing themselves in hula, and both sexes are following the art on a democratic basis. Whatever is said of the lower place of women in traditional hula, it must be remembered that the presiding deities of hula have always been predominantly female—Laka, Hi'iaka, Kapo, and Pele.

Hula instruction and the *halau* of today fall into several categories. The hula most familiar to tourists is the commercial hula of nightclubs and hotels. The dancers of such modern hula are those who are paid and often belong to entertainers' unions. Others learn hula simply for self-enrichment and recreation. The lighter forms of hula are attractive, if well performed, and the professional dancers who perform for tourists are contributing both to the enjoyment of visitors and to the economy of the State of Hawaii.

However, there exists in Hawai'i a serious devotion to hula of the older style that is taught in a number of *halau*. This hula strives to recapture the spirit of the ancient dance either by attempting to reproduce, as much as possible, the dances in their ancient forms or by using traditional hula as the basis for deliberately innovative hula that adopts quite honestly the techniques of modern choreography and creative costume design.

The renaissance of Hawaiian culture that began in the 1960s and made rapid advances in the 1970s has encouraged a return to the older hula forms. It is refreshing also to see in recent years the increased public appreciation of the traditional dances. An enthusiastic response can be witnessed on such occasions as the annual hula and chant competition held each Kamehameha Day or at performances such as those associated with the Merry Monarch Festival celebrating King Kalakaua, who was Hawai'i's greatest 19th-century champion of the hula.

This interest has helped spark enthusiasm for the older dances and provides an additional catalyst for the revival of Hawaiian cultural forms.

Dr. Nathaniel B. Emerson was a great contributor to Hawaiian culture insofar as he worked for its preservation. Stories like that of

Pele and Hi'iaka were transmitted for centuries prior to Emerson by word of mouth and by means of hula, for the Hawaiians had no written language before the missionaries introduced an alphabet. They relied, instead, on their excellent memories, which were aided by rigorous cultivation of the ability to perform word-perfect recitations. Emerson was well aware of the steady loss of old tradition that followed the missionaries' arrival in Hawai'i, and he labored many years to preserve in written form Hawaiian lore and language material that otherwise would have disappeared upon the deaths of the last carriers of the oral tradition.

The old-time Hawaiians were naturally reluctant to part with sacred, traditional knowledge, but Emerson was a very persistent man. In his preface to this book he speaks of the years he spent tediously collecting and refining the literary form of these precious Hawaiian chants. The material was secured by what he calls *viva voce,* that is, by word of mouth. Much of what he collected was first published in Honolulu newspapers.

Nathaniel Emerson was born at Waialua, Oahu, on 1 July 1839. His parents, the Reverend and Mrs. John S. Emerson, were members of the fifth company of missionaries that sailed from New Bedford, Massachusetts, in 1831 to minister the gospel to the Hawaiians. Emerson's father served as pastor of the native church at Waialua, and this gave the young Emerson a rare opportunity to observe and learn from the Hawaiian people at first hand. The Emersons did not protect their children from daily contact with the Hawaiians as did many of their fellow missionaries. Rather, they seemed to encourage direct Hawaiian contact and even adopted the Hawaiian priest Hewahewa, who had served Kamehameha I as a great *kahuna,* or priest. Hewahewa died shortly before the young Nathaniel was born, but much of his knowledge must have been transmitted by Emerson senior to his son, Nathaniel.

During the American Civil War Emerson enlisted on the northern side in the First Regiment of the Massachusetts Volunteer Infantry, and while in service he was wounded. At Gettysburg he narrowly missed death when a shell fragment tore off the back of his cap.

After the war, Emerson resumed his education both in Hawai'i and America, graduating with the degree of medical doctor. Later he married Sarah Eliza Peirce, who was to become Hawai'i's first woman physician.

In the course of his medical duties in Hawai'i, Emerson served among the leper patients at Moloka'i as inspector of leper stations for the Hawaiian Government Board of Health. He returned to Honolulu and, after further government service, resumed private medical practice in 1890. Later he took the post of police surgeon, and this brought him into direct contact with many Hawaiians. He was unrelenting in seeking knowledge from his patients or any other person who could provide information on Hawai'i's past. After a very useful life as physician and scholar, he died at sea between Seattle and San Francisco in 1916.

In his lifetime Emerson published three books and several scholarly articles, all of which are invaluable. His major contributions are *Unwritten Literature of Hawaii: The Sacred Songs of Hula* (published in 1909 and reprinted by the Charles E. Tuttle Company in 1965) and *Pele and Hiiaka: A Myth from Hawaii.* The latter was printed for Emerson by the *Honolulu Star-Bulletin Limited* in 1915. Because of its very limited edition, it was soon assigned to the rare-book category; for decades it was virtually unobtainable.

The present reprint will surely be welcomed by librarians, teachers, students, and other people interested in Hawaiiana. It will contribute much to hula practice and to a general appreciation of Hawai'i's landscape. Indeed, those who enter the sacred realm of Pele and Hi'iaka, which is now Hawai'i's Volcanoes National Park, can use this book to get a better understanding of this wonderful region. We can all be thankful to Dr. Emerson for his labors, but we must never forget the genius of the original composers. *Pele and Hiiaka: A Myth from Hawaii* remains their work.

A few things need to be said in regard to this reprint edition. Emerson saw fit to give us the Hawaiian language text with his translations. We must realize that he was writing Hawaiian at a time when the macron for an elongated vowel and the hamza for the glottal closure were little used. Critical as such marks are, it has not been possible to attempt a revision of the Hawaiian portions of this book. A dictionary and some knowledge of Hawaiian can make good this shortcoming for those wishing to pursue the printed Hawaiian text.

This reprint is from the first and only edition. There are some minor revisions made from notes left by Dr. Emerson and made available by Mr. Robert E. Van Dyke of Honolulu. Mr. Van Dyke also loaned a typescript copy of Dr. Emerson's original manuscript for study. I am indebted to that extraordinary lady of hula and song, Mrs. Winona Beamer, and to Mr. Neil Hannahs (both of Kamehameha Schools) for looking over this introduction and for making welcome comments.

The original illustrations of the 1915 edition were unsuitable for reproduction. A new set of scenes relating to Hawai'i's volcanic landscape was photographed by this writer.

TERENCE BARROW, PH.D.

Honolulu, Hawai'i

PREFACE

THE story of Pele and her sister Hiiaka stands at the fountain-head of Hawaiian myth and is the matrix from which the unwritten literature of Hawaii drew its life-blood. The material for the elaboration of this story has, in part, been found in serial contributions to the Hawaiian newspapers during the last few decades; in part, gathered by interviews with the men and women of the older regime, in whose memory it has been stored and, again, in part, it has been supplied by papers solicited from intelligent Hawaiians. The information contained in the notes has been extracted by *viva voce* appeal to Hawaiians themselves. These last two sources of information will soon be no longer available.

Merely as a story, this myth of Pele and her kindred may be deemed to have no compelling merit that should attract one to its reading. The cycle of world-myth already gathered from the rising to the setting of the sun, from the north pole to the south pole, is quite vast enough, and far in excess of the power of any one scholar to master and digest. It contains enough pretty stories, in all conscience, to satisfy the demands of the whole raft of storiologists and penny-a-liners, ever on the alert to cram the public with new sensations, without making it necessary to levy upon Hawaii for her little contribution.

It is not from a disposition to pander to any such appetite that the writer has drudged through many long years in collecting and giving literary shape to the material herein presented. The people who settled the Hawaiian group of islands are recognized as having occupied a unique station, one so far removed from the center and vortex of Polynesian activity as to enable them to cast a highly important side-light on many of the problems yet unsolved, that are of interest to ethnologists and philologists and that still enshroud the Polynesian race.

Hawaii rejoiced in a Kamehameha, who, with a strong hand, welded its discordant political elements into one body and made of it a nation. But it was denied a Homer capable of voicing its greatest epic in one song. The myth of the volcanic queen, like every other important Hawaiian myth, has been handled by many poets and raconteurs, each from his own point of view, influenced, no doubt, by local environment; but there never stood

forth one singer with the supreme power to symphonize the jar-
ring notes and combine them into one concordant whole. This
fact is a tribute to the independent attitude of Hawaii's geo-
graphical units as well as to its scattered minstrelsy.

This book does not offer itself as a complete history of Pele;
it does not even assume to present all the oli, mele, and pule that
deal with the great name of Pele. There were important events
in her life that will receive but incidental mention. Of such is
the story of Pele's relations with the swine-god Kama-pua'a. As
indicated in the title, the author confines his attention almost
wholly to the story of Pele's relations with Prince Lohiau of
Haena, in which the girl Hiiaka became involved as an accessory.

It was inevitable that such a myth as that of Pele should draw
to it and, like an ocean-reef, become the stranding ground of a
great mass of flotsam and jetsam poetry and story. Especially
was this true of those passional fragments of Hawaiian mele and
oli, which, without this, would not easily have found a concrete
object to which they might attach themselves.

It matters not whether the poet-philosopher, deep pondering
on the hot things of love, hit upon Pele as the most striking and
appropriate character to serve his purpose and to wear his garment of passionate song and story, or, whether his mind, working
more objectively, took Nature's suggestion and came to realize
that, in the wild play of the volcanic forces, he had exemplified
before him a mighty parable of tempestuous love. Certain it is
that the volcano was antecedent to the poet and his musings,
and it seems more reasonable to suppose that from it came
the first suggestion and that his mind, as by a flash of inspiration, began its subjective work as the result of what he saw
going on before his eyes.

The Hawaiian to whose memory was committed the keeping
of an old time mele regarded it as a sacred trust, to be transmitted in its integrity; and he was inclined to look upon every different and contradictory version of that mele as, in a sense, an
infringement of his preserve, a desecration of that sacred thing
which had been entrusted to him. It resulted from this that such
a thing as a company of haku-mele (poets or song-makers) conferring together for the purpose of settling upon one authorita-
tive version of a historic mele was an impossibility.

It is a misfortune when the myth-cycle of any people or country
is invaded for exploitation by that class of writers whose sole
object is to pander, or cater—to use a softer term—to the public

taste for novelty and sensation, before that cycle has been canvassed and reported upon by students who approach it in a truthful yet sympathetic spirit. In other words: plain exposition should come before sensational exploitation. To reverse the order would be as undesirable as to have Münchausen gain the ear of the public before Mungo Park, Livingston, Stanley, Cook, or Vancouver had blazed the way and taken their observations.

Fortunately for Hawaii, the spirit of the times has set its face like a flint against this sort of sensation-mongering, and if a Münchausen were now to claim the public ear he would have the searchlight of scientific investigation turned upon him as pitilessly as it was done in the case of an alleged claim to the discovery of the north pole.

It is a satisfaction to the author, after having accomplished his pioneer work of opening up a new domain, to bid the public enter in and enjoy the delicious lehua parks once claimed by the girl Hiiaka as her own; and he can assure them that there yet remain many coverts that are full of charm which are to this day unravaged by the fires of Pele.

Thanks, many thanks, are due from the author—and from us all—to the men and women of Hawaiian birth whose tenacious memories have served as the custodians of the material herein set forth, but who have ungrudgingly made us welcome to these remainder biscuits of mythological song and story, which, but for them, would have been swallowed up in the grave, unvoiced and unrecorded.

N. B. EMERSON.

INTRODUCTION

ACCORDING to Hawaiian myth, Pele, the volcanic fire-queen and the chief architect of the Hawaiian group, was a foreigner, born in the mystical land of Kuai-he-lani, a land not rooted and anchored to one spot, but that floated free like the Fata Morgana, and that showed itself at times to the eyes of mystics, poets and seers, a garden land, clad with the living glory of trees and habitations—a vision to warm the imagination. The region was known as Kahiki (Kukulu o Kahiki), a name that connotes Java and that is associated with the Asiatic cradle of the Polynesian race.

Pele's mother was Haumea, a name that crops up as an ancestor in the hoary antiquity of the Hawaiian people, and she was reputed to be the daughter of Kane-hoa-lani.

Pele was ambitious from childhood and from the earliest age made it her practice to stick close to her mother's fireplace in company with the fire-keeper Lono-makua, ever watchful of his actions, studious of his methods—an apprenticeship well fitted to serve her in good stead such time as she was to become Hawaii's volcanic fire-queen. This conduct drew upon Pele the suspicion and illwill of her elder sister Na-maka-o-ka-ha'i, a sea-goddess, who, fathoming the latent ambition of Pele, could not fail to perceive that its attainment would result in great commotion and disturbance in their home-land.

Her fears and prognostications proved true. Namaka, returning from one of her expeditions across the sea, found that Pele, taking advantage of her absence, had erupted a fiery deluge and smothered a portion of the home-land with aä.

It would have gone hard with Pele; but mother Haumea bade her take refuge in the fold (*pola*) of Ka-moho-alii's malo. Now this elder brother of Pele was a deity of great power and authority, a terrible character, hedged about with tabus that restricted and made difficult the approach of his enemies. Such a refuge could only be temporary, and safety was to be assured only by Pele's removal from her home in the South land, and that meant flight. It was accomplished in the famed mythical canoe Honua-i-a-kea.

The company was a distinguished one, including such godlike beings as Ka-moho-alii, Kane-apua, Kane-milo-hai and many other relations of Pele, the youngest, but not the least important, of whom was the girl Hiiaka, destined to be the heroine of the story here unfolded and of whom it was said that she was born into the world as a clot of blood out of the posterior fontanelle (*nunoi*) of her mother Haumea, the other sisters having been delivered through the natural passage.

The sailing course taken by Pele's company brought them to some point northwest of Hawaii, along that line of islets, reefs, and shoals which tail off from Hawaii as does the train of a comet from its nucleus. At Moku-papápa Pele located her brother Kane-milo-hai, as if to hold the place for her or to build it up into fitness for human residence, for it was little more than a reef. Her next stop was at the little rock of Nihoa that lifts its head some eight hundred feet above the ocean. Here she made trial with the divining rod Paoa, but the result being unfavorable, she passed on to the insignificant islet of Lehua which clings like a limpet to the flank of Niihau. In spite of its smallness and unfitness for residence, Pele was moved to crown the rock with a wreath of kau-no'a, while Hiiaka contributed a chaplet of lehua which she took from her own neck, thus christening it for all time. The poet details the itinerary of the voyage in the following graphic lines:

KE KAAO A PELE I HAAWI IA KA-MOHO-ALII I KA HAALELE ANA IA KAHIKI

Ku makou e hele me ku'u mau poki'i aloha,
Ka aina a makou i ike ole ai malalo aku nei,
A'e makou me ku'u poki'i, kau i ka wa'a;
No'iau ka hoe a Ka-moho-alii;
A'ea'e, kau i ka nalu—
He nalu haki‿kakala,
He nalu e imi ana i ka aina e hiki aku ai.
O Nihoa ka aina a makou i pae mua aku ai:
Lele a'e nei makou, kau i uka o Nihoa.
O ka hana no a ko'u poki'i, a Kane-apua,
O ka hooili i ka ihu o ka wa'a a nou i ke kai:
Waiho anei o Ka-moho-alii ia Kane-apua i uka o Nihoa.
No'iau ka hoe a Ka-moho-alii
A pae i ka aina i kapa ia o Lehua.

TRANSLATION

PELE'S ACCOUNT TO KAMOHOALII OF THE DEPARTURE FROM KAHIKI

We stood to sail with my kindred beloved
To an unknown land below the horizon;
We boarded — my kinsmen and I — our craft,
Our pilot well skilled, Ka-moho-alii.
Our craft o'ermounted and mastered the waves;
The sea was rough and choppy, but the waves
Bore us surely on to our destined shore—
The rock Nihoa, the first land we touched;
Gladly we landed and climbed up its cliffs.
Fault of the youngster, Kane-apua,
He loaded the bow till it ducked in the waves;
Ka-moho-alii marooned the lad,
Left the boy on the islet Nihoa
And, pilot well skilled, he sailed away
Till we found the land we christened Lehua.

When they had crowned the desolate rock with song and wreath, Ka-moho-alii would have steered for Niihau, but Pele, in a spasm of tenderness that smiles like an oasis in her life, exclaimed, "How I pity our little brother who journeyed with us till now!" At this Ka-moho-alii turned the prow of the canoe in the direction of Nihoa and they rescued Kane-apua from his seagirt prison. Let the poet tell the story:

Hui (a) iho nei ka wa'a a Ka-moho-alii
E kii ana i ko lakou pokii, ia Kane-apua, i Nihoa.
Pili aku nei ka wa'a o Ka-moho-alii i uka nei o Nihoa,
Kahea aku nei i ko lakou pokii, ia Kane-apua,
E kau aku ma ka pola o ka wa'a.
Hui iho nei ka ihu o ka wa'a o Ka-moho-alii —
He wa'a e holo ana i Niihau,
Kau aku nei o Ka-moho-alii i ka laau, he paoa, (b)

(a) *Hui*, an elided form of *huli*, the *l* being dropped.
(b) *Paoa*. One Hawaiian says this should be *pahoa*. (Paulo Hokii.)
The Paoa mentioned in verse eight was a divining rod used to determine the suitability of any spot for Pele's excavations. The land must be proof against the entrance of sea water. It also served as a spade in excavating for a volcanic crater.

When a suitable place was finally discovered on Hawaii, the Paoa staff was planted in Panaewa and became a living tree, multiplying itself until it was a forest. The writer's informant says that it is a tree known to the present generation of men. "I have seen sticks cut from it," said he, "but not the living tree itself."

E imi ana i ko lakou aina e noho ai, o Kauai:
Aole na'e i loa'a.
Kau mai la o Ka-moho-alii i ka`laau, he paoa;
O Ahu (c) ka aina.
Ia ka ana iho nei o lakou i Alia-pa'akai,
Aole na'e he aina.

TRANSLATION

Ka-moho-alii turned his canoe
To rescue lad Kane from Nihoa.
Anon the craft lies off Nihoa's coast;
They shout to the lad, to Kane-apua,
Come aboard, rest with us on the pola. (d)
Ka-moho-alii turns now his prow,
He will steer for the fertile Niihau.
He sets out the wizard staff Paoa,
To test if Kauai's to be their home;
But they found it not there.
Once more the captain sails on with the rod,
To try if Oahu's the wished for land:
They thrust in the staff at Salt Lake Crater,
But that proved not the land of their promise.

Arrived at Oahu, Ka-moho-alii, who still had Pele in his keeping, left the canoe in charge of Holoholo-kai and, with the rest of the party, continued the journey by land. The witchery of the Paoa was appealed to from time to time, as at Alia-pa'akai, Puowaena (Punchbowl Hill), Leahi (Diamond Head), and lastly at Makapu'u Point, but nowhere with a satisfactory response. (The words of Pele in the second verse of the kaao next to be given lead one to infer that she must for a time have entertained the thought that they had found the desired haven at Pele-ula— a small land-division within the limits of the present city of Honolulu.) Let the poet tell the story:

Ke ku nei makou e imi kahi e noho ai
A loa'a ma Pele-ula:
O Kapo-ula-kina'u ka wahine;

(c) *O Ahu.* The particle *o* is not yet joined to its substantive, as in Oahu, the form we now have.

(d) *Pola,* the raised platform in the waist of the canoe, a place of honor.

A loaʻa i ka lae kapu o Maka-pu'u.
Ilaila pau ke kuleana;
Imi ia Kane-hoa-lani,
A loa'a i ka lae o Maka-hana-loa.—
He loa ka uka o Puna:
Elua kaua i ke kapa hookahi.
Akahi au a ike—haupu mau, walohia wale:
E Kane-hoa-lani, e-e!
E Kane-hoa-lani, e-e!
Aloha kaua!
Kau ka hokú hookahi, hele i ke ala loa!
Aloha kama kuku kapa a ka wahine!
He wahine lohiau, naná i ka makani;
He makani lohiau, haupu mai oloko!

TRANSLATION

We went to seek for a biding place,
And found it, we thought, in Pele-ula—
Dame Kapo—she of the red-pied robe—
Found it in the sacred cape, Maka-pu'u;
The limit that of our journey by land.
We looked then for Kane-hoa-lani
And found him at Maka-hana-loa.
Far away are the uplands of Puna;
One girdle still serves for you and for me.
Never till now such yearning, such sadness!
Where art thou, Kane-hoa-lani?
O Father Kane, where art thou?
Hail to thee, O Father, and hail to me!
When rose the pilot-star we sailed away.
Hail, girl who beats out tapa for women—
The home-coming wife who watches the wind,
The haunting wind that searches the house!

The survey of Oahu completed, and Kamoho-alii having resumed command of the canoe, Pele uttered her farewell and they voyaged on to the cluster of islands of which Maui is the center:

Aloha, Oahu, e-e!
E huli ana makou i ka aina mamua aku,
Kahi a makou e noho ai.

Farewell to thee, Oahu!
We press on to lands beyond,
In search of a homing place.

Repeated trial with the divining rod, Paoa, made on the western part of Maui as well as on the adjoining islands of Molokai and Lanai proving unsatisfactory, Pele moved on to the exploration of the noble form of Hale-a-ka-la that domes East Maui, with fine hope and promise of success. But here again she was dissatisfied with the result. She had not yet delivered herself from the necessity of protection by her kinsman, Ka-moho-alii: "One girdle yet serves for you and for me," was the note that still rang out as a confession of dependence, in her song.

While Pele was engaged in her operations in the crater of Hale-a-ka-la, her inveterate enemy Na-maka-o-ka-ha'i, who had trailed her all the way from Kahiki with the persistency of a sea-wolf, appeared in the offing, accompanied by a sea-dragon named Ha-ui.

The story relates that, as Na-maka-o-ka-ha'i passed the sand-spit of Moku-papápa, Kane-milo-hai, who, it will be remembered, had been left there in charge as the agent of Pele, hailed her with the question: "Where are you going so fast?"

"To destroy my enemy, to destroy Pele," was her answer.

"Return to Kahiki, lest you yourself be destroyed," was the advice of Kane-milo-hai.

Pele, accepting the gage thrown down by Na-maka-o-kaha'i, with the reluctant consent of her guardian Ka-moho-alii, went into battle single-handed. The contest was terrific. The sea-monster, aided by her dragon consort, was seemingly victorious. Dismembered parts of Pele's body were cast up at Kahiki-nui, where they are still pointed out as the bones of Pele (*na iwi o Pele.*) (She was only bruised). Ka-moho-alii was dismayed thinking Pele to have been destroyed;—but, looking across the Ale-nui-haha channel, he saw the spirit-form of Pele flaming in the heavens above the summits of Mauna-loa and Mauna-kea. As for Na-maka-o-ka-ha'i, she retired from the battle exultant, thinking that her enemy Pele was done for: but when she reported her victory to Kane-milo-hai, that friend of Pele pointed to the spirit body of Pele glowing in the heavens as proof that she was mistaken. Namaka was enraged at the sight and would have turned back to renew the conflict, but Kane-milo-hai dissuaded her from this foolhardy undertaking, saying, "She is invincible; she has become a spirit."

The search for a home-site still went on. Even Hale-a-ka-la was not found to be acceptable to Pele's fastidious taste. According to one account it proved to be so large that Pele found herself unable to keep it warm. Pele, a goddess now, accordingly bade adieu to Maui and its clustering isles and moved on to Hawaii.

HE KAAO NA PELE, I HAALELE AI IA MAUI

Aloha o Maui, aloha, e!
Aloha o Moloka'i, aloha, e!
Aloha o Lana'i, aloha, e!
Aloha o Kaho'olawe, aloha, e!
Ku makou e hele, e!
O Hawaii ka ka aina
A makou e noho ai a mau loa aku;
Ke ala ho'i a makou i hiki mai ai,
He ala paoa ole ko Ka-moho-alii,
Ko Pele, ko Kane-milo-hai, ko Kane-apua,
Ko Hiiaka—ka no'iau—i ka poli o Pele,
I hiki mai ai.

TRANSLATION

PELE'S FAREWELL TO MAUI

Farewell to thee, Maui, farewell!
Farewell to thee, Moloka'i, farewell!
Farewell to thee, Lana'i, farewell!
Farewell to thee, Kaho'olawe, farewell!
We stand all girded for travel:
Hawaii, it seems, is the land
On which we shall dwell evermore.
The route by which we came hither
Touched lands not the choice of Paoa;—
'Twas the route of Ka-moho-alii,
Of Pele and Kane-milo-hai,
Route traveled by Kane-apua, and by
Hiiaka, the wise, the darling of Pele.

Pele and her company landed on Hawaii at Pua-kó, a desolate

spot between Kawaihae and Kailua. Thence they journeyed
inland until they came to a place which they named Moku-aweo-
weo—not the site of the present crater of that name, but—situated where yawns the vast caldera of Kilauea. It was at the
suggestion of Ku-moku-halii and Keawe-nui-kau of Hilo that
the name was conferred. They also gave the name Mauna-loa
to the mountain mass that faced them on the west, "because,"
said they, "our journey was long."

Night fell and they slept. In the morning, when the elepaio
uttered its note, they rose and used·the Paoa staff. The omens
were favorable, and Pele decided that this was the place for her
to establish a permanent home.

The people immediately began to set out many plants valuable
for food; among them a variety of kalo called aweü, well suited
for upland growth; the ulu (*bread-fruit*); the maiä (banana);
the pala-á (an edible fern); the awa (*Piper methysticum*) and
other useful plants.

The land on the Hilo side of Kilauea, being in the rain belt,
is fertile and well fitted for tillage. The statement, however,
that Kilauea, or its vicinity, became the place of settlement for
any considerable number of people cannot be taken literally.
The climatic conditions about Kilauea are too harsh and untropi-
cal to allow either the people or the food plants of Polynesia to
feel at home in it. The probability is that instead of being gathered about Kilauea, they made their homes in the fat lands of
lower Puna or Hilo.

Pele, on her human side at least, was dependent for support
and physical comfort upon the fruits of the earth and the climatic
conditions that made up her environment. Yet with all this, in
the narrative that follows her relations to humanity are of that
exceptional character that straddle, as it were, that border line
which separates the human from the superhuman, but for the
most part occupy the region to the other side of that line, the
region into which if men and women of this work-a-day world
pass they find themselves uncertain whether the beings with
whom they converse are bodied like themselves or made up of
some insubstantial essence and liable to dissolve and vanish at
the touch.

A mountain trail, Haena, Kaua'i.

CHAPTER I

PELE IN THE BOSOM OF HER FAMILY

Once, when Pele was living in the pit of Kilauea, she roused up from her couch on the rough hearth-plate and said to her sisters, "Let us make an excursion to the ocean and enjoy ourselves, open the opihi shells and sea-urchins, hunt for small squid and gather sea-moss."

To this all joyfully assented, saying, "Yes, let us go."

The sisters formed quite a procession as they tramped the narrow downhill path until they came to the hill Pu'u-Pahoehoe—a place in the lower lands of Puna. Pele herself did not visibly accompany them on this journey; that was not according to her custom: she had other ways and means of travel than to plod along a dusty road. When, however, the party arrived at the rendezvous, there, sure enough, they found Pele awaiting them, ready for the business in hand.

In the midst of their pleasurings Pele caught sight of Hopoe and Haena as they were indulging in an *al fresco* dance and having a good time by the Puna sea. She was greatly pleased and, turning to her sisters, said, "Come, haven't you also got some dance that you can show off in return for this entertainment by Hopoe and her companion?"

They all hung their heads and said, "We have no hula."

Hiiaka, the youngest, had stayed behind to gather lehua flowers, and when she came along laden with wreaths, Pele said to her, jestingly, "I've just been proposing to your sisters here to dance a hula in response to that of Hopoe and her fellow, but they decline, saying they have not the art. I suppose it's of no use to ask you, you are so small; but, perhaps, you've got a bit of a song."

"Yes, I have a song," Hiiaka answered, to the surprise of all.

"Let us have it, then; go on!" said Pele.

Then the little girl, having first decorated all of her sisters with the wreaths, beginning with Pele, sang as follows:

> Ke ha'a la Puna i ka makani;
> Ha'a ka ulu hala i Keaau;
> Ha'a Haena me Hopoe;
> Ha'a ka wahine,
> Ami i kai o Nana-huki, la—
> Hula le'a wale,
> I kai o Nana-huki, e-e!

Puna's a-dance in the breeze,
The hala groves of Keaau shaken:
Haena and Hopoe are swaying;
The thighs of the dancing nymph
Quiver and sway, down at Nana-huki—
A dance most sightly and pleasing,
Down by the sea Nana-huki.

Pele was delighted. "Is that all you have?" she asked.
"I have somthing more," said the girl.
"Let us hear it then."
Hiiaka put even more spirit into the song as she complied:

O Puna kai kuwá i ka hala;
Pae ka leo o ke kai;
Ke lu, la, i na pua lehua.
Nana i kai o Hopoe,
Ka wahine ami i kai
O Nana-huki, la;
Hula le'a wale,
I kai o Nana-huki, e-e.

The voice of Puna's sea resounds
Through the echoing hala groves;
The lehua trees cast their bloom.
Look at the dancing girl Hopoe;
Her graceful hips swing to and fro,
A-dance on the beach Nana-huki:
A dance that is full of delight,
Down by the sea Nana-huki.

At the conclusion of this innocent performance—the earliest mention of the hula that has reached us—Hiiaka went to stay with her friend Hopoe, a person whose charm of character had fascinated the imagination of the susceptible girl and who had already become her dearest intimate, her inspiring mentor in those sister arts, song, poesy and the dance.

Pele herself remained with her sister Hiiaka-i-ka-pua-enaena (Hiiaka-of-the-fire-bloom), and presently she lay down to sleep in a cave on a smooth plate of pahoehoe. Before she slept she gave her sister this command: "Listen to me. I am lying down to sleep; when the others return from fishing, eat of the fish, but don't dare to wake me. Let me sleep on until I wake of myself. If one of you wakes me it will be the death of you all. If you must needs wake me, however, call my little sister and let her be the one to rouse me; or, if not her, let it be my brother Ke-o-wahi-maka-o-ka-ua—one of these two."

When Ke-o-wahi-maka-o-ka-ua, who was so closely related to Pele that she called him brother, had received this command and had seen her lapse into profound sleep he went and reported the matter to Hiiaka, retailing all that Pele had said. "Strange that this havoc-producer should sleep in this way, and no bed-fellow!" said Hiiaka to herself. "Here are all the other Hiiakas, all of equal rank and merit! Perhaps it was because my dancing pleased her that she wishes me to be the one to rouse her."

The cavern in the hill Pahoehoe in which Pele lay and slept, wrapped in her robe (*kapa-ahu*), remains to this day.

In her sleep Pele heard the far-off beating of hula drums, and her spirit-body pursued the sound. At first it seemed to come from some point far out to sea; but as she followed, it shifted, moving to the north, till it seemed to be off the beach of Waiakea, in Hilo; thence it moved till it was opposite Lau-pahoehoe. Still evading her pursuit, the sound retreated till it came from the boisterous ocean that beats against the shaggy cliffs of Hamakua. Still going north, it seemed presently to have reached the mid channel of Ale-nui-haha that tosses between Hawaii and Maui.

"If you are from my far-off home-land Kahiki, I will follow you thither, but I will come up with you," said Pele.

To her detective ear, as she flitted across the heaving waters of Ale-nui-haha, the pulsing of the drums now located itself at the famous hill Kauwiki, in Hana; but, on reaching that place, the music had passed on to the west and sounded from the cliffs of Ka-haku-loa.

The fugitive music led her next across another channel, until in her flight she had traversed the length of Moloka'i and had come to the western point of that island, Lae-o-ka-laau. Thence she flew to cape Maka-pu'u, on Oahu, and so on, until, after crossing that island, she reached cape Kaena, whose finger-point reaches out towards Kaua'i. In that desolate spot dwelt an aged creature of myth, Pohaku-o-Kaua'i by name, the personal representative of that rock whose body-form the hero Mawi had jerked from its ocean bed ages before, in his futile attempt to draw together the two islands Kaua'i and Oahu and unite them into one mass.

Pele, arguing from her exasperation, said, "It must be my old grandfather Pohaku-o-Kaua'i who is playing this trick with the music. If it's he that's leading me this chase, I'll kill him."

The old fellow saw her approach and, hailing her from a distance, greeted her most heartily. Her answer was in a surly mood: "Come here! I'm going to kill you to-day. So it's you that's been fooling me with deceitful music, leading me a wearisome chase."

"Not I, I've not done this. There they are, out to sea; you can hear for yourself." And, sure enough, on listening, one could hear the throbbing of the music in the offing.

Pele acknowledged her mistake and continued her pursuit, with the parting assurance to the old soul that if he *had* been the guilty one, it would have been his last day of life.

The real authors of this illusive musical performance were two little creatures named Kani-ka-wí and Kani-ka-wá, the former a sprite that was embodied in the nose-flute, the latter in the hokeo, a kind of whistle, both of them used as accompaniments to the hula. Their sly purpose was to lure Pele to a place where the hula was being performed.

Pele now plunged into the water—from this point at least she swam—and, guided by the call of the music, directed her course to the little village of Haena that perched like a gull on the cape of the same name, at the northernmost point of the island of Kaua'i. It was but a few steps to the hall of the hula—the *halau* —where throbbed the hula drums and where was a concourse of people gathered from the whole island.

CHAPTER II

PELE MEETS AND FASCINATES LOHIAU

As Pele drew near to the rustic hall where the hula was in full blast, the people in the outskirts of the assembly turned to look in wonder and admiration at the beauty and charm of the stranger who had appeared so unexpectedly and whose person exhaled such a fragrance, as if she had been clad with sweet-scented garlands of maile, lehua and hala. One and all declared her to be the most beautiful woman they had ever looked upon. Where was she from? Surely not from Kaua'i. Such loveliness could not have remained hidden in any nook or corner of the island, they declared.

Instinctively the wondering multitude parted and offered a lane for her to pass through and enter the halau, thus granting to Pele a full view of the musicians and performers of the hula, and, sitting in their midst, Lohiau,—as yet seemingly unconscious of her presence,—on his either hand a fellow drummer; while, flanking these to right and left, sat players with a joint of bamboo in either hand (the kaekeeke). But drummer and kaekeeke-player, musicians and actors—aye, the whole audience—became petrified and silent at the sight of Pele, as she advanced step by step, her eyes fixed on Lohiau.

Then, with intensified look, as if summoning to her aid the godlike gifts that were hers as the mistress of Kilauea, she reached out her hand and, in a clear tone, with a mastery that held the listeners spell-bound, she chanted:

> Lu'ulu'u Hanalei i ka ua nui,
> Kaumaha i ka noe o Alaka'i,
> I ka hele ua o Manu'a-kepa;
> Uoi ku i ka loa o Ko'i-alana,
> I ka alaka'i 'a a ka malihini, e!
> Mai hina, mai hina au,
> Mai palaha ia o-e.
> Imi wale ana au o kahi o ke ola,
> O ke ola nei, e-e!

TRANSLATION

Tight-pressed is Hanalei's throng,
A tree bent down by heavy rain,

Weighted with drops from the clouds,
When rain columns sweep through Manu'a-kepa,
This throng that has lured on the stranger,
Nigh to downfall, to downfall, was I,
Laid flat by your trick—aye yours!
My quest was for comfort and life,
Just for comfort and life!

The silence became oppressive. In the stillness that followed
the song expectant eyes were focused upon Prince Lohiau, awaiting his reply to the address of the stranger who stood in their
midst. No one knew who she was; no one imagined her to be
Pele. That she was a person of distinction and rank was evident
enough, one whom it was the duty and rare privilege of their
chief to receive and entertain.

Presently there was wrinkling of foreheads, an exchange of
glances, prompting winks and nods, inclinations of the head, a
turning of the eyes—though not a word was spoken—; for his
friends thought thus to rouse Lohiau from his daze and to prompt
him to the dutiful rites of hospitality and gallantry. Paoa, his
intimate friend, sitting at Lohiau's right hand, with a drum between his knees, even ventured to nudge him in the side.

The silence was broken by Pele:

> Kalakú Hilo i ka ua nui;
> Kapu ke nu, ke i,
> I ka puá o ka leo,
> I ka hamahamau—hamau kakou—
> I ka hawanawana;
> I ke kunou maka;
> I ka awihi maka;
> I ka alawa iki.
> Eia ho'i au, kou hoa,
> Kou hoa, ho'i, e-e!

TRANSLATION

> Bristling, frumpy, sits Hilo,
> Drenched by the pouring rain,
> Forbidden to murmur,
> Or put forth a sound,
> Or make utt'rance by speech:

˙Must all remain breathless,
Nor heave an audible sigh,
Withholding the nod, the wink,
And the glance to one side.
I pray you behold me now:—
Here stand I, your guest,
Your companion, your mate!

Lohiau, once roused from his ecstacy, rose to the occasion and with the utmost gallantry and politeness invited Pele to sit with him and partake of the hospitalities of the halau.

When Pele had seated herself on the mat-piled dais, Lohiau, following the etiquette of the country, asked whence she came.

"I am of Kaua'i," she answered.

"There is no woman of Kaua'i your equal in beauty," said Lohiau. "I am the chief and I know, for I visit every part of the whole island."

"You have doubtless traveled about the whole island," answered Pele; "yet there remain places you are not acquainted with; and that is where I come from."

"No, no! you are not of Kaua'i. Where *are* you from?"

Because of his importunity, Pele answered him, "I am from Puna, from the land of the sunrise; from Ha'eha'e, the eastern gate of the sun."

Lohiau bade that they spread the tables for a feast, and he invited Pele to sit with him and partake of the food. But Pele refused food, saying, "I have eaten."

"How can that be?" said he, "seeing you have but now come from a long journey? You had better sit down and eat."

Pele sat with him, but she persistently declined all his offers of food, "I am not hungry."

Lohiau sat at the feast, but he could not eat; his mind was disturbed; his eyes were upon the woman at his side. When they rose from the table he led her, not unwilling, to his house, and he lay down upon a couch by her side. But she would favor him only with kisses. In his growing passion for her he forgot his need of food, his fondness for the hula, the obligations that rested upon him as a host: all these were driven from his head.

All that night and the following day, and another night, and for three days and three nights, he lay at her side, struggling with her, striving to overcome her resistance. But she would grant him only kisses.

And, on the third night, as it came towards morning, Pele said to Lohiau, "I am about to return to my place, to Puna, the land of the sunrise. You shall stay here. I will prepare a habitation for us, and, when all is ready I will send and fetch you to myself. If it is a man who comes, you must not go with him; but, if a woman, you are to go with the woman. Then, for five days and five nights you and I will take our fill of pleasure. After that you will be free to go with another woman."

In his madness, Lohiau put forth his best efforts to overcome Pele's resistance, but she would not permit him. "When we meet on Hawaii you shall enjoy me to your fill," said she. He struggled with her, but she foiled him and bit him in the hand to the quick; and he grasped the wound with the other hand to staunch the pain. And he, in turn, in the fierceness of his passion, planted his teeth in her body.

At this, Pele fluttered forth from the house, plunged into the ocean and—was gone.

CHAPTER III

LOHIAU COMES TO HIMSELF—HIS DEATH—THE THREAT OF PAOA

When Lohiau came to himself, as from a dream, he looked for the woman who had lain at his side, but her place was vacant and cold. He went out into the open air, but she was nowhere to be found, and he turned back into the empty house.

Lohiau's stay with Pele in the sleeping house had prolonged itself beyond all reason and his friends became concerned about him; and as night after night and day after day passed and they neither saw nor heard anything of him, their concern grew into alarm. Yet no one dared enter the house. Lohiau's sister, however, made it her business to investigate. Opening the door of the house, she entered, and, lo, there hung the body of her brother, suspended from a rafter, his malo about his neck. Life had been gone for many hours and the body was cold. Her screams brought to her aid a group of Lohiau's friends who at once lifted their voices in unison with hers, bewailing their chief's death and denouncing the woman who had been with him as the guilty cause.

Paoa was the most outspoken in his imprecations. Stripping off his malo, he stood forth in the garb of nature and declared he would not resume his loin cloth until he had sought out the woman and humiliated her by the grossest of insults. "I will not gird my loins with a malo until I have kindled a fire in Pele's face, pounded her face as one pounds a taro, consumed her very eyes." This was the savage oath with which Paoa pledged his determination to avenge the death of his friend, his chief, Lohiau. With universal wailing, amid the waving of kahilis, with tender care and the observance of all due rites, his people anointed the dear body of their chief with perfumed oil, wrapped it in scented robes of choicest tapa, and laid it to rest in the sepulcher.

The favorite dog of Lohiau, who was greatly attached to his master, took his station at the grave and would not be persuaded to leave. Poha-kau, a cousin of Pele,—himself a kupua and possessed of superhuman powers,—having journeyed from Hawaii to Haena, found the faithful creature keeping his lonely vigil at the grave and he brought the dog with him to Pele.

"Your man is dead; Lohiau is dead," said he. "But this animal—do you recognize him?—I found watching by the grave in Haena."

"Yes, that is the dog I saw with Lohiau," answered Pele; and she hid the dog away in her secret place.

CHAPTER IV

PELE AWAKES FROM HER SLEEP

While the scene we have described was being enacted on Kaua'i, the spirit of Pele, returning from its long flight, hovered over the sleeping body at Lau-pahoehoe. Above it waved the kahilis, about it were gathered the sisters and other relatives, quietly sobbing. Though it was many days since Pele had lain down to sleep, and though they feared the consequences if she continued thus, they dared not disturb her. When that was proposed, the sister in charge objected. "If it must be done, we shall have to send for Hiiaka the beloved."

Some of them suggested that Pele must be dead, she had remained so long without motion. But Hiiaka-of-the-lightning-flash scouted the idea: "How can that be? The body shows no signs of decay."

The girl Hiiaka saw the messenger that had been despatched to fetch her, while as yet she was in the dim distance,—it was her nurse, Paú-o-pala'e,—and there came to her a premonition of what it all meant, a vision, a picture, of the trouble that was to come; yet. overmastering her, was a feeling of affection and loyalty for her elder sister. Standing outside the house, that she might better watch the approach of Paú-o-pala'e and be on hand to greet her, she voiced her vision in song:

> A ka lae ohi'a i Papa-lau-ahi,
> I ka imu lei lehua o Kua-o-ka-la—
> Lehua maka-nou i ke ahi—
> A wela e-e, wela la!
> Wela i ke ahi au,
> A ka Wahine mai ka Lua, e-e!

TRANSLATION

> From the forest-tongue at Papa-lau-ahi
> To the garlands heaped at Back-o'-the-sun,
> The beauteous lehuas are wilted,
> Scorched, burnt up, aye burnt,
> Consumed by the fire of the Woman—
> The fire that flows from the Pit.

As the messenger, in the vibrating sunlight, thridded her way among the tree clumps and lava-knobs, which now concealed her and now brought her into full view, Hiiaka, with gaze intent to gain such snap-shots of her as these obstructions did not forbid, continued her song:

> No ka Lua paha ia makani, o ka Pu'u-lena,
> Ke halihali i ke ala laau,
> Honi u ai ke kini i kai o Haena—
> Haena aloha!
> Ke kau nei ka haili moe;
> Kau ka haili moe i ke ahiahi:
> He hele ko kakahiaka:
> Mana'o hele paha au e-e.
> Homai ka ihu a hele a'e au;
> Aloha oe a noho iho, e-e!

TRANSLATION

From the Pit, doubtless, breathes Pu'u-lena,
With its waft of woodland perfume—
A perfume drunk in with rapture
On the beach of belovéd Haena.
There wafts to me this premonition,
This vision and dream of the night:
I must be gone in the morning:
I foresee I must travel to-morrow.
A farewell kiss ere I journey;
Farewell, alas, to thee who remainest!

Her hostess, Hopoe, would not take the song or the farewell of Hiiaka seriously. "You are simply joking," she said, "letting your gloomy imagination run away with you. Who in the world is driving you away, as if you had worn out your welcome?"

The messenger, Paú-o-pala'e, when she had saluted Hiiaka, said, "I come from your sisters. They want to see you."

Arrived at Lau-pahoehoe, (a) Hiiaka found her sisters in great consternation, fearing for the life of Pele if she were allowed to continue her long sleep. Her spirit, it is true, had come back to her body; but it was merely hovering about and had not entered and taken possession, so that there were no signs of animation or life. It seemed to be waiting for the voice of Hiiaka, the belovéd, to summon it back and to make it resume consciousness.

Hiiaka demanded to know the cause of the wailing.

"We are lamenting our sister, the head of the family. You can see for yourself; she is dead."

After carefully examining the body of Pele, Hiiaka stoutly declared, "She is not dead. That is evident from the absence of corruption." Then, sitting close to Pele's feet, she sang:

O hookó ia aku oe
O ka hana ana a ke akua:
I kai o Maka-wai
Ke kiké la ka pohaku:
Wáhi kai a ke 'kua—
He akua, he kanáka;
He kanáka no, e-e!

(a) This Laupahoehoe is to be distinguished from that in Hilo.

Content you now with your god-work:
Down by the sea at Maka-wai
The rocks have smitten together;
The sea has opened a channel.
Goddess you were, now human,
Return to your human clay!

Pele slept on and gave no sign of waking. Hiiaka then chanted this serenade:

E ala, e ala, e ala!
E ala, e Hi-ka-po-kuakini!
E ala, e Hi-ka-po-kuamáno!
E ala, e ke Akua, e ke Alo!
E ala, e ka Uwila nui,
Maka ehá i ka lani, la!
E ala, e, e ala!

Awake now, awake, awake!
Wake, Goddess of multiple god-power!
Wake, Goddess of essence most godlike!
Wake, Queen of the lightning shaft,
The piercing fourth eye of heaven!
Awake; I pray thee awake!

The effect was magical: Pele's bosom heaved; breath entered her lungs; a fresh color came to her face, and spread to the tips of her ears. She sighed, stretched herself and sat up: she was herself again.

CHAPTER V

PELE MAKES A PROPOSITION TO HER SISTERS

That same day Pele and the other sisters returned to Kilauea, while Hiiaka went back to resume her visit with Hopoe, each party reaching its destination at about the same time. Early the next morning Pele called to her sister Hiiaka-i-ka-ale-i (Hiiaka-of-the-choppy-sea) and said, "I want you to go on an errand for me."

"No doubt I shall agree to go when you have told me what it is," was the answer of the young woman.

"You are to journey to Kaua'i and escort hither our lover—yours and mine. While on the way you are not to lie with him; you are not to touch noses with him; you are not to fondle him or snuggle close to him. If you do any such thing I will kill both of you. After your return, for five days and five nights, I will have him to myself, and after that he shall be your lover."

On hearing this, the young woman hung her head and wept.

Pele then made the same proposal to each of the other sisters in turn. Not one of them would consent to undertake the mission. They knew full well the perils of the undertaking: the way was beset with swarms of demons and dragons, with beings possessed with powers of enchantment; and Pele did not offer to endow them with the power that would safeguard them on their journey.

Pele, finding herself foiled on this tack, as a diversion, said, "Let us refresh ourselves and have some luau." The sisters immediately set to work, and, when they had made up the bundles of delicate taro leaves and were about to lay them upon the fire, Pele called to Paú-o-pala'e and bade her go straightway to Haena and fetch Hiiaka, "And you are to be back here by the time the luau is cooked."

Now the girl, whose full name was Hiiaka-i-ka-poli-o-Pele, was the youngest of the sisters, and, by reason of her loveliness and accommodating disposition, she was Pele's favorite. She was, moreover, gifted with a quick intuition and a clairvoyant perception of distant happenings and coming events. At the time of the conversation between Pele and the seven sisters, Hiiaka was sporting in the ocean with her surf-board in the company of Hopoe. While thus engaged, the whole matter of the proposed journey to Haena came to her as in a vision. In the midst of her surfing she turned to Hopoe and said, "I perceive that I am about to undertake a long journey; and during my absence you will remain here in Puna waiting my return."

"No! What puts such a notion into your head?" said Hopoe.

"Yes, I must go," insisted Hiiaka. Then they mounted a roller, and, as their boards touched the beach, there stood the messenger of Pele; and this was the message: "Gird on your paú and come with me to Kilauea. Your sister commands it."

As the two jogged on their uphill way, an impulse seized Hiiaka, and she gave voice to a promonition, a shadow of coming trouble, as it were, and, standing in the road at Mokau-lele, she sang:

> He uä kui lehua ko Pana-ewa;
> He uä ma kai kui hala ko Puna, e!
> Aloha e, aloha wale Koloa, e-e!
> Na mau'u i moe o Malei.

TRANSLATION

> Pana-ewa's rain beats down the lehuas,
> A rain by the sea smites the halas of Puna.
> My love, my pity go out to Koloa;—
> Her fare, wilted herbs at Malei.

Hiiaka—true poet that she was, and alive to every colorable aspect of nature—as she trudged on her way, came upon a sight that touched her imagination; two birds were sipping together in loving content of the water that had collected in the crotch of a tree, in which also was growing an awa plant.—Such nature-planted awa was famed as being the most toxic of any produced in Puna.—Her poetic mind found in the incident something that was in harmony with her own mood, and she wove it into a song:

> O ka manu múkimukí,
> Ale lehua a ka manu,
> O ka awa ili lena
> I ka uka o Ka-li'u;
> O ka manu ha'iha'i lau awa o Puna:—
> Aia i ka laau ka awa ona o Puna,
> O Puna, ho'i, e-e!

TRANSLATION

> O bird that sips with delight
> the nectar-bloom of lehua,
> Tasting the yellow-barked awa
> That climbs in Ka-liu's uplands;
> O bird that brews from this leafage
> Puna's bitter-sweet awa draught;—
> Puna's potentest awa grows
> Aloft in the crotch of a tree;—
> Most potent this awa of Puna !

CHAPTER VI

HIIAKA CONSENTS TO PELE'S PROPOSITION

Hiiaka arrived at the Pit in good time to partake with the others of the frugal feast ordered by Pele. At its conclusion, Pele turned to the girl Hiiaka and put the question in her blunt way, "Will you be my messenger to fetch our lover—yours and mine—from Kaua'i? Your sisters here"—she glanced severely about the group—"have refused to go. Will you do this for me?"

The little maid, true to her sense of loyalty to the woman who was her older sister, the head of the family, and her alii, to the surprise and dismay of her other sisters, answered, "Yes, I will go and bring the man."

It was a shock to their sense of fitness that one so young should be sent on an errand of such danger and magnitude; but more, it was a reproof that slapped them in the face to have this little chit accept without hesitation a commission which they had shrunk from through lack of courage. But they dared not say a word; they could but scowl and roll the eye and shrug the shoulder.

"When you have brought our lover here," continued Pele, "for five nights and five days he shall be mine; after that, the tabu shall be off and he shall be yours. But, while on the way, you must not kiss him, nor fondle him, nor touch him. If you do it will be the death of you both."

In spite of the gestured remonstrances of the group, Hiiaka, in utter self-forgetfulness and diplomatic inexperience, agreed to Pele's proposition, and she framed her assent in a form of speech that had in it the flavor of a sacrament:

> Kukulu ka makia a ka huaka'i hele moe ipo:
> Ku au, hele, noho oe.
> E noho ana na lehua lulu'u,
> Ku'u moku lehua i uka o Ka-li'u, e.
> Li'uli'u wale ka hele ana
> O ka huaka'i moe ipo.
> Aloha mai ka ipo—
> O Lohiau ipo, i Haena.

TRANSLATION

Firm plant the pillar, seal of our love-pact;
Here stand I, begirt for this love-quest;
You shall abide, and with you my groves —
Lehua and hala —heavy with bloom.
The journey is long and toilsome the task
To bring our fine lover to bed.
Hark! a love-hail — from beloved Lohiau !
Beloved Lohiau of Haena!

(I am impelled by my admiration for this beautiful song to give another version of it:)

Ku kila ke kaunu moe ipo;
Ku au, hele, noho oe, a no-ho,
A noho ana i na lehua o Lu-lu'u,
O ka pae hala, moku lehua, i uka o Ka-li'u.
Li'u-li'u ho'i, li'u-li'u wale
Ka hele ana o ka huaka'i moe ipo.
Aloha mai ka ipo,
O Lohiau ipo, e!

TRANSLATION

Fixed my intent for the lover-quest:
Here I stand to depart; you remain,
And with you my bloom-clad lehuas,
And the palm-groves that wave in Ka-li'u.
Long, wearisome long, shall the journey be
To find and to bring our lover —
That dearest of lovers, Lohiau!

Hiiaka would sleep on it. Her start was to be in the morning. The next day, while Hiiaka was climbing the long ascent up the crater-pali, her sisters, anxious and appreciating the danger of the undertaking, were quietly weeping outside the cave; but they dared not utter a word that might come to the ears of Pele. They began, however, to beckon and signal to Hiiaka to return. She saw them and turned back, uttering the following plaint:

E ku ana au e hele;
E lau ka maka o ua nei ino;

E ka po'e ino, o lakou nei, e:
E mana ana, ka, ia'u e hele;
E hele no au, e-e!

TRANSLATION

While I stand ready for travel,
You bad lot! 'Tis you that I mean!
This weight of travel you'd lay on me;
These bad ones sit with impudent stare:
And so it is I that must go!

The opposition of the sisters was based largely on Hiiaka's youth and inexperience. The girl did not understand nor give them credit for this generous regard for herself; she saw only their disobedience and disloyalty to Pele's command.

Pele, impatient at her vacillation, broke out on her savagely: "Here you are again! Be off on your journey! You shall find no food here, no meat, no raiment, no roof, no sisterly greeting, nothing, until you return with the man. It would have been useless to dispatch these homely women on this errand; it seems equally useless to send a beautiful girl like you."

To this outburst Hiiaka retorted:

Ke hanai a'e la ka ua (*a*) i ka lani:
Maka'u au i ka ua awa i ka uka o Kiloi.
Iná (*b*) ia ia la, he loiloi, (*c*), e —
I loiloi no oe elua (*d*) oiwi —
Loiloi iho la, e-e!

TRANSLATION

The rain doth replenish the heavens;
I dread the fierce rain of upland Kiloí.
Behold now this one, the fault-finder!
You, in two shapes, are hard to please —
Aye, in either shape, hard to please!

(*a*) *Ua,* rain. It is suggested this may refer—sarcastically—to the watery secretion in Pele's eyes, as found in old people.

(*b*) *Ina,* here means consider.

(*c*) *Loiloi.* If a chief was not pleased or satisfied with a gift, loiloi would express his state of mind.

(*d*) *Elua oiwi,* literally, two shapes. Pele had many metamorphoses.

"I am not grumbling or finding fault with you (*loiloi*): it was simply because you turned back that I spoke to you. Do you call that reproaching you?"

Hiiaka, though a novice in diplomacy, as shown by her instant and unconditional acceptance of Pele's proposition, having once got her second breath, now exacted of Pele a condition that proved her to be, under the discipline of experience, an apt pupil in the delicate art of diplomacy. "I am going to bring our lover, while you remain at home. If during my absence you go forth on one of your raids, you are welcome to ravage and consume the lands that are common to us both; but, see to it that you do not consume my forests of lehua. And, again, if the fit does come upon you and you must ravage and destroy, look to it that you harm not my friend Hopoe."

Pele readily agreed to Hiiaka's reasonable demand, thinking thus to hasten her departure. To the inexperienced girl the terms of the agreement seemed now complete and satisfactory, and, in the first blush of her gratification, Hiiaka gave expression ·to her pleasure:

Ke kau aloha wale mai la ka ua, e-e;
Ka mauna o ka haliü kua, a-a.
I ku au a aloha oe, ka Lua, e-e!
Aloha ia oe, e-e!

TRANSLATION

Kindly falls the rain from heaven;
Now may I turn my back and travel:
Travel-girt, I bid farewell to the Pit;
Here's a farewell greeting to thee.

Even now Hiiaka made an ineffectual start. Some voice of human instinct whispered that something was wanting, and she again faced her sister with a request so reasonable that it could not be denied:

Ke ku nei au e hele:
Hele au a ke ala,
Mihi mai e-e:
Mana'o, ho'i mai no au,
Ia oe la, ia o-e.
La'i pohu mai la

Lalo o ka Lua, e:
I elua mai la, pono au.
Olelo I ke aka,
Ka hele ho'okahi, e;
Mamina ka leo —
He leo wale no, e-e!

TRANSLATION

My foot still shod for travel,—
I made a misstart on my journey;
I've come to repair my neglect.
A need, a request, brings me back,
To plead in thy presence once more:
Joy springs up within;
There's calm in the Pit.
Give me but a travel-mate:
That would content me.
Who travels alone has
For speech-mate his shadow.
Futile is speech, with
No answering voice —
Empty words, only a voice.

(The exigencies of the narrative have induced me, in the above song, to couple together two mele which the story-tellers have given us as belonging to two separate incidents in Hiiaka's fence with Pele.)

"Your request is reasonable," said Pele; "to travel alone is indeed to converse with one's shadow. You shall have a companion."

Pele designated a good-natured waiting woman as her attendant, who had the poetical name of Paú-o-pala'e (or Paú-o-palaá). This faithful creature heartily accepted the trust, that of *kahu*—a servant with the pseudo responsibility of a guardian—and, having expressed her fealty to her new mistress, she at once took her station. Thus everything seemed arranged for a start on the eventful journey.

The terms and conditions of Hiiaka's going were not even yet to the satisfaction of her watchful sisters and relatives. One matter of vital importance had been omitted from the outfit: Pele had not bestowed upon Hiiaka the *mana*, power and au-

thority, to overcome and subdue all the foes that would surely
rise up to oppose and defeat her. With wild gestures they signalled to Hiiaka once more to return.

Hiiaka's answering song, though pointed with blame, gives
proof that her own intuitions were not entirely at fault:

A ka luna, i Pu'u-onioni,
Noho ke anaina a ke 'Kua.
Kilohi a' ku'u maka ilalo,
I ka ulu o Wahine-kapu:
He o'ioina Kilauea,
He noho-ana o Papa-lau-ahi, e.
Ke lau-ahi mai la o Pele ia kai o Puna:
Ua one-á, oke-á, kai o Maláma, e.
E málama i ka iki kanaka,
I ka nu'a kanáka;
O kakou no keia ho-akua—
Akua Mo'o-lau, e!
O Mo'o-lau ke ala, e!

TRANSLATION

From the crest of Tremble(a) Hill
I look on the concourse of gods,
At ease on the gossip-ground,
The seat of Wahine-kapu,
Rest-station to Kilauea,
Its pavement of lava-plate:
Such plates Pele spreads in Puna—
Hot shards, gray sands at Maláma.
Succor and life for small and great!
Be it ours to play the god; our way
Beset by demons four hundred!

The communication between Hiiaka and her sisters had, on
their part, been carried on mostly by means of gesture and sign-
language. But on this return of Hiiaka the whole family of
brothers and sisters were so moved at the thought of the danger to Hiiaka that they spoke out at last and frankly advised
Hiiaka to go before Pele and demand of her the gift of spiritual
power, *mana,* that she might be able to meet her enemies on

(a) The wavering of indecision.

equal terms at least, so that she need not feel powerless in their presence. But nothing came of this move at the time, for at this moment out came Pele from her cave, and, seeing Hiiaka standing with the others, she addressed her sharply and said: "What! You still here? Why are you not on the way to fetch our man?"

Face to face with Pele, Hiiaka's courage oozed away and she promised to make another start in the morning. When on this new start she had come near the top of the ascent, she turned about and sang:

> Punohunohu i ka lani
> Ka uahi o ka lua;
> He la'i ilalo o Kilauea;
> Maniania 'luna o Wahine-kapu.
> I kapu, la, i ke aha ka leo, e?

TRANSLATION

> The pit-smoke blankets the heavens;
> Clear is the air in Kilauea,
> Tranquil Wahine-kapu's plain—
> The Woman, why silent her voice?

Hiiaka now made common cause with the group of sisters and relatives who were bent on securing for her justice and fair treatment. Among them, taking council together, sat Ka-moho-alii, Kane-milo-hai, Kapo and Pohakau(a). By this action Hiiaka took a new attitude: while not coming out in open defiance to her sister, she virtually declared her determination no longer to be domineered over by Pele.

In the council that took place it was determined that Ka-moho-alii, who stood high in Pele's regards and whose authority was second only to hers, was the proper one to approach Pele in the matter of conferring upon Hiiaka the necessary mana. When, therefore, Pele put to Hiiaka the question why she had returned, why she was not on her journey, Ka-moho-alii spoke up and said, "It is because of fear she has returned. She sees danger by the way. You have not given her the mana to protect her from the

---

(a) This Pohakau was the friend, previously mentioned, who had brought to Pele the faithful dog that lay fasting and mourning at Lohiau's grave. Pohakau remained at Pele's court; the dog Pele hid away in her own secret place.

dragons and monsters that infest the road. *O Mo'o-lau ke ala, e:* The way is beset by dragons four hundred."

"Ah, that is the trouble?" said Pele. Then she called upon the Sun, the Moon, the Stars, Wind, Rain, Thunder, Lightning —all the heavenly powers—to aid and safeguard Hiiaka and she authorized her to exercise the powers of these heavenly beings. The gods, thereupon, ratified this act of Pele; and at last the way was made clear for Hiiaka's departure.

CHAPTER VII

HIIAKA STARTS ON HER JOURNEY

The refusal of her sisters to undertake the mission to fetch Lohiau had angered Hiiaka. Her intrepid fealty to Pele, their oldest sister and their alii, laughed to scorn the perils of the journey. She could not and, for a time, would not bring herself to understand their prudential attitude. Pele was their alii, and it was rank disloyalty in them to shirk any danger or to decline any command Pele might think fit to impose. In judging the conduct of her sisters, it did not at first enter the head of Hiiaka that motives of sound worldly prudence justified them in declining for themselves an errand full of danger, or in putting obstacles in the way of her going on the same errand: she saw in it only a failure to rise to the level of her own loyalty.

The situation, then, was heavily charged with estrangement, and when the woman in Hiiaka could not refrain from one more farewell, the color and tone of voice and song had in them the snap of electricity:

> Ke ku nei au e hele, a noho oe;
> A noho ana na Wahine o Lu-lu'u
> E ka pae(*a*) moku lehua
> I uka o Ka-li'u, la.
> Li'uli'u wale ka hele ana
> O ka huaka'i moe ipo.
> Aloha mai ka ipo,
> O Lohiau ipo, e-e!

(*a*) One critic says it should be *po'e*.

Here stand I begirt for travel;
You must tarry at home, and these........
These....women....who sit downcast.
Oh, care for my parks of lehua—
How they bloom in upland Ka-li'u!
Long is the way and many the day
Before you shall come to the bed of love,
But, hark! the call of the lover,
The voice of the lover, Lohiau!

At the utterance of this name Pele brightened and called to Hiiaka, "Yes, that is the name of our man. I purposely kept it back until you should have reached the water-shed (*kaupaku* (a) *o ka hale o kaua*, literally the ridgepole) of our house, intending then to reveal it to you; but you have divined the man's name. Go on your journey. Nothing shall avail to block your road. Yours is the power of woman; the power of man is nothing to that."

On reaching the plateau of Wahine-kapu Hiiaka received a spiritual message telling her that Lohiau — the object of her errand—was dead. She at once turned towards Pele and commemorated the fact in song:

I Akani-hia,
I Akani-kolea,
I Pu'u-wa'a-hia,
I Pu'u-manawa-le'a,
I Pu'u-aloha, la:
He mea e ke aloha o ke kane, e.
Ke haale iho nei au e hanini, e;
E uwé au, e!

Let us sound it aloud—
Far as the plover's flight;
With full breath shout it,
And with a full heart,
Big with affection.

(a) *Kaupaku o ka hale o kaua.* A hidden reference to sexual intercourse.

Ah, wondrous the love for a man!
The feelings that strive,
As these tears, to rush out—
I can not repress them!

Pele did not know this name-song of Lohiau until she heard it recited by Hiiaka. This it was that led Hiiaka to come back within easy hearing distance:

Ke uwá ia mai la e ka ua;
Ke kahe ia mai la e ka wai:
Na lehua i Wai-a'ama, la, lilo,
Lilo a'u opala lehua
I kai o Pi'i-honua, la;
Mai Po'i-honua no a Pi'i-lani.

TRANSLATION

It sobs in the rain;
It moans in the rushing tide.
Gone is my grove of lehuas—
My rubbish grove, that stood
By the pilfering waters—flown,
He has flown, like its smoke, to heaven.
'Tis there I must seek him!

"How absurd of you," said Pele; "you were not sent on an expedition to heaven, but to bring a man who is here on earth. If you fly up to heaven, you will pass him by and leave him here below."

Hiiaka and her faithful companion—Pau-o-pala'e—had gotten well away from the vast pit of Kilauea, with its fringe of steam-cracks and fumaroles that radiate from it like the stays of a spider-web, and they were nearing the borders of Pana-ewa, when Hiiaka's quick ear caught the sound of a squealing pig. Her ready intuition furnished the right interpretation to this seemingly insignificant occurrence:

A loko au o Pana-ewa,
Halawai me ka pua'a
A Wahine-oma'o,
Me ku'u maka lehua i uka,

Me ka Malu-ko'i (*b*) i ka nahele,
E uwé ana i ka laau.
Alalá ka pua'a a ka wahine—
He pua'a kanaenae,
He kanaenae mohai ola—
E ola ia Pele,
I ka Wahine o ka Lua, e-e!

TRANSLATION

In the heart of Pana-ewa—
Lehuas were heavy with bud,
The dim aisles solemn with shadow —
I met with a suckling pig,
The pet of Wahine-oma'o,
A wailing voice in the wilderness:
'Twas the creature wail of the thing,
Foredoomed as an offering, this
Wailing thing was a sacrifice,
An appeal to Pele for life,
To the Woman who dwells in the Pit.

At this moment a young woman of attractive person appeared on the scene and, prostrating herself to the earth, said, "O, Pele, behold my offering, which I bring to thee in fulfillment of the pledge made by my parents, that I should first seek thee, O Pele, before I come to my marriage bed. Accept this suckling which I offer to thee, O Pele."

"I am not the one you are seeking: I am not Pele," said Hiiaka. "Pele is over yonder in the Pit."

The woman was persistent and begged that Hiiaka would not despise her offering. After undeceiving her, Hiiaka carefully instructed her, lest she make some fatal mistake in her approach to the jealous goddess: "When you come to the Pit you must be careful in your approach to Pele. The least departure from the etiquette she demands would be the cause of your death. Do not imagine that the fine large woman sitting at the door is Pele, nor that any one of the women seated within is she. You must pay no attention to these. Look for the figure of a wrinkled old woman lying bundled up on the hearth: that is Pele: make the offering to no one else but to her."

(*b*) *Malu-ko'i*, dark and gloomy.

"Alas for me," said Wahine-oma'o. "You will be gone a long way from this place by the time I shall return to seek you. I shall not be able to find you."

"You will find us here," replied Hiiaka assuringly.

Hiiaka used her power to bring the woman at once to her destination. Following the instructions given her, Wahine-oma'o was quickly transported into the presence of Pele and, having made her offering in due form, was about to retire, when Pele called her back and said, "Did you not meet some women going from here as you came this way?"

"I met some women," she answered.

"Make haste and come up with them," said Pele. "The younger woman is very dear to me. Attach yourself to her as a friend."

"That I will do," said Wahine-oma'o. Then, moved by an impulse that came to her (the work, it is said, of Hiiaka), she said to Pele, "I had imagined you to be a beautiful woman, Pele. But, lo, you are old and wrinkled; and your eyes are red and watery." Thus saying, Wahine'oma'o took her departure and almost immediately found herself again with Hiiaka.

"You have made quick time," Hiiaka said. "How did you get on?"

"I followed your instructions and presented my offering to the woman who was lying on the hearth. She asked me if I had met you, and when I said yes, she told me to look after you as a friend."

"Is that all?"

"She also told me to watch you, to observe how you behaved towards the man—whether you kissed him or had any dalliance with him."

"And did you say anything to Pele?"

"U-m, I bantered her about her looks; told her she was a very ill-favored woman, while the women attending her were very handsome."

Hiiaka laughed at this naive account.

Night shut down upon them at Kuolo, a place just on the border of Pana-ewa. Paú-o-pala'e proposed that they should seek a resting place for the night with the people of the hamlet. Hiiaka would not hear to it: "Travelers should sleep in the open, in the road; in that way they can rise and resume their journey with no delay." (*O ka po'e hele he pono ia lakou e moe i ke alanui, i ala no a hele no.*)

CHAPTER VIII

THE GIRL PA-PULEHU—THE FEAST

In the morning while it was still dark, they roused and started afresh. Their way led through lehua groves of the most luxuriant growth, the bloom of which crimsons the landscape to this day, exuding a honey that is most attractive to the birds of heaven. The cool still air wafted to their ears the hum of voices which was soon explained when they came upon a bevy of girls who were busily plucking the bright flowers to string into wreaths and garlands, in anticipation of some entertainment. This rural scene made an appeal to the poet in Hiiaka which she could not resist:

> A Wai-akea, i ka Hilo-hana-kahi,
> Ala i ka wa po iki,
> I ka lehua lei o Hilo, o Hi-lo;
> E pauku ana no ka hala me ka lehua.
> Maikai Hilo, o Hilo-hana-kahi!

TRANSLATION

> At Wai-akea, in Hilo—
> The Hilo of Hana-kahi—
> They rise in the early morning
> To weave fresh wreaths of lehua,
> Inbeading its bloom with hala—
> Gay Hilo of Hana-kahi!

At sight of Hiiaka's party, the lively flower-girls made a rush, as if to capture and appropriate their friendly acquaintance for individual possession. The most vivacious and forward of the whole party was Pa-pulehu, their leader, a buxom young woman, of good family, who at once took possession of Hiiaka for herself, crowned and bedecked her with wreaths and garlands, with many expressions of enthusiastic admiration: "This is *my* friend! —What a beauty!—How the scarlet lehua becomes her!—Just look, girls!—And now you are to come and be my guest.—The feast is set for this very day.—But you are all welcome."

The unrestrained gush of the young woman's rattling talk was quite in contrast to the selected words of Hiiaka.

Now Pa-pulehu was of a large and important family, embracing numerous friends and relations, and, having ample means, her hospitalities were unstinted. The report spread quickly, "Pa-pulehu has a distinguished guest come to visit her. There is to be a feast this afternoon. All are invited."

The tables were spread with a great variety of fish, meats, fruits and vegetables. The parents and guardians of the girl, nevertheless, came to her and inquired, "What is there that this young woman, your friend, would specially like to eat?" Paú-o-pala'e took it upon her to answer, that the one thing that would be most acceptable to Hiiaka would be a dish of luau. Thereupon a large quantity of young and delicate taro leaves were prepared for the table.

When they were gathered at the tables, Hiiaka sitting in the place of honor, Paú-o-pala'e, at her request, bade all the people incline their heads and close their eyes. Then Hiiaka called upon her allies, the Sun, the Moon, the Stars, the elements and all the gods to come to the feast and partake; and when the prayer was ended and they opened their eyes—lo, the tables spread for Hiiaka were empty! Hiiaka had not been seen to take into her hands any of the food that was spread before her. It had vanished away as a drop of water evaporates in the heat of the sun.

The feast being concluded, Hiiaka rose, bade good bye to the people and resumed her journey, taking with her Pa-pulehu.

This girl Pa-pulehu was of genuine flesh and blood, with no blend of divine ichor in her veins, such as enriched the blood of Hiiaka; nor had she, like Wahine-oma'o and Paú-o-pala'e, been strengthened and made more resistant to spiritual and physical foes—a privilege granted to those who had enjoyed a close approach to Pele as attendants and worshippers. This weakness in her nature had its influence in determining the fate to which her history now quickly leads.

Their journey still lay through Puna. They were at Kalalau, not far from Haena (at the place where, centuries afterwards, Kamehameha was struck with that well-nigh fatal blow by an outraged fisherman). Some fishermen were hauling in their nets full of fish. The sight was too much for Pa-pulehu. "I hunger for fish," she xeclaimed. "These fish belong to my father. Oh, if I only were at home! how I would eat until I was satisfied!"

Hiiaka thought it best to indulge the appetite of this novice in her service. From a little knoll overlooking the ocean, she descried the canoe of a fisherman named Pahulu floating in the offing, but already well stocked with fish. Hiiaka used her power and drove away the school of fish that would have come to his net. The man himself was so intent on his work that he had no eyes for what was passing on shore; but his assistant exclaimed, "Look at the beautiful woman standing on the shore and watching us!"

"I must keep my eyes on my nets," the fisherman replied.

Thereupon Hiiaka attracted his attention with a song:

> Nani ku a ka Hilo pali-ku!
> O ka au-hula ana o Ka-lalau,
> O ka au alana loa i kai, e!
> Ho mai he i'a, na ka pehu o uka, ea.

TRANSLATION

> A standing wonder, Hilo cliffs!
> How daring this Ka-lalau swimming,
> Far out to sea on a floating plank!
> Pray grant us, O man, of your fish—
> Fish for the herb-swollen rustic.

This brought the two fishermen ashore who thereupon willingly parted with some of their fish to Hiiaka, coupling the gift, however, with a proposition insulting to the honor of the two women. The fishermen, imagining they had the two women under their power, were soon after seen lying in the open embracing two figures of stone which they, in their insane infatuation, fancied were the two women, thus exposing themselves to the jeers and derision of their fellows.

Pa-pulehu cooked and ate the fish, but her manner of eating was lacking in due punctilio, in that she did not dispose properly of the unconsumed parts—the tails, fins, bones and scales—of the fish. She should have burned or buried them; instead she left them lying about in a slovenly way. This neglect was highly offensive to Pele and caused her to withdraw from Pa-pulehu the protection she otherwise would have given her.

CHAPTER IX

HIIAKA CHOOSES THE ROUTE THROUGH PANA-EWA

Two routes offered themselves for Hiiaka's choice, a makai road, circuitous but safe, the one ordinarily pursued by travelers; the other direct but bristling with danger, because it traversed the territory of the redoubtable witch-mo'o, Pana-ewa. Hiiaka had deigned to appeal to the girl Pa-pulehu, she being a kamaaina (*a*), as if for information. When Hiiaka announced her determination to take the short road, the one of danger that struck through the heart of Pana-ewa, Pa-pulehu drew back in dismay and expostulated: "That is not a fit road for us, or for any but a band of warriors. If we go that way we shall be killed." She broke forth with lamentations, bewailing her coming fate and the desolation that was about to visit her family.

As they advanced Wahine-oma'o descried a gray scare-crow object motionless in the road ahead of them. She thought it to be the blasted stump of a kukui tree. Hiiaka recognized its true character, the witch-form taken as a disguise by a mo'o. It was a scout sent out by Pana-ewa; in real character a hag, but slimed with a gray excrement to give it closer resemblance to a mouldering tree-stump. The deceiving art of magic did not avail against Hiiaka. She rushed forward to give the death stroke to the foul thing, which at once groveled in the dirt in its true form.

Night overtook them in a dense forest. While the others lay and slept, Hiiaka reconnoitered the situation. The repose of the wilderness was unbroken save for the restless flitting of a solitary bird that peered at Hiiaka obtrusively. It was a spy in the employ of Pana-ewa and its actions roused the lively suspicions of Hiiaka, eliciting from her an appropriate incantation:

> Ka wai mukiki ale lehua a ka manu,
> Ka awa ili lena i ka uka o Ka-li'u,
> Ka manu aha'i lau awa o Puna:
> Aia i ka laau ka awa o Puna.
> Mapu mai kona aloha ia'u—
> Hoolaau mai ana ia'u e moe,
> E moe no au, e-e!

(*a*) *Kamaaina,* a resident, one acquainted with the land.

O honey-dew sipped by the bird,
Distilled from the fragrant lehua;
O yellow-barked awa that twines
In the upper lands of Ka-li'u;
O bird that brews from this leafage
Puna's bitter-sweet awa draught;—
Puna's potentest awa grows
Aloft in the crotch of the trees.
It wafts the seduction to sleep,
That I lock my senses in sleep!

It was a subtle temptation that suggested the awa cup as a relief for her troubles. Hiiaka had need that all her faculties should give her their best service. For her to have slept at this time would have been fatal. Her song well expressed it:

E nihi ka hele i ka uka o Puna;
Mai ako i ka pua,
O lilo i ke ala o ka hewahewa.
Ua huná ia ke kino i ka pohaku,
O ka pua na'e ke ahu nei i ke alanui—
Alanui hele o ka unu kupukupu, e-e;—
Ka ulí-a!
A kaunu no anei oe o ke aloha la?
Hele a'e a komo i ka hale o Pele;
Ua huahua'i i Kahiki; lapa uila,
Pele e, hua'i'na ho'i!

Heed well your way in upland Puna;
Pluck never a single flower;
Lest you stray from the path.
The shape lies hid neath a stone,
The path is one carpet of flowers,
The blocks of stumbling overgrown.
Quick follows the downfall!
Is there a compact between us of love?
Fly, voice, assail the ear of Pele!
Erupt, Kahiki, with lightning flash!
Now, Pele, burst forth in thy might!

Pana-ewa entrusted the work of reconnoisance and scouting for information to two of his creatures named Ke-anini and Ihi-kalo, while he lay down and slept. Having done their work, the two scouts waked the drowsy monster in the middle of the night with the information that four human beings, women, had entered his domain and were coming towards him. "Where are they?" he asked.

"Out in this direction (pointing), and they are moving this way."

"Well, this day of fasting has gone by. What a pity, however, that the poi in my calabash has turned sour, but the taro is sweet. Eye-balls! what juicy, delicious morsels! The day of privation turns out to be a day of feasting." Thus muttered the cannibal monster, gloating like Polyphemus·in his cave at the prospect of a feast.

Hiiaka kept her own courage at the fine point of seeming in-difference, she also inspired her companions with the same feel-ing by the calm confidence displayed in her singing:

> Pau ke aho i ke kahawai lau o Hilo:
> He lau ka pu'ŭ, he mano ka iho'na;
> He mano na kahawai o Kula'i-po;
> He wai Honoli'i, he pali o Kama-e'e,
> He pali no Koolau ka Hilo-pali-ku;
> He pali Wailuku, he one ke hele ia;
> He one e ke'ehia la i Wai-olama.
> He aka ka wi a ka wai i Pana-ewa—
> O Pana-ewa nui, moku-lehua,
> Ohi'a kupu hao'eo'e i ka ua,
> Lehua ula i ka wi' ia e ka manu.
> A ua po, e, po Puna, po Hilo
> I ka uahi o ku'u aina.

By Pana-ewa.—

> "Ola ia kini! ke a mai la ke ahi, e-e!"

TRANSLATION

> One's strength is exhausted, climbing, climbing
> The countless valleys and ridges of Hilo,—
> The streams without number of Ku-la'i-po,
> The mighty water of Hono-li'i,
> The precipice walls of Kama-e'e,
> And the pali of Ko'olau:

Na Pali coast, Kaua'i.

Such a land is Hilo-pali-ku.
The banks of Wailuku are walls;
The road to its crossing but sand;
Sandy the way at Wai-o-lama.
How cheery the purl of these waters!—
Great Pana-ewa — her parks of lehua,
Scraggy in growth yet scarlet a-top,
Its nectar wrung out by the birds!
Black night covers Puna and Hilo,
A pall from the smoke of my home land!
(By Pana-ewa).
"Here's food for me and mine!
Behold the blaze of the ovens!"

(The last two lines are said to be the utterance of Pena-ewa who feigned
to regard the fires as those of his own people, who, in anticipation of an
easy victory, had made ready their ovens to receive the bodies of Hiiaka
and her party.)

Hiiaka bravely answered Pana-ewa:

O Pana-ewa, ohi'a loloa,
Ohi'a uliuli i ka uä,
I moku pewa ia
E ka laau o kepakepa,
A ka uka i Haili la.
Ilihia, ilihia i ka leo —
He leo wale no, e!

TRANSLATION

Pana-ewa, a tall ohi'a,
The fruit red-ripe in the rain,
Is vilely slashed with the stick
Of the mountaineer.
It stands in upland Haili:
Terriffic — the voice is terriffic;
Yet it's merely a voice!

"The voice was threatening only because my servants reported
that some people were trespassing. That set my tongue agoing
about poi - - - and - taro. - - - After all it's a question of
strength. Your valor it is that must win for you a passage
through this land of mine."
This was Pana-ewa's ultimatum.

Hiiaka accepted the defiance of Pana-ewa by chanting a solemn kahoahoa, which was at once a confident prediction of victory and an appeal to the gods:

Kua loloa Keäau i ka nahele hala;
Kua huluhulu Pana-ewa i ka laau:
Inoino ka maha, ka ohi'a o La'a, e;
Ku kepakepa ka maha o ka laau,
U-á po'ohina i ka wela a ke Akua;
U-a-uahi Puna o ka oloka'a pohaku ia,
I ka huná pa'a ia e ka Wahine.
Nanahu ahi ka ka papa o Oluea;
Momoku ahi Puna, hala i Apua;
Ulu-á ka nahele me ka laau:
Ka ke kahiko ia o Papa-lau-ahi.
Ele-i(*a*) kahiko, e Ku-lili-kaua;
Ka ia,(*b*) hea (*c*) hala o Ka-li'u;
E ne (*d*) ka La, ka malama;
Onakaka ka piko (*e*) o Hilo i ke one,
I hu-lá (*f*) ia aku la e, hulihia i kai.
Ua wawahia, ua nahahá,
Ua he-helelei ka papa i Pua-le'i, e!

TRANSLATION

Long is the reach of Keäau's palms;
Bristly-backed Pana-ewa's woodlands;
Spoiled are the restful groves of La'a;
Ragged and patchy the tree-clumps —
Gray their heads from the ravage of fire.
A blanket of smoke covers Puna —
All paved with the dump from Her stone-yard.
The Goddess' fire bites Olu-eä —
One cinder-heap clean to Apua;

(*a*) *Ele-i.* One Hawaiian says this rare word means blue-black, shiny black (J. W. P.); another says it means rich, choice, select (T. J. P.)

(*b*) *Ka,* to remove, clean up entirely, as in bailing a canoe.

(*c*) *Hea,* destroyed, flattened out.

(*d*) *Ne,* an elided poetical form of nele, meaning gone, blotted out.

(*e*) *Piko,* the navel. The belly, or piko, of a fish was the choicest part. "I ka piko no oe, lihaliha." Eat of the belly and you shall be satiated. (Old saying.)

(*f*) *Hu-la.* (Notice the accent to distinguish it from hula.) To dig up, as a stone out of the ground.

Food for Her oven are wildwood and brush —
The finish that to Lau-ahi's glory:
Her robe now is changed to jetty black,
At the onset of Ku-lili-kaua,
Ka-liu's palms plucked root and branch.
The Sun and the Moon are blotted out;
Hilo is shaken to its foundation,
Its lands upheaved, despoiled to the sea,
Shattered, fissured, powdered, reduced;
Its plain is ashes and dust!

The battle that ensued when Panaewa sent to the attack his nondescript pack of mo'o, dragonlike anthropoids, the spawn of witchcraft, inflamed with the spite of demons, was hideous and uncanny. Tooth and claw ran amuck. Flesh was torn, limbs rent apart, blood ran like water. If it had been only a battle with enemies in the open Hiiaka would have made short work of the job. Her foes lay ambushed in every wood and brake and assumed every imaginable disguise. A withered bush, a bunch of grass, a moss-grown stone, any, the most innocent object in nature, might prove to be an assailant ready to spit venom or tear with hook and talon. Hiiaka had need of every grain of wit and every spark of courage in her nature. Nothing could withstand her onset and the billows of attack against her person were broken as by a solid rock. Some described her as wielding a flaming battle-ax and hurling missiles of burning sulphur. They might well be deceived. The quickness of her every motion was a counterfeit of the riving blade or blazing fire-ball. Some assert that, in her frenzy, she tore with her teeth and even devoured the reeking flesh until her stomach rose in rebellion. Such a notion seems incompatible with the violence of her disgust for the reptilian blood that besmeared her from sole to crown.

Paú-o-pala'e, using her magical paú as a besom of destruction, was transformed into a veritable Bellona; and Wahine-oma'o displayed the courage of an amazon. These both escaped serious injury. The unhappy fate of Pa-pulehu realized that girl's premonition. She fell into the hands of the enemy and, as if to fulfill the prediction of Pele, became "food for the gods of Pana-ewa."

As Hiiaka glanced heavenward, she saw the zenith filled with cloud-forms—Kane, Kanaloa, Ka-moho alii, Poha-kau and others, encouraging her with their looks.   The sight, while it cheered, wrung from her a fervent prayer:

Kela pae opua i ka lani, e,
Ke ka'i a'e la mauka o Poha-kau.
He kaukau, aloha keia ia oe,
Ia oe no, e-e-e!

Yon group of god-forms, that float
And sail with the clouds heaven-high,
Mustered and led by Poha-kau;
This prayer is a love-call to you!.

"Our sister is in trouble," said Ka-moho-alii, "let us go to her assistance!"   Such was the call of Ka-moho-alii when he saw his little friend and quondam protegé Hiiaka in trouble, and theirs were the god-forms that sailed through the sky to reenforce her.

CHAPTER X

HIIAKA'S BATTLE WITH PANAEWA

The bird-spies sent out by Pana-ewa brought back contradictory reports.   The first pair reported that Hiiaka was being worsted.   Soon after another pair, garbling the facts, said "Our people are lying down, but they are still alert and keep their eyes open.   As for Hiiaka, she has fallen into a deep sleep."

The situation was far from satisfactory and Pana-ewa despatched another pair of birds to reconnoitre and report.   It was not yet morning and the night was dark; and they accordingly took the form of kukui(a) trees, thinking thus to illuminate the scene of operations.   The intelligence they brought was confounding: "Our people," they said, "are all dead, save those who have the form of kukui trees·   Hiiaka lies quietly sleeping in the road."

This account, though strictly in accord with the facts, was so disconcerting to Pana-ewa that he burst forth in a rage, "Slaves, liars! you're deceiving me.   I'll wring your necks!" and he reached out to execute his threat.   The birds eluded him and found safety in flight.

_____

(a)   *Kukui,* the tree whose nuts furnished torches.

Pana-ewa' now saw that it was necessary to take the field in person at the head of his regular forces, composed of the Namú and Nawá. The disguise he chose for himself was that of an ohia-lehua tree. No sooner had he taken that form than he found himself unable to move hand or foot. A parasitic network of i-e-i-e embraced his body and a multitude of aërial roots anchored him to the spot. It was the craft of the sleeping girl that had done this. He had to content himself with the unwarlike guise of the kukui tree.

While Hiiaka slept, her faithful servitor Paú-o-pala'e kept open eye and detective ear to what was going on in the star-lit forest about them At the first glimmering of dawn her keen sense felt rather than heard a murmurous rustle that broke the stillness and a movement, as if the forest itself were advancing and closing in upon them. This oncoming of the enemy was in such contrast to the onset of the yelping pack on the previous day as to be most impressive. The sound that touched her keen sense was not the joyous twitter and stir of nature preparing to greet a new day; it was rather the distant mutter of the storm, soon to be heard as the growl of the tempest, or the roar and snarl of an enraged menagerie of wild beasts.

The woman felt her responsibility and, with the double intent of summoning to their aid the friendly gods and of waking Hiiaka, she lifted a solemn prayer:

> Kuli'a, e Uli,[1] ka pule kala ma ola;
> Kuli'a imua, i ke kahuna;[2]
> Kuli'a i ke Alohi-lani.[3]
> E úi aku ana au
> I kupua oluna nei, e?
> Owai kupua oluna nei, e?
> O Ilio-uli[4] o ka lani;

---

(1) *Uli,* an elder sister of Pele, a character much appealed to by sorcerers.

(2) *Kahuna,* in this case probably Hiiaka.

(3) *Alohi-lani,* literally, the brightness of heaven; a term applied to the residence or heavenly court of both Uli and Kapo. In verses 36 and 37 it is distinctly mentioned as the abode of Kapo-ula-kina'u: "E ho'i, e komo i kou hale, O Ke-alohi-lani."

(4) *Ilio-uli,* literally, a dog of dark blue-black color. The primitive Aryans, according to Max Muller, poetically applied the term "sheep" to the fleecy white clouds that float in the sky. The Hawaiian poet, in the lack of a nobler animal, spoke of the clouds as *ilio,* dogs. With this homely term, however, he coupled—by way of distinction—some ennobling adjective.

O Ilio-ehu,[5] o Ilio-mea,[6] o ka lani;
O Ku-ke-ao-iki,[7] o Ku-ke-ao-poko,[8]
O Ku-ke-ao-loa[9] o ka lani;
O Ku-ke-ao-awihiwihi[10] ula o ka lani;
Ua ka ua, kahi wai, a na hoalii;[11]
O nei ka pali ma Ko-wawá;[12]
O Kupina'e,[13] o Ku-wawá;
O Ku-haili-moe;[14]
O Ha'iha'i-lau-ahea;[15]
O Mau-a-ke-alii-hea;[16]
Kánaka[17] loloa o ka mauna —
O Ku-pulupulu[18] i ka nahele,
O na Akua mai ka wao kele;
O Kuli-pe'e-nui[19] ai ahua;
O Kiké-alana;[20]
O Ka-uahi-noe-lehua;
O ke Kahuna i ka puoko[21] o ke ahi;

---

(5)   *Ilio-ehu,* literally, a white dog.

(6)   *Ilio-mea,* literally, a dog—cloud—of a warm pinkish hue.

(7)   *Ku-ke-ao-iki, Ao-iki,* small clouds that stand ranged about the horizon.

(9)   *Ao-loa,* long clouds—stratus?—such as are seen along the horizon.

(10) *Ao-awihiwihi-ula,* a cloud-pile having a pinkish, or ruddy, tint.

(11) *Hoalii,* the relatives of Hiiaka.

(12) *Ko-wawa,* a notched *pali* that formed part of the wall enclosing the caldera of Kilauea—on its Kau side.

(13) *Kupina'e,* echo, here personified and endowed with the attributes of a superhuman being.

(14) *Ku-haili-moe,* one of the forms, or characters, of god Ku, representing him as a smoother and beautifier of the landscape.

(15) *Ha'iha'i-lau-ahea,* a goddess who had to do with the flame of fire. Her share in the care of a fire, or, perhaps, of Pele's peculiar fire, seems to have been confined to the base of the flame.

(16) *Mau-a-ke-alii-hea,* a being who had special charge of the flame-tip.

(17) *Kanaka loloa o ka mauna,* this included Ku-pulupulu and his fellows.

(18) *Ku-pulupulu* ,described as a hairy being, the chief god of canoe-makers, who had his residence in the wildwoods.

(19) *Kuli-pe'e-nui.* This much-used term is the embodiment in a word of the wild, lumbering, progress of a lava-flow, or lava-tongue. Translating the figure into words, my imagination pictures a huge, shapeless monster, hideous as Caliban drunk, wallowing, sprawling, stumbling along on swollen disjointed knees—a picture of uncouth desolation.

(20) *Kike-alana,* the formulation in a word of the rending and crashing sounds—rock smiting rock—made by a lava-flow.

(21) *Kahuna i ka, puoko o ke ahi.* The word Kahuna is used here where the word akua or kupua would seem to have served the purpose of the meaning, which, as I take it, is the spirit, or genius, of flame.

O I'imi,[22] o Lalama.[23]
Ku'i ke ahi, ka hekili;
Nei ke ola'i;
Olapa ka uila.
Lohe o Kane-hekili;[24]
Ikiiki ka maláma ia Ka-ulua.[25]
Elua wahine i hele i ka hikina a ka La —
O Kumu-kahi,[26] laua o Ha'eha'e:[27]
Ha'eha'e ka moe
O Kapo-ula-kina'u,[28] he alii;
E ho'i, e komo i kou hale,
O Ke-alohi-lani;
E auau i kou ki'owai kapu,
O Ponaha-ke-one;
E inu i kou puawa hiwa,
Awa papa(a) a ke Akua,
I kanaenae no Moe-ha-úna-iki,[29] e;
Hele a'e a komo
I ka hale o Pele.
Ua huahua'i Kahiki, lapa uwila:
Pele e, hua'i'na ho'i!
Hua'i'na a'e ana
Ka mana o ko'u Akua iwaho la, e!
O kukulu ka pahu[30] kapu a ka leo;

----

(22) *I'imi*, derived seemingly from *imi*, to seek.

(23) *Lalama*, derived seemingly from *lala*, a branch; or possibly, from *lama*, a flambeau.

(24) *Kane-hekili*. Thunder is always spoken of as under the control of god Kane.

(25) *Ka-ulua*, the name of one of the months in the cool season of the year; one can not say positively which month is intended, for the reason that the nomenclature varied greatly in the different islands, and varied even on the same island.

(26) *Kumu-kahi*, the name of a hill in Puna on the easternmost cape of Hawaii; also the name of a monolith once set up there; in this connection the name of the female kupua who acted as keeper of the Sun's eastern gate. This name is almost always coupled with that of . . .

(27) *Ha'eha'e*, of whom the same account can be given as above.

(28) *Kapo-ula-Kina'u*, one of the family. The epithet *ula-kina'u* is used in allusion to the fact that her attire, red in color, is picked out with black spots. The name Kapo alone is the one by which she is usually known.

(a) The awa papa had a small root, but it was of superior quality.

(29) *Moe-ha-una-iki*, literally, the sleep with a gentle snore—such sleep as follows the use of awa. The poet personifies this sleep. To such lengths does the Hawaiian poetic imagination go.

(30) *Pahu kapu a ka leo*. One—who ought to know—tells me this means the ear; as if the ear were the drum on which the voice played.

Ho'okikí(31) kanawai:
He kua(32) á kanawai;
He kai oki'a(33) kanawai;
He ala muku(34) no Kane me Kanaloa;
He ki(35) ho'iho'i kanawai,
No Pele, no ko'u Akua la, e!

TRANSLATION

Stand in the breach, O Uli;
Give heed to this plea for life;
To the front at the call of thy priest;
Come in the splendor of heaven!
I entreat these powers on high.
And who are these beings of might?
Ye somber Clouds that rampart the sky;
Ye warm Clouds and ye that gleam ruddy;
Ye Clouds that guard heaven's border;
Ye Clouds that mottle the heavenly vault;
Ye Clouds that embank the horizon;
Ye cloud-piles aglow in the sunlight.
Descend, O Rain; O Water, pour—
Torrential rush of the princes!
Rent be the wall of the crater;
Let its groans reëcho and fly!
Come, Ku who fashions the landscape;
She who crushes the leaves of aheä;
Goddess who guards the outer flame-tip;
Ye tall ones who dwell in the forest;
Ku, the hirsute god of the wilds;
With his fellows who carve the canoe;

---

(31) *Ho'okiki kanawai*, to enforce, to carry out the law.

(32) *He kua a kanawai.* It was said of Pele that her back was hot like fire, and that a bundle of taro leaves laid thereon was cooked and turned into luau. It was an offense punishable by death for any one to stand at her back or to approach her by that way.

(33) *He kai oki'a kanawai*, literally, an ocean that separates. Exclusiveness, to live apart, was the rule of Pele's life. This principle is enforced with further illustration in the next line:—

(34) *He ala muku no Kane me Kanaloa.* Even to the great gods Kane and Kanaloa the path of approach to Pele was cut off by the edict, thus far shalt thou come and no further.

(35) *He ki ho'iho'i kanawai.* The *ki* is said, to my surprise, to be the thong with which a door was made fast, *ho'iho'i*, in the olden times of Hawaii. I cannot but look upon this statement with some suspicion.

Come bent-kneed terrace-consumer,
With crash and groan of lava-plate;
And reeking smoke that glooms the forest.
Come, Lord of the ruddy flame;
Fire-tongues that search and spread;
Fire-shafts that smite and crash.
Let earthquake groan and lightning flash.
Kane the god of lightning shall hear
And warm this frigid month Ulua·
Two women go to the Sun's east gate
To rouse goddess Kapo from sleep —
She of the black-spotted red robe.
O Kapo, reënter your Sun-temple
And bathe in your sacred water-pool —
Round as a gourd, scooped in the sand;
Drink from your black polished awa cup
Dark awa that's offered to the gods,
To placate the goddess of gentle snore;
Then enter the house of Pele.
Pele once burst forth at Kahiki;
Once again, O Pele, break forth;
Display thy power, my God, to the world;
Let thy voice sound out like a drum;
Reütter the law of thy burning back;
That thy dwelling is sacred, apart;
That Kane and Loa have limits;
That fixed and firm are Pele's laws!
For Pele, great Pele, is my God!

The sisters, uncles, aunts and other kindred of Hiiaka heard this prayer of Paú-o-pala'e distinctly enough, and so did Pele; and when they saw that she appeared indifferent and made no move, they muttered among themselves. Then Ku-ili-kaua, a man of war and a leader in battle, spoke up and, addressing Ka-moho-alii, said "Why is it that she does not send warriors to the assistance of her sister? The girl has fought most bravely all day and is worn out; and there she lies fast asleep."

Ka-moho-alii thereupon bade Kilioe-i-ka-pua and Olu-wale-i-malo, two handsome lads who were very dear to Pele (*mau keiki punahele a Pele*)—her sons in fact—to go in to Pele and ask her sanction to their going to the aid of Hiiaka.

When these two boys came into Pele's presence they found

her poking the fire with a stick (*hoelo kapuahi*). With a fine show of confidence, they at once went and seated themselves in Pele's lap, one on her right thigh and one on her left. Pele's looks softened as she contemplated them, tears gathered in her eyes and she said, "What is the thought in the heart? Speak." (*Heaha ka hua i ka umauma? Ha'i'na.*)

"Your commands·" (*O ka leo,*(*a*) literally, the voice.)

At this Pele stood up and, leaving her own home-hearth, went over and took her station in the fire-pit of Hale-ma'u-ma'u. Then, pointing to the east, she said:

O ka leo o ke kanáka hookahi, mailuna mai;
Mailoko mai o ka leo o ka manu.(*b*)
O huli kai-nu'u(*c*) a Kane;
E wehe ka lani, hamama ka honua;
O wela Kahiki-ku me Kahiki-moe;
Ala mai o Ka-moho-alii
E moe ana iloko o ke ao polohiwa.
E Ku e, e ho'i ka amama(*d*) i ka lani;
E Ku e, e ho'i ke ola ia Hiiaka-i-ka-poli-o-Pele,
A ola loa no, a-a!

(*a*) *Leo,* the voice; articulate speech. *Leo o ka kanaka hookahi.* This one supreme man was Kane. The poet evidently had in mind the myth which is embodied in a certain *Kumu-lipo,* or song of creation: Kane, the supreme one, looking from heaven, saw Chaos, or the god of Chaos, *Kumu-lipo,* spread out below and he called to him to send his voice—*leo*—to the east, to the west, to the north and to the south. Kumo-lipo, thus roused from inaction, despatched the bird *Halulu,* who flew and carried the message to the east, to the west, to the north and to the south.

It was such a voice of utterance as this (*leo*) that the two boys who went in before Pele desired. These two messenger-boys, by the way, are, in another account, spoken of as birds.

The purpose of Kane in sending out this *leo* seems to have been to rouse into activity the earth-strata, *na papa honua.*.

(*b*) *Ka manu,* the bird Halulu, above mentioned.

(*c*) *Kai-nu'u a Kane.* This expression is an allusion to god Kane's surf-riding, which is often mentioned in Hawaiian mythology. *Huli* refers to the curling or bending over of the breaker's crest; *Nu'u* to the blanket of white and yeasty water that follows as the wake of the tumbling wave. The Hawaiians who are best informed in these matters have only vague ideas on the whole subject.

(*d*) *Amama,* a word frequently used at the end of a prayer in connection with the word *noa* (free), as in the expression *amama, ua noa.* The evident meaning is it (the tabu) is lifted, it is free. I conjecture that the word *amama* is derived from, or related to, the word *mama,* light, in the sense of levitation.

TRANSLATION

The voice from above of a man supreme
Flies east, flies west, in the cry of a bird:
Curl over, thou yeasty billow of Kane!
Be rent, O Heaven, and quake, O Earth!
Kahiki's pillars, flame ye and burn!
Ka-moho-alii doth wake and rise
From his couch on banks of purple cloud·
To heaven return with thy tabu, O Ku!
Salvation, O Ku, for Hi'iaka—
Hi'iaka the darling of Pele!
Immortal life to her!

At this the gods of war sprang into array, as if unleashed by
the words of Pele. At their head marched Ku-lili-ai-kaua, a
veteran who had followed Pele in her voyage from Kahiki.
With him, went Ke-ka-ko'i, a guide (*hookele*) well acquainted
with the forest trails. In the van strode three weird figures
(Ka-maiau, Ka-hinihini and Mápu) bearing conchs, to which
they ever and anon applied their lips and sent forth resounding
blasts. But even more thrilling and inspiring than the horns
of Triton was the vòice of these gods of war as they chanted
their war-song:

MELE KA'I KAUA

Hulihia ka mauna, wela i ke ahi ;
Wela mo'a-nopu ka uka o Kui-hanalei,(*a*)
I ke a pohaku Pu'u-lena(*b*) e lele mai iuka.
O Ke-ka-ko'i(*c*) ka hookele mai ka Lua ;
O Ka-maiau(*d*) kani pololei, kani le'ale'a ;
O ka Hinihini(*e*) kani kua mauna ;
O ka Mápu(*f*) leo nui, kani kóhakohá ;

(*a*) *Kui-hanalei,* a region in Puna, not far from the caldera of Kilauea,
said to be covered now with pahoehoe and aa.

(*b*) *Pu'u-lena,* a wind that blows in the region of the volcano.

(*c*) *Ke-ka-ko'i* (literally ,the ax-maker), the name of the guide and
path-finder to the company.

(*d*) *Ka-maiau,* their trumpeter who carried a conch.

(*e*) *Hinihini,* a poetical name for a land-shell, probably one of the genus
Achatinella, which was popularly believed to give a shrill piping note.

(*f*) *Mapu,* one of the trumpeters.

O hulihia i ka ale ula,(g) i ka ale lani,(h)
I ka pu-ko'a,(i) i ka a'aka(j)—
I ke ahu a Lono(k) e!
E lono anei, e hookuli?
E hookuli i ka uwalo, e!
Eü, e hele no e!
Hé-he-hé-e-e!

TRANSLATION

The Mount is convulsed, it belches flame;
Fire-scorched is upland Kui-hanalei—
A hail of stones shot out with sulphur-blasts.
Ka-ko'i guides the warrior-van;
The rousing peals of pearly conch
And thrilling notes of woodland shells
Stir every heart with tuneful cheer.
Heaven's blue is turmoiled with fire-clouds —
Boiling fountains of flame and cinder —
Such the form we give to our message:
Will he heed it, or turn a deaf ear?
Ah, you see, he scorns our entreaty.
Be valiant! now forward to battle!
Hé-he-hé-e-e!

Thus chanting their battle-mele (*mele ka'i kaua*), these gods
of an old-time mythology marched, or flew, with resolute purpose to their task of rescuing Hiiaka and her little band and of
ridding the land, at one and the same stroke, of their old in-
trenched foe, Pana-ewa. Heaven and earth stirred at their onset·
The visible signs of their array were manifest in columns of
seething fire-shot clouds that hovered like vultures over the
advancing army. Arrived at striking distance, they let loose
their lightning-bolts and sounded their thunder-gongs. Earth

(g) *Ale ula*, a cloud of steam and smoke, such as accompanied an
eruption.

(h) *Ale lani,* the patches of blue sky between masses of clouds.

(i) *Pu-ko'a*, a column of steam and smoke bursting up from a volcanic
eruption.

(j) *A'aka*, a column of lapillae, accompanied by hot vapor and smoke,
such as jet up from a volcanic crater or fissure.

(k) *Lono*, a message; to hear a message, i.e., to receive it. The expression *ahu a lono* is at first a little puzzling. It means the visible bulk,
or sign, of the message.

and heaven at once became turmoiled in one confused whirl of warring elements.

The warriors of Pana-ewa, who — in imitation of their chief — had for the most part taken the guise of trees and other natural objects, found themselves from the first fettered and embarrassed by a tangle of parasitic vines, so that their thrusts against Hiiaka were of little avail. Now comes the onset of the Pele gods in the tempest-forms of hurricane, lightning, hail, and watery cloud-bursts that opened heaven's flood-gates· Against these elemental forces the dryad-forms of Pana-ewa's host could not stand for a moment. Their tree-shapes were riven and torn limb from limb, engulfed in a swirling tide that swept them down to the ocean and far out to sea.

Two staunch fighters remained, Kiha, who had chosen to retain the honest dragon-form; and Pua'a-loa, a creature, like Kama-pua'a, in the demi-shape of a boar, whom Pana-ewa, at the scent of disaster, had thrust into the confinement of a secret cave. This manner of retreat saved the twain from the immediate disaster by flood but not from the vengeance of Pele's army. Detected in their lairs, they were slain and their petrified bodies are pointed out to this day in verification of this story.

The fate of Pana-ewa himself was most tragical. He no sooner had taken the form of a kukui tree than he found himself overlaid and entangled with meshes of parasitic growth; he could neither fight nor fly. The spot on which he stood sank and became a swamp, a lake, a sink; the foundations on which its bottom rested were broken up and fell away. Pana-ewa, swallowed up in the gulf, was swept out to sea and perished in the waves· Kane-lu-honua had broken up the underlying strata and made of the place a bottomless sink.

(A reef is pointed out in the ocean opposite Papa'i which is the remains of the body of the mo'o Pana-ewa.)

The part taken by Hiiaka in this last act of her deliverance was hardly more than that of a spectator. She had but to look on and witness the accomplishment of her own salvation. Having been roused from the refreshment of sleep by the long-drawn recitative of Paú-o-pala'e's prayer-mele (see pp. 37-40), she did her best to cheer her two companions with assurances of coming deliverance and, gathering her little brood about her, after the manner of a mother-hen, figuratively, bade them cling to her, nestle under her wings, lest they should be swept away in the flood of waters that soon began to surge about them — a flood which carried far out to sea the debris of battle — as already described·

The victory for Hiiaka was complete. Hawaii for once, and for all time, was rid of that pestilential, man-eating, mo'o band headed by Pana-ewa who, from the time of Pele's coming, had remained entrenched in the beautiful forest-land that still bears the name—Pana-ewa.

CHAPTER XI

HIIAKA HAS VARIOUS ADVENTURES—THE SHARK MAKAU-KIU

At one stroke, the benign action of the heavenly powers had freed a fair land from a pestilential mo'o band, disinfected it of the last shred and fragment of their carcases and ushered in a reign of peace in the wooded parks and tangled forests of Pan-ewa. Hiiaka could afford to celebrate her victory by recuperating her powers in well-earned repose. While she thus lay in profound sleep on the purified battle-field, her two companions busied themselves in preparing such simple refreshment as the wilderness afforded. The *piece de resistance* of this dinner of herbs was luau, the favorite food of the Pele family.

When the women had finished the task of collecting, sorting, making into bundles and cooking the delicate leaves of kalo, Hiiaka still slept. Paú-o-pala'e thereupon took her station at the feet of her mistress and chanted the dinner-call in the form of a gentle serenade:

E ala, e ala, e!
E ala, e Hika'a-lani;
E ala, e Ke-ho'oilo-ua-i-ka-lani;
E ala, e Ho'omaú,
Wahine a Makali'i, la!
E ala, e!

TRANSLATION

O Daughter of heaven,
Awake, awake!
Hiiaka, awake!
Sender of winter rain,
Guardian of womanly rites,
Spouse of God Maka-li'i,
Awake thee, awake!

"The luau must be burnt to a crisp," Hiiaka said as she sat up.

As Hiiaka and her companions again wended their way through the forest, it was evident that its innocent creatures had unjustly suffered in company with their guilty invaders and time had not yet sufficed for the exercise of that miracle of tropic repair which quickly heals and covers the damage done by a tempest. Broken limbs, fallen trees and twisted vines still blocked the narrow trails, while here and there an uprooted forest giant, in unseemly fashion, obtruded a Medusa-head of tawny roots in place of its comely coronal of leaves·

In their journey they came at length to a place, Maka'u-kiu, where the road seemingly ended abruptly in a precipice with the ocean dashing wildly at its base. The alternative open to their choice was, to seek out some round-about inland way, or to take the shorter route and swim the ocean-made gap· The two women, Wahine-oma'o taking the lead, proposed, as a diversion, to swim the ocean and thus avoid a long and wearisome detour. Hiiaka strenuously vetoed the proposition; but the two women, not yet trained to subordinate their will and judgment to the decision of the leader, persisted. Hiiaka, thereupon, took a stem of the ti plant and, peeling off its rusty bark, left it white and easily visible. "I will throw this stick into the water," said she, "and if it disappears we will not make of this an *au-hula-ana;*(a) but if it remains in sight, then we will swim across this wild piece of water·"

It seemed to Hiiaka that her companions displayed a masculine stubbornness and unreasonableness, a criticism which she uttered in her chanting way:

(a) *Au-hula-ana.* This is the term applied to such a break in a seaside trail as is above described. The word *hula* indicates the billowy toss of the ocean or of the swimmer's body while making the passage. The term, following Hawaiian usage, is employed either as a noun or as a verb.

Au ma ka hula-ana!
Kai-ko'o ka pali!
Pihapiha o Eleele,
Ke kai o Maka'u-kiu!
Aole au e hopo i ka loa
O Hono-kane-iki.
I Kane, la, olua;
I wahine, la, wau, e!

TRANSLATION

To swim this tossing sea,
While waves are lashing the cliff
And the ocean rages high,
At Eleele, the haunt of the shark!
I balk not the length of the road
By Hono-kane-iki.
Be you two stubborn as men!
Let me be guideful as woman.

Hiiaka then threw the peeled stick into the ocean and in a
moment it was snatched out of sight. "There! If we were to
swim we would be seized and eaten by Maka'u-kiu."

"When you tossed the stick into the ocean, the sea-moss covered and concealed it, and you thought it was the work of a
shark," was the reply of Wahine-oma'o. Again they made
ready to plunge into the sea. Hiiaka threw another stick and
that too was instantly swallowed; whereupon she chanted again:

Hookukú ka au-hula-ana o ka pali!
Ke pu'e 'a la e ke kai a nalo ka auki;
He i'a ko lalo, he i'a, o Maka'u-kiu —
O Maka'u'kiu, ho'i, e!

TRANSLATION

Have done with this fool-hardy swim!
The ocean just gulps down the stick!
A monster fish dwells in the depth —
That monster shark, Maka'u-kiu;
Aye, the shark-god Maka'u-kiu!

The women were not yet convinced and still persisted, a stubbornness that drew from Hiiaka another remonstrance:

Me he uahi máhu, la,
Ko lalo o Kaka-auki,
I Maka'u-kiu.
He kiu, he alele aloha,
Eia i o'u nei, e!

TRANSLATION

A seething whirl of ocean-mist
Marks the place where I cast the stick:
'Tis the work of the lurking shark.
Your loving guard, your faithful spy —
That is my service to you!

At these words the huge form of the shark rose to the surface, and the women, convinced at last, leaped out of the water and abandoned their purpose· Hiiaka now gave battle to the shark and that was the end of one more power of evil.

CHAPTER XII

THE ROUT OF THE MAHIKI

The location of the adventure with the shark-god Maka'u-kiu(a) was at the mouth of Waipi'o valley, a region where Hawaii's storm-coast forms an impassable rampart, save as it is cut by this and its twin valley, Wai-manu. These valleys take head in a wild forest region, the home of mist, rain and swamp. Adjoining this and part of the same watershed is the region known as Mahiki-waena, a land which the convenience of traffic required should be open to travel. It was the haunt of a ferocious horde of mo'o called mahiki(b) from their power to leap and spring like grass-hoppers.

When Hiiaka proposed to pass through this region in the

(a) *Maka'u-kiu*, afeared-o-a-spy.
(b) *Ma-hi-ki (mahiti, mawhiti)*, to leap, to skip, to spring up suddenly The Maori Comp. Dict. E. Tregear.

ordinary course of travel, the head of the Mahiki insolently denied her the right of way, suggesting as an alternative the boisterous sea-route around the northern shoulder of Hawaii. Hiiaka's blood was up. The victory over the hosts of Pana-ewa and the more recent destruction of Maka'u-kiu had fired her courage. She resolved once for all to make an end of this arrogant nuisance and to rid the island of the whole pestilential brood of imps and mo'o. Standing on a height that overlooked Wai-pi'o, she chanted a mele which is at once descriptive of the scene before her and at the same time expressive of her determination:

MELE UHAU

A luna au o Wai-pi'o,
Kilohi aku k'uu maka ilalo;
Hele ho'i ke ala makai o Maka'u-kiu;
Hele ho'i ke ala mauka o Ka-pu-o'a —
Pihapiha, he'e i ka welowelo,
I ka pu'u Kolea, i ka ino, e —
Ino Mahiki:
Ua ike ka ho'i au, he ino Mahiki,
He ino, he ino loa no, e!

TRANSLATION

As I journeyed above Wai-pi'o
Mine eyes drank in that valley —
The whole long march as far as from
The sea-fight at Maka'u-kiu
Till the trail climbs Ka-pu-o'a.
There soggy the road and glairy,
And there do flaunt and flourish,
On Plover Mount, the cursed Mahiki.
For I am convinced that that crew
Are bad, as bad as bad can be!

Hiiaka's march to encounter the Mahiki was interrupted for a short time by an incident that only served to clinch her resolution. An agonizing cry of distress assailed her ear. It came from a dismantled heap of human flesh, the remains of two men who had been most brutally handled — by these same Mahiki, perhaps — their leg and arm-bones plucked out and they left to welter in their misery· It was seemingly the cruel infliction of the Mahiki. The cry of the two wretches could not be disregarded:

> E Hiiaka-i-ka-poli-o-Pele, e,
> E ki'i mai oe ia maua;
> E ka hookuli i ka ualo, e!
> Ka opu aloha ole, e-e!

TRANSLATION

> O Hiiaka-of-Pele's-heart,
> Come thou and assist us.
> Turn not a deaf ear to our cry!
> Be not of hard and unfeeling heart!

Hiiaka, with a skill that did credit to her surgery, splinted the maimed limbs, inserting stems from her favorite ti plant to take the place of the long bones that had been removed. She left them seated in comfort at the roadside at Pololú.

The Mahiki, on seeing Hiiaka advance into their territory, threw up the dirt and dust in their front, to express their contempt for such an insiginficant body of trespassers· Hiiaka, paying no attention to their insolence, pressed on. Her purpose was to strike directly at Mo'o-lau, the leader of the horde, to whom she addressed this incantation:

> A loko au o Mahiki,
> Halawai me ke Akua okioki po'o.
> Okioki ino, la, i kona po'o;
> Kahihi a'e la i kona naau;
> Hoale mai ana i kona koko i o'u nei.
> E Lau e, Lau e-e!
> No'u ke ala, i hele aku ho'i, e-e!

TRANSLATION

> I enter the land of Mahiki;
> I counter the head-hunting witch.
> See me pluck the head from her body;
> See me tear out her very heart,

Till her blood surges round me in waves —
Blood of the monster that's legion.
Mine is the common right of way:
The traveler's right to the road!

At dark Hiiaka camped in the road and during the night a
female ku-pua named Lau-mihi, whom the Mahiki chief had sent
as a spy to watch Hiiaka, was seen standing on a high place to
one side of them. Hiiaka at once flew at her and put an end
to her.

Now began a fierce battle between Hiiaka and the Mahiki
dragon and his forces. They fought till both sides were exhausted and then, as if by mutual consent, stopped to rest.

Hiiaka perceived that the battle was to be even more fiercely
contested than that at Pana-ewa. She bade Paú-o-pala'e to take
good care that no ill came to Wahine-oma'o. Looking up into
the heavens, Hiiaka saw her relatives and friends Poha-kau,
Ka-moho-alii, Kane-milo-hai, and a large concourse of other gods,
including Kane, Kanaloa, Ku and Lono, watching her, evidently
greatly interested in her performances. They assured her of
their protection. At this Hiiaka was much encouraged and gave
utterance to her feelings in this kanaenae:

A Moolau, i ka pua o ka uhiuhi,
Helele'i mai ana ka pua o Ko'o-ko'o-lau·
Lohi'a e na mo'o liilii—
Na mo'o liilii ke ala
E kolo i ke kula,
E iho i kai o Kawaihae, la.
Hea a'e la ka mo'o liilii:
E hakaká kaua; paio olua auane'i.
He 'kau Mo'o-lau, o Mo'o-lau akua, e!

TRANSLATION

In the wilds of Mo'o-lau,
The uhiuhi's time for bloom —
The petals fall of Koolau's flower:
The little dragons have found the way
By which they can crawl to the plain,
Go down to the sea at Kawaihae.

The little demons now announce
That you and I shall battle wage:
We two, indeed, must fight, they say—
A god is Mo'o-lau, a host of gods!

At this the great dragon Mo'o-lau bestirred himself. His attack was direct, but he divided his host into two columns so as to envelope Hiiaka and attack her on each flank. Hiiaka saw them approaching through the jungle and chanted the following rallying song:

MELE HO'-ULUULU

A Mo'o-lau, i ka pua o ka uhiuhi,
Pala luhi ehu iho la
Ka pua o ke kauno'a i ka la;
Na hale ohai i Kekaha, o Wa'a-kiu;—
E kiu, e kiu ia auane'i kou ahiahi;
E maka'i ia olua auane'i.
He akua Mo'o-lau, o Mo'o-lau akua, e!

TRANSLATION

In the jungle of Mo'o-lau,
The uhi-uhi's season of bloom;
The flower of the rootless kau-no'a
Is wilted and bent in the sun;
My bower in Kekaha's invaded:
Some creature is playing the spy.
I, in turn,—be warned—will spy out
Your quiet and rest of an evening:
This to you, you, god Mo'o-lau!

Pele, perceiving that the crisis of the conflict had now come, called upon all the male and female relatives of Hiiaka (*hoaiku*) to go to her assistance; "Go and help your sister Hiiaka. There she is fighting desperately with Mo'o-lau—fighting and resting, fighting and resting, well nigh exhausted. Go and help her; all of you go. It's a fight against Mo'o-lau."

When the battalion of gods moved against the mo'o, it was a rout and a slaughter. Then the cry arose: "No fight has been made against the Mahiki dragon; he yet survives." There-

upon they turned their attack against that old dragon and his
guards. Hiiaka then celebrated the double victory in this paean:

> Kaiko'o Pu'u-moe-awa, wawá ka laau;
> Nei o Pu'u-owai ma, e:
> Nahá ka welowelo; he'e na'e ho'i, e!
> E Pu'u-owai ma, e, ke holo la!
> E Miki-aloalo, e, nawai ka make?
> Ke i-o nei, e!

TRANSLATION

> A roar as of surf on the hill Moe-awa:
> The tumult resounds through the forest:
> Pu'u-owai and his band lead the rout,
> Your battallions are torn into tatters—
> You are running, Captain Owai!
> And you, Captain Spry, whose the defeat?
> The answer is made by the shouting!

Hiiaka's chief weapon of attack seems to have been her magical paú· With this as a besom she beat them down as a husband-
man might beat down a swarm of locusts. The Mahiki and the
Mo'o-lau had ceased to exist as organized bodies. But from the
rout and slaughter of the armies many individuals had escaped
with their lives, and these had hid themselves away in caves
and secret places, some of them even, presuming apparently
upon their power of disguise, had taken refuge in the remote
scattered habitations of the people. Such an inference seems
to be justified by the language of the mele now to be given:

NOTE.—The gods that came to the assistance of Hiiaka such times as
circumstances pinched her and whose spiritual power at all times re-
enforced her feeble humanity were limited in their dominion to certain
vaguely defined provinces and departments. Thus, if there was any sea-
fighting to be done, it fell to the shark-god, the Admiral Ka-moho-alii, to
take charge of it. On the other hand, the conduct of a battle on *terra firma*
would be under the generalship of Kane-milo-hai; while to Kana-loa belonged the marshalling of the celestial hosts, the moon and the stars. But
the orb of day, the Sun, belonged to Lono. Hence, if the fighting was during
the hours of daylight, Lono would logically assume the command. The
rule of the great god Ku was also exercised principally by day. It was he
who arranged the calendar and settled the order of the seasons, the days
and the nights. The subdivisions and departmental complications under
these general divisions were numerous.

Lilo i Puna, lilo i Puna,
Lilo i Puna, i ke au a ka hewahewa;
Popo'i aku ka i na hale:
Ua piha na hale i ke 'kua —
O Kini Akua o Wai-mea,
O ka Lehu Akua o Maná.
Kini wale Wai-mea
I ka pihe o ke 'kua o Uli, e.
Po wale Mahiki;
A ia Mahiki ke uwá la no, e!

TRANSLATION

Scattered through Puna, scattered through Puna,
Is the rout of the vagrant imps:
They swarm in the dwellings of men;
The houses are lousy with demons —
Wai-mea's myriads of godlings,
Thy four hundred thousand, Maná·
Wai-mea thrills with the snarl of witch-gods:
Night's shadows brood over Mahiki;
The uproar keeps on in Mahiki.

CHAPTER XIII

HIIAKA LOOPS BACK IN HER JOURNEY

Hiiaka, having thus far, as it would seem, journeyed along the western coast of Hawaii, now loops back in her course and travels in the direction of Hilo by the way of Hamakua, for the seeming purpose of completing her work of extermination. Like a wise general, she would leave no enemies in her rear.

When they came into the neighborhood of Wahine-oma'o's home, that girl spoke up and said, "I think we had better take another road. If we keep to this one, which passes by my door, my parents, who will be watching for me, will see me and will want me to remain with them·" This she said by reason of her great desire to continue in Hiiaka's company. True enough, when they caught sight of her old home, there sat her mother Puna-hoa and her father Kai-pala-oa.

"There they sit," said the girl. "If they recognize me they will want to keep me."

Hiiaka bade Wahine-oma'o fall in behind her, hunch her shoulders, bend forward her head and walk with short infirm steps in imitation of an old woman. Hiiaka, on coming close to the old people, using the language of song, asked directions as to the road:

> E Puna-hoa i Kai-pala-oa,
> I na maka o Nana-kilo ma
> E nonoho mai la, e,
> Auhea ka ala, e?

TRANSLATION

> O Puna-hoa and Kai-pala-oä,
> You with the clear-scanning eyes,
> Sitting at rest before me,
> Point me out now the road.

"The road is plain enough; you are taking the right way. . . . We are looking at that young woman of your party — she has such a strong resemblance to our missing daughter, save her way of shuffling and holding her head."

On reaching the outskirts of the village of Hilo, Hiiaka found a rickety foot-bridge, consisting of a single narrow and wobbly plank, liable to turn at every step and precipitate the passenger into the tumbling waters below — and this was the only passage across the rocky chasm of the Wai-luku(a) river. This precarious crossing was the work of two sorcerers, degenerate nondescripts, who had the audacity to levy toll for the use of their bridge, in default of which the traveler suddenly found himself precipitated into the raging water. By virtue of their necromantic powers, they had the presumption to claim spiritual kinship with Hiiaka, a bond the woman could not absolutely repudiate.

"Here comes our mo'o-puna,(b) called out Pili-a-mo'o to his companion.

"Well, what of it? She will have to pay her fare the same as anyone else," replied Noho-a-mo'o· "Only on that condition shall she cross by our bridge."

On Hiiaka's attempting to cross without paying toll, the two sorcerers would, following their own practice, have disarranged the treacherous plank and precipitated her and her party into the raging stream.

"Well said," Noho-a-mo'o replied; "provided she will consent to it."

Hiiaka now called to them in the language of song:

> Kahuli-huli,(c) e-e,
> Ka papa o Wai-luku!
> Kahuli o Apua,
> Ha'a mai o Mau-kele:
> He ole ke kaha kuai ai, e-e!
> Homai ka ai,
> Homai ho'i ka ai, e-e!
> I ai'na aku ho'i, e-e!

TRANSLATION

> Cranky, cranky the bridge,
> Bridge across the Wai-luku!
> Upset is Apua;
> Maukele declares that
> The barter of food is naught.
> Give us then of your food;
> Give us something to eat;
> Let us partake of your meat.

To this unusual demand they replied, "Indeed, do you imagine we will do any such thing as that? It is not for us to give to you; you must give us the fare before you cross on our bridge. We don't give away things for nothing."

Hiiaka replied by repeating her request in nearly the same words:

> Ka-huli-huli, e-e,
> Ka papa o Wai-luku.
> He ole ke kaha kuai i'a, e!

(a) *Wai-luku,* water of destruction.

(b) *Mo'o-puna,* a grandchild, nephew or niece.

(c) *Kahuli-huli. Kahuli,* or its intensive, *kahuli-huli,* primarily means to upset, to overturn. A secondary meaning, much employed in the argot of hula folk, is to hand over, to pass this way; as when one guest at table might say to a neighbor, "hand me the salt (if you please)."

Ho-mai ka i'a;
Ho-mai ana, ho'i, ka i'a,
I ai'na aku, ho'i, e-e!

TRANSLATION

Unstable the bridge,
Bridge that spans the Wai-luku.
This barter of fish is a fraud·
Give us of your fish;
Grant us kindly some meat;
Give us something to eat.

Hiaaka repeated her demands in varying form with no other
effect than to make the toll-keepers more stubborn in their
ridiculous demands. Not even when Hiiaka, as if to cap the
climax of their absurdity, ended her demand with this ironical
request:

Ho-mai, ho'i, ka wai, e;
I inu ia aku, ho'i, e!!

TRANSLATION

Give us of this water,
Give us water to drink!

Hiiaka now openly denounced the two sorcerers as being
simply mo'o in disguise, entirely wanting in those generous feelings that belong to godhood. "These creatures are simply mo'o.
If I attack them, they will run for their lives·"

The people, failing to recognize Hiiaka as their deliverer,
spiritless from long habituation to the fraudulent dominion of
these imposters, fearful also of their vengeance, stoutly opposed
Hiiaka, affirming that Pili-a-mo'o and Noho-a-mo'o were gods
in reality, having great power and capable of doing many wonderful things. They declared their readiness to back their opinion
with their property, yes, with their lives. They were at length
persuaded, however, to accept as decisive the test proposed by
Hiiaka, namely, that, if they fled when attacked, they should
cease to be regarded as gods and should be dealt with as imposters.

True to Hiiaka's prediction, the mo'o, in abject fear, turned and fled for their lives at her first threatening move and she now called upon the people to pursue and destroy them:

Kaumaha ka aï o Hilo i ka lehua
Mai ka Nuku-o-ka-manu(a) a Puna-hoa, e.
Hoa ia iho la kau kanáka
I pa'a, o pahe'e auane'i;
Hina i ka Lua-kanáka.
He kanáka! He mau akua, e!

TRANSLATION

The neck of Hilo is heavy,
Weighted with wreaths of lehua
From Bird-beak clean down to the feet.
Catch and bind these robbers of men;
Bind them fast, lest they slip through your hands
And escape to the robber-pit —
These mortals, who call themselves gods!

The meaning of the figure in the first two verses, though obscure, seems to be that Hilo, so rich in natural beauty, is by that very fact robbed of the energy to defend herself and cast off the incubus that oppresses her.

As the creatures fled from Hiiaka's pursuit, their human disguise fell from them and their real character as mo'o was evident.

"We've committed a great blunder," said Pili-a-mo'o to his mate. "It looks as if she meant to kill us. Let us apologize for our mistake and conciliate her with fair words·"

Noho-a-mo'o agreed to this and, turning to Hiiaka, made this wheedling speech:

Kupu maikai a'e la
Ka wahine o ka Lua;
Uä ia iho la e ka ua,
A kilinahe ka maka o ka lehua ma-uka.
Ma-uka oe e hele ai,
Ma ka hoauau wai.
E waiho ke ala no maua,
No na kupuna, e.

(a) *Nuku-o-ka-manu*, literally, the beak of the bird; said to be a cape in the neighborhood of Hilo.

She has grown a fine figure,
Our girl from the Fire-pit.
The plentiful rain has made bright
This bud of upland lehua·
Pray choose your road farther inland;
That way will offer good fordage —
This road leave to your ancient kin.

Hiiaka spared not, but pursued them to their cavernous rock-heaps in which they thought to hide themselves, and, having seized them, rent them asunder jaw from jaw. Thus did Hiiaka add one more to the score of her victories in the extermination of the mo'o.

CHAPTER XIV

HIIAKA MEETS MOTHER-GRUNDY

It was at this point of the journey that Hiiaka lost the attendance of her sympathetic companion and faithful servant, Paú-o-pala'e. She was persuaded to unite her fortunes with those of a man from Kohala named Pa-ki'i; and we must leave unanswered the question, how she finally settled with Pele this apparent desertion of the trust with which she had been charged, that of acting as aide, kahu, to Hiiaka. Wahine-oma'o now remains as the sole companion of Hiiaka in her future adventures.

On resuming the journey they came before long to the broad stream of Honolii, which was ·swimming deep and, in the lack of other means of crossing, they bundled their clothes, held them above their heads with one hand and easily made the opposite shore by swimming with the aid of the other hand.

At the sight of this performance, the ghost-god, Hina-hina-ku-i-ka-pali and her companion, in a spirit of pure fault-finding and Mother-Grundyism, exclaimed:

Popó ke kapa o ka wahine,
Au kohana wai, hoauau wai o Honoli'i.
E kapu oe, he mau alii;
He mau alii no, o Hina-hina-ku-i-ka-pali.

TRANSLATION

The women bundle their garments
And, naked, they swim the stream,
The water of Hono-li'i —
An action quite unseemly:
'Tis a slur on your noble rank,
I too am a chief, my name
Hina-hina-gem-of-the-cliff·

"For shame!" said Hiiaka. "These ghost-gods have been spying on our nakedness, and now they make sport of us."

A great fear came upon the ghosts, that the dread goddess would seize them and pinch out their atomy spark of existence. In their terror, they flew home and, perched on the shoulders of their mother, besought her to interpose in their behalf and appease Hiiaka by a suitable offering of luau.

"There burns a fire," said Wahine-oma'o, as they drew near the house.

"The fire of the ovens built by the ghosts," Hiiaka answered. "They have saved themselves from death."

By the time they reached the house the luau was done to a turn and the tables were spread. Wahine-oma'o made an oblation to the gods and then ate of the viands. Hiiaka did not partake of the food.

Hiiaka now spent several days at Hono-kane, in Kohala, anxiously awaiting the departure of some canoe, by which she might pass over to the island of Maui. While thus absorbed, in a sentimental mood, looking one day across the ocean at the misty outline of the distant land, she saw a man of remarkable appearance strike out from one headland of the bay to swim to the opposite point. Her admiration for his physical beauty and his daring performance drew from her a song:

I i au, e au ma kai o ka hula ana.
Kai-ko'o a'e la lalo o ka pali;

Pího-pihó a'e; lele ke kai o Maka'u-kiu;
Au hopohopo ana i ka loa o Hono-kane-iki.
I kane oe a i wahine au.

TRANSLATION

My heart beats high at your venture —
To buffet the raging sea!
Wild heave the waves 'neath the cliff-wall.
To be whelmed by Ocean's might —
The ocean of Maka'u--kiu!
My heart forgets to beat at sight
Of your rashness, Hono-kane!
Would you were the man, the woman I!

Hono-kane heard, of course, the words that were uttered in his praise and, being a man of chivalrous instincts as well as of honor, he invited Hiiaka and Wahine-oma'o to enjoy the hospitalities of his home.

As they sat at a feast spread in her honor, Hiiaka, as was her wont, bowed her head in prayer with closed eyes, and the others did likewise and when they opened their eyes and looked, the portion that had been set before Hiiaka was gone, spirited away.

In the evening it was announced that a canoe was to sail in the early morning on a voyage to Maui, whereupon Hiiaka secured the promise of a passage for herself and Wahine-oma'o·

CHAPTER XV

THE VOYAGE TO MAUI

Hiiaka's voyage across the Ale-nui-haha channel, considered merely as a sea adventure, was a tame experience. There was no storm, no boistrous weather, sea as calm as a mill-pond, nothing to fillip the imagination with a sense of excitement or danger; yet it was far from being an agreeable experience to the young woman who was now having her first hand-to-hand tussle with the world.

They had spent the night at the house of one Pi'i-ke-a-nui. In the early morning their host and a younger man — apparently his son — named Pi'i-ke-a-iki, made ready their canoe to sail for Maui. Hiiaka, assuming that passage would be granted both of them, in accordance with a promise made the previous day, stood ready against the hour of departure. At the last moment, the younger man, having assisted Wahine-oma'o to her seat in the bow next to himself, called to his elder, "Pi'i-ke-a-nui, why don't you show your passenger to her seat, the one next you?"

"I won't do it," Pi'i-ke-a-nui answered groutily. "I find that the canoe will be overloaded if we take passengers aboard and all our landlord's freight will get wet."

The real reason for this *volte-face* on the part of the old sailor was that he had made an unseemly proposition to Hiiaka the night before and she had repelled him.

Wahine-oma'o, thereupon, left her seat and the canoe started without them. It was not more than fairly underway, however, when a violent sea struck the craft and swamped it, and all the loose freight was floating about in the ocean.

"There, you see! We'd 'ave had better luck with the women aboard·" Such was the exclamation of Pi'i-ke-a-iki.

It did not take long to convince the old man Pi'i-ke-a-nui, who was captain of the canoe, that he had invited this disaster on himself, the agent of which, as he rightly suspected, was none other than the distinguished-looking young woman who now stood on the beach watching him in his predicament with unperturbed countenance.

The two men floated their canoe, collected their baggage and came ashore. When they had got the stuff dry and stowed in the waist of the craft, they escorted the women aboard, seating Wahine-oma'o, as directed by the captain, in the bow near Pi'i-

ke-a-iki and Hiiaka in the after part, within arm's length of
Pi'i-ke-a-nui, and they put to sea.

The canoe was a small affair, unprovided with that central
platform, the pola, that might serve as the cabin or quarter deck,
on which the passengers could stretch themselves for comfort·
In her weariness, Hiiaka, with her head toward the bow, re-
clined her body against the top rail of the canoe, thus eking out
the insufficiency of the narrow thwart that was her seat; and
she fell asleep, or rather, entered that border-land of Nod, in
which the central watchman has not yet given over control of
the muscular system and the ear still maintains its aerial recon-
noissance.

The wind, meanwhile, as it caromed aft from the triangular
sail of mat, coquetted with her tropical apparel and made paú and
kihei shake like summer leaves.

The steersman, in whom that precious factor, a chivalrous
regard for woman, was even of less value than is common to
the savage breast, in the pursuit of a fixed purpose, began to
direct amorous glances at the prostrate form before him and
to the neglect of his own proper duties. Presently he left his
steering and stole up to Hiiaka with privy paw outstretched.
Hiiaka roused from her half-dreamy state on the instant, and
the man sprang back and resumed his paddle.

Hiiaka, with the utmost coolness, expressed in song her remonstrance and sarcastic rebuke for this exhibition of inhospitable rudeness:

> A Hono-ma-ele au, i Hono-ka-lani,
> Ike au i ka ua o ko'u aina,
> E halulu ana, me he kanaka la —
> Ka ua ku a-o-a i kai.
> Haki kaupaku o ka hale i ka ino, e!
> Ino Ko'o-lau, ino Ko'o-lau, e-e!

TRANSLATION

> With pillowed neck I lay, face to heaven:
> The rain, I found, beat on my bed;
> Came a tremor, like tread of a man —
> The slap of a rain-squall at sea;
> Within, the roof-tree broken down,
> My house exposed to the storm,
> My garden of herbs laid waste!

Makapuʻu, at the eastern end of Oʻahu.

The young man added his protest: "Yes, his whole conduct is, indeed, shameful, scandalous. He hasn't the decency to wait till he gets ashore."

In the midst of this unpleasantness it was a comfort to hear the strong cheerful voice of her former companion Paú-o-pala'e calling to her across the stretch of waters. It will be remembered that their roads had parted company sometime before Hiiaka had left the big island. The separation had made no change, however, in their mutual affection:

> O hele ana oe, e ka noe, e ka awa,
> E na ki a Wahine-kapu,
> E ka ua lele a'e maluna
> O Ka-la-hiki-ola, la:
> O hele ana, e!

TRANSLATION

> Like a cloud you fleet by,
> On the wings of the storm —
> Vision of womanly tabu —
> Of the rain-clouds that sweep
> O'er the Hill-of-good-luck:
> May you speed on your way!

Hiiaka replied to her kahu's mele in these words:

> A noho ana,
> E na hoaiku,
> E na hoa haele,
> I uka o Ka-li'u-la,
> I Moe-awakea.

TRANSLATION

> Kinsmen, allies, travel-mates,
> You rest in upland Ka-li'u;
> There taste you midday repose.

Perhaps it was that Hiiaka failed to manifest in her carriage and deportment the dignity and tabu that hedges in an alii or an akua; perhaps the rough hearted Pi'i-ke-a-nui, sailor-fashion, deemed himself outside the realm of honor which rules on land.

However that might be, as Hiiaka lay decently covered against
the cold wind that drew down the flank of Hale-a-ka-la, this
rude fellow, regardless of every punctilio, stole up to Hiiaka
and repeated his former attempt· Hiiaka caught his hand in
mid air and administered this rebuke:

> O Ka-uwiki, mauna ki'eki'e,
> Huki a'e la a pa i ka lani:
> He po'o-hiwi no kai halulu;
> Au ana Moku-hano i ke kai —
> He maka no Hana,
> O maka kilo i'a.
> O kou maka kunou, a,
> Ua hopu-hia.

TRANSLATION

> Ka-uwiki, famous in story,
> While buffeting ocean's blows,
> Aspires to commerce with heaven.
> Moku-hano's palms, that float
> Like a boat in the water,
> Are watchful eyes to Hana,
> Alert for the passing school:
> Your wanton vagrant eye
> Is caught in the very act.

The canoe grated on the shingly beach. The two young
women, rejoiced to be free at last from the enforced proximity
of ship-board, sprang ashore and with speedy steps put a distance
between themselves and the canoe-house. "That's right," called
out the steersman. "Make haste to find a bath. We'll join you
in a short time."

CHAPTER XVI

KAPO-ULA-KINA'U, A RELATIVE OF HIIAKA — THE MAIMED GIRL MANA-MANA-IA-KALU-EA

The canoe-men, having used their utmost expedition in landing the freight and hauling up the canoe and getting it under cover, hastened to meet the two women at the rendezvous they had suggested. But they were nowhere to be found. They had disappeared as completely as though the earth had swallowed them up· When Pi'i-ke-a-nui asked the people of the village as to the whereabouts of the two young women who had just now landed as passengers from the canoe, they one and all denied having set eyes upon them.

Hiiaka had planned a visit with her sister Kapo; but, on reaching Wailuku, the house was empty; Kapo and her husband Pua-nui had but just started to make a ceremonious call on Ole-pau, a famous chief of the district. The receding figure of Kapo was already hazy in the distance, so that it seemed more than doubtful if the words of Hiiaka's message reached the ears for which they were intended:

He ahui hala(*a*) ko Kapo-ula-kina'u,(*b*)
Ko ka pili kaumaha;
I ka pili a hala, la, ha-la!
Hala olua, aohe makamaka o ka hale
E kipa aku ai la ho'i i ko hale,
I kou hale, e-e!

TRANSLATION

The clustered hala is Kapo's shield,
An omen portending disaster.

(*a*) *Hala.* The fruit of the hala was so · often worn in the form of a wreath by Kapo that it came to be looked upon almost as her emblem. To ordinary mortals this practice savored of bad luck. If a fisherman traveling on his way to the ocean were to meet a person wearing a lei of this description he would feel compelled to turn back and give over his excursion for that day. In this instance Kapo was on her way to visit a sick man— a bad omen for him.

(*b*) *Kapo-ula-kina'u.* This was the full name of Kapo, who was one of the goddesses of the kahunas who practiced anaana (*po'e kahuna anaana*). *Ula-kina'u* is a term applied to a feather cloak ·or cape made of yellow feathers which had in them black spots.

The traveler came in your absence;
Both of you gone, no one at home —
No lodge for the traveler within,
No hospitality within!

Here is another version of this mele by Hiiaka (furnished by Pelei-oholani)· As the version previously given is confessedly imperfect, in part conjectural, there having been several hiatuses in the text, I think it well to give an authorized version, though very different:

He ahui hala na ka makani:(*a*)
Hala ka ua,(*b*) noho i na pali, e —
I ka pali aku i Pua-lehei,(*c*) e.
Loli iho la, pulu elo i ka ua, e.
Aohe makamaka e kipa aku ai
I kou hale, e;
E noho ana i ke kai o Kapeku;
E hoolono i ka uwalo, e!

TRANSLATION

A hala bunch, snatched by the wind
That blows from the medicine man,
Pushing the rain to Pua-lehei:
Cold is the traveler and soaking wet,
No friend to give welcome and cheer;
House empty — gone to the seashore;
No one to heed my entreaty.

As Hiiaka passed along the cliff that overlooks the wave-swept beach at Hono-lua, a pitiful sight met her eye, the figure of a woman crippled from birth — without hands. Yet, in spite of her maimed condition, the brave spirit busied herself gathering shell-fish; and when a tumbling wave rolled across the beach she made herself a partner in its sport and gleefully retreated, skipping and dancing to the words of a song:

(*a*) *Makani.* The reference is to the halitus, spirit, or influence that was supposed to rest upon and take possession of one obsessed, even as the tongues of fire rested upon the multitude in Pentecostal times. Kapo herself had this power.

(*b*) *Ua,* literally, rain, is by a much employed figure of speech used to mean the guests or people of a house. Thus, if one sees a great number of guests arriving to share the hospitality of a house, he might say, *"kuaua ua nui ho'i keia e hele mai nei."*

(*c*) *Pua-lehei,* a pali mauka of Wai-he'e.

Aloha. wale ka i'a lamalama o ku'u aina, la,
Ka i'a kahiko pu no me ka wahine.
Lilo ke hoa, ko'eko'e ka po;
Akahi kona la o aloha mai, e-e!
Aloha Kona, ku'u aina i ka pohu, e-e!

TRANSLATION

How dear the torch-caught fish of my home-land,
The fish embraced by the women folk!
Gone one's companion, chill grows the night:
Love cheered for a day, then flew away.—
Oh Kona, thou land of peace and of calm!

Search for the hidden meaning of this oli has brought out a
marvellous diversity of opinion. The chief difficulty lies in the
interpretation of the second verse: *Ka i'a kahiko pu no me ka
wahine*, and centers in the expression *kahiko pu*. One able critic
finds in it an allusion to the coöperation of women with the men
in the work of fishing. *Kahiko* is a word of dignity meaning
finely apparelled. The addition of the preposition *pu* amplifies
it and gives it almost the meaning of wrapped together. It
seems probable also that the word *i'a*, literally fish, is to be taken
in an esoteric sense as a euphemism for man. Putting this interpretation upon it, the meaning of the expression *kahiko pu*
becomes clear as being wrapped together, as in the sexual
embrace·

Wahine-oma'o was greatly fascinated by the pathos and
romance of the situation and declared she would like to have
her for an aikane, an intimate friend·

Hiiaka replied, "Maimed folk seem to be very numerous in
these parts."

The maimed girl kept up her fishing, her light-hearted dancing and singing:

Ua ino Hono-kohau; he Ulu-au nui ka makani;
Ke ha'iha'i la i ka lau o ka awa·
La'i pono ai ke kai o Hono-lua,
E hele ka wahine i ke kapa kahakai,
Ku'i-ku'i ana i ka opihi,
Wa'u-wa'u ana i kana limu,
O Mana-mana-ia-kaluea,
Ka wahine ua make, e-e!

TRANSLATION

Rough weather at Hono-kohau;
The Ulu-au blows a gale;
It snaps off the leaves of the awa,
But the sea lies calm at Hono-lua
And the woman can fish along shore,
Pounding her shell-fish, rubbing her moss —
This maiméd girl Kalu-é-a,
The girl that is dead.

As the wild thing ran from the dash of an incoming wave, by some chance the gourd that held her fish slipped from her and the retreating water carried it beyond her reach, a loss that she lightly touched in her song:

Ha'a ka lau o ka i'a;
Ha'a ka lima i ke po'i;
Ha'a ke olohe(a) i ke awakea:
Kina'i aku la i ke kai, la.
Lilo ka i'a, lilo ka i'a
I ka welelau o ku'u lima,
A lilo, e-e!

TRANSLATION

My fish are adance on the waves:
My hand just danced from the basket:
The skilled(a) one dances at noontide
And deafens the roar of ocean.
Gone are my fish, lost out of hand,
Snatched clean away from my hand-stumps;
They are gone, gone, gone from my hand!

There was a shark lurking in the ocean and when Mana-mana-ia-kalu-ea saw it she uttered a little song:

O ka i'a iki maka inoino,
Ihu me'ume'u o ka moana;
Ke a'u lele 'ku o kai,
I ka puo'a o kai uli, e.
Auwé, pau au i ka manó nui, e! !

(a) *Olohe,* an expert in the hula.

TRANSLATION

Little fish with wicked eye;
Snub-nosed fish that swims the deep;
Sworded fish that darts and stabs
Among the blue sea coral-groves —
Alas, the shark has done for me,
The mighty shark, mine enemy!

Wahine-oma'o could not repress her admiration for the girl and her desire to have her as an aikane (an intimate friend); and she was full of regret that their presence on the cliff had driven away the fish and interfered with the girl's occupation.

"The figure you see dancing down there is not a human body; it is only a spirit," said Hiiaka.

"What!"

"Yes, only a spirit, and I'll prove it in this way," she plucked a hala drupe from a wreath about her neck; — "I'll throw this down to her; and if she flies away, it will prove she is a spirit; but, if she does not disappear, it will prove her to be a human body."

Hiiaka threw the hala, and the moment the poor soul saw it fall in front of her she vanished out of sight. But in a short time she reappeared and, seizing the hala with her fingerless hand-stumps, she pressed it to her nose with an extravagant display of fondness and, looking up to Hiiaka, she chanted:

No luna ka hala, e;
Onini pua i'a i ke kai.
No Pana-ewa ka hala e;
No Puna ka wahine —
No ka Lua, e-e!

TRANSLATION

The hala, tossed down from the cliff,
Ruffs the sea like a school of sprats:
The hala's from Pana-ewa,
The Woman's homeland is Puna —
That wonderful Pit of Puna!

The loss of her fish still weighed upon the mind of Mana-

mana-ia-kaluea. Sitting down on a convenient rock, she mourned
aloud:

> Aloha wale ka pali o Pi-na-na'i,
> Ka lae iliili ma-kai o Hono-manú, e!
> He u ko'u, he minamina, e-e,
> I ka lilo ka i'a i ka poho o ka lima —
> A lilo, e-e!

TRANSLATION

> How dear the cliff of Pi-na-na'i,
> And the pebbly cape at Hono-manú! —
> How I mourn for the loss of my fish!
> They were swept from the reach of my hand;
> They are gone, forever gone!

Mana-mana-ia-kalu-ea, sitting on the rock, wrapped in her
own little garment of trouble, seemed for the moment quite
oblivious to the presence of Hiiaka, who was intently watching
her. Suddenly she looked up and, with brightening eye, exclaimed, "I know where you are from:"

> A Pu'u-lena, i Wahine-kapu i pua, e,
> A ilalo o Hale-ma'u-ma'u, e:
> Nolaila, e; nolaila paha, e!

TRANSLATION

> The land of Wahine-kapu,
> The land of the Pu'u-lena,
> Exhaled from the depths of the Pit —
> The fire-pit Hale-ma'u-ma'u —
> It comes to me: that is your home!

Hiiaka had conceived a strong prejudice against the girl almost
from the first, but now she softened and, turning to Wahine-
oma'o, said, "If you really want this girl for an aikane, I think
it can be managed. The only trouble will be to hold her after
she is caught."

Hiiaka, using her magical power, caught the spirit of Mana-
mana-ia-kalu-ea and, in the lack of a more suitable receptacle,
they wrapped it carefully in the free end of Wahine-oma'o's
loin-cloth and went on their way, traveling towards Wailuku.

CHAPTER XVII

HIIAKA RESTORES TO LIFE MANA-MANA-IA-KALU-EA

As they drew near Wailuku, they crossed a sandy plain dotted with tumuli. At once the captive spirit of Mana-mana-ia-kalu-ea became restless, as if eager to be free. "We are nearing the place where rests its body," explained Hiiaka. Wahine-oma'o by soft words and gentle touch did her best to soothe the perturbed thing.

It might almost be said that the captive spirit of Mana-mana-ia-kalu-ea was the guide (acting like the magnetic needle to point the way) to the home where the as-yet uncorrupted body of the girl still lay, mourned over by her parents..

It was with much prayer and the use of persuasive force that Hiiaka compelled the seemingly reluctant spirit to reenter its bodily tenement and to take up its abode there. As it passed from its point of entrance at the toe up into the chest its progress was marked by a kindling warmth that gave the assurance that the spirit was resuming its empiry over the whole body.

The first request made by the girl, on regaining full consciousness, was that her parents would prepare a feast as a thank-offering to Hiiaka, her physician, her deliverer. The special articles on which she was most insistent were luau and baked aoaoa.(a)

When it came to the final dressing of the luau for the table, namely the stripping off of the outer leafy covering from the scalding hot mass within — an operation which the girl insisted on doing with her own newly restored hands — Hiiaka watched her critically; for the proper etiquette of the function was most punctilious. But Hiiaka could find no fault with her technique: there was no slip, no solecism, no blowing on her fingers to relieve the scalding heat, as she stripped off the wrappings of the bundles.

When the feast was set and all were gathered about the tables, at Hiiaka's command all bowed their heads with closed eyes and she offered up her prayer to the gods of heaven. At the conclusion of her prayer, when they looked, lo, the portion of the feast set apart for the gods had vanished without leaving a trace

---

(a) Aoaoa, an imitative word, meaning dog.

behind. On this occasion Hiiaka was seen to eat of the food that was provided for her.(*b*)

The line of travel now chosen by Hiiaka was that along the northern or Koolau side of the island of Maui and led them at first through a barren stretch of country called a kaha, the food-supply of which came from a distance. It was here that Wahine-oma'o began to complain bitterly of hunger and exhaustion from the lack of food, and she besought Hiiaka to intercede with the people of a neighboring fishing village to give them some-thnig to eat.

"How is this, that you are a-hungered so soon after the feast of which you have partaken? This is a kaha," said Hiiaka, "and you must know that food does not grow in this place. They have only fish from the sea. Nevertheless, I will venture the request." This she did in the language of song:

> Ke kahulihuli a ka papa o Wailuku;
> He ole ke kaha kuai ai, e:
> Ho-mai he ai;
> Ho-mai ana ua ai, e!

TRANSLATION

> As trembles the plank at Wailuku
> (So trembles the fate of the king):
> There's no market where to buy meat;
> Give the stranger, then, something to eat:
> Give us, I pray, of your meat.

Some of the people derided them, saying, "Mahaoi!" — what impudence! Others, with kindness in their tones, explained, "This is a barren place; and all of our food comes from a great distance." The churlish ones, however, kept up their taunts: "You won't get any food in this place. Go up there;" and they pointed in the direction of Iao valley, where was the residence of King Ole-pau.

During the whole of the day, while tramping through this

(*b*) The most acceptable *bonne bouche* that could be offered to Pele, or to Hiiaka, by way of refreshment, was the tender leaf of the taro plant. We of this day and generation eat it when cooked under the name of lu-au. In the old old times, when the gods walked on the earth, it was acceptable in the raw state under the name of *paha;* but, when cooked, it was called *pe'u*. The word luau seems to be modern.

region, Hiiaka had observed from time to time a ghostly object flitting across the plain within hearing distance and in a direction parallel to their course. Though this spirit was not visible to ordinary mortal eye, Hiiaka recognized it as the second soul of Ole-pau, the very chief to whom the people of the fishing village had bid her make her appeal for food. Hiiaka, putting two and two together, very naturally came to the conclusion that this vagrant *kino wailua* was, in the last resort, responsible for this denial of hospitality to herself and her companion. Acting on this conclusion, Hiiaka made a captive of the vagrant soul and determined to hold it as a hostage for the satisfaction of her reasonable demands.

On coming within speaking distance of the house where lived the woman Wai-hinano, who ostentatiously played the part of kahu and chief adviser to Ole-pau, Hiiaka made known her wish, concluding her appeal with ominous threats against the life of the king, in case her demands were not met:

E Wai-hinano, wahine a ka po'ipo'i,(*a*) e,
Ua make ke alii,(*b*) ka mea nona nei moku.
He pua'a kau(*c*) ka uku no Moloka'i;
He ilio lohelohe(*d*) Lana'i;
A pale ka A-a ka Kanaloa;(*e*)
He puo'a kai Molokini:
Huli ka ele(*f*) o na Hono;

(*a*) *Po'ipo'i.* *Po'i uhane,* soul catching, was one of the tricks of Hawaiian black art and sorcery.

(*b*) There seems to be a disagreement in the different versions as to who is the king with whom Hiiaka is now contending, whether Ole-pau or Ka-ula-hea. For historical reasons I deem it to be Ole-pau, unless, indeed, the two names represent the same person.

(*c*) *Kau,* offered, literally put upon the altar.

(*d*) *Lohelohe,* By some inadvertence, this word was wrongly written as *kohekohe,* and I was cudgelling my wits and searching heaven and earth, and all the dictionaries, to learn the meaning of this artifact, this false thing. After having vainly inquired of more than a score of Hawaiians, one man, wiser than the rest, suggested that it should be lohelohe, not kohekohe, meaning underdone, or half-baked dog. The word-fit was perfect; the puzzle was solved.

(*e*) *Kanaloa,* a name given to Kaho'olawe, the island that faces East Maui, lying opposite to Lahaina, and acts as a sort of buffer against the blasts of the south wind, allusion to which is made, as I believe, in the word *A-a,* in the same line.

(*f*) *Ele.* Some critics vlaim that *ka* and *ele* properly form one word (*kaele*), meaning overturned. The grammatical construction of the sentence forbids this claim, and favors the interpretation I have given it. The figure is that of a canoe whose black body has turned turtle.

Haki kepakepa na moku;
Pa'iauma(g) ka aina;
Uwé kamali'i, uwé ka hanehane —
Ke uwé la i ka pili,(h)
I ke kula o Ka-ma'o-ma'o;(i)
Ka'a kumakena o Maui, e!
Ia wai Maui?

TRANSLATION

O Waihinano, thou soul-grabber,
Dead is the king of this island;
Moloka'i shall offer a boar;
Lana'i's a half-baked dog;
Kanaloa fends off the A-a;
Molokini buffets the waves.
The ship of state turns turtle:
What wailing and beating of breast!
Wild anguish of child and of ghost
O'er the sandy plain of Kama'o.
The districts are frenzied with grief —
Tearing of hair and breaking of teeth —
One wail that lifts to heaven.
Who shall be heir to this Maui land?

To this the sorceress, Waihinano, answered pertly:

Ia Ole-pau, ia ka Lani, ke Alii,
Ka-uhi-lono-honua;
O Ka-uhi-kapu ia a Kama,
A Kama-lala-walu:
O ke alii kahiko i hanau ia ai a Kiha —
O Ka-ula-hea nui o ka Lani:
Iaia Maui.

(g) *Pa'iauma.* This is a word that has presented some difficulties in the discovery of its meaning. The reference, I believe, is to breast-beating practiced by persons distracted with grief. *Uma,* the final part of the word, I take to be the shortened form of *umauma,* the bosom.

(h) *Pili,* to meet, the point or line of meeting, the boundaries of a land, therefore, the whole land.

(i) *Ka-ma'o-ma'o,* the name given to the sandy plain between Kahului and Wailuku, Maui.

To Ole-pau, the heavenly, the King,
In line from deep-rooted Kauhi —
Sacred Kauhi of Kama was he —
Kama, the sire of eight branches —
Of the ancient stock of Kiha,
And Ka-ula-hea, the great king:
Maui belongs to him.

To this Hiiaka retorted:

Ua make ia:
Ke ha'i mai nei na Wahine
I ka Hikina La ma Puna,
O na Wahine i ka La o Ha'eha'e,
O na Wahine i ka La o Ku-ki'i,
Ako lehua o Kua-o-ka-la,
Walea wai o ka Milo-holu,
Kui pua lei o Ma-li'o —
O Pele-honua-mea i ka Lua;
O Hiiaka i ka alawa maka o Wakea:
Ke i mai nei Haumea,
He kalawa ka ma'i a puni:
Ua make!

The sentence of death is affirmed
By the women — the gods — who tend
On the rising Sun of Puna,
Are Sun-guards at Ha'e-ha'e,
Pluck lehua-bloom at Kuki'i,
Rejoice in the stream Milo-holu
String the flower-wreaths of Mali'o —
Confirmed by Pele, God of the Pit —
Once heir to the sacred South-land,
And by Hiiaka, her shadow,
Gleam shot from the eye of Wakea.
Thus saith the goddess Haumea:
Great torment, fever and swelling
Shall scorch and rack him to death!

The woman Wai-hinano replied to Hiiaka with great spirit and temper:

Aole e make ku'u alii ia oe:
Ke hoole mai nei na 'kua wahine o ia nei,
O Ha-pu'u,(*a*) laua o Ka-lei-hau-ola,(*b*)
O na 'kua nana i lapu Hawaii a puni:
Oia ho'i ka i a ke Akua:
Ke hoole mai nei, aole e make!

TRANSLATION

My king shall not die by your arts:
His witch-gods deny you the power —
Ha-pu'u and Ka-lei-hau-ola; —
They peopled Hawaii with ghosts:
The voice of the gods, the king's gods,
Declares that he shall not die!

The situation was peculiar: while Ka-ula-hea (in the narrative sometimes called Ole-pau) lay asleep, his second soul, *kino wailua,* deserting its post of duty as life-guard over the bodily tenement, had stolen away in pursuit of its own pleasures. It was this very *kino wailua* that Hiiaka had seen flanking her own route, as it flitted through the fields, and which she had caught and now held fast in her hand like a fluttering moth, a hostage answerable for his misbehaviour and disregard of the rites of hospitality. Its possession gave Hiiaka complete power over the life of the king. It was no empty vaunt when Hiiaka again declared in song:

Aohe kala i make ai;
Ua pu-á ia na iwi;
Ua akua(*c*) ka ai a ka ilo!

TRANSLATION

King death has gripped him ere this;
His bones already are bundled;
The worms — they batten like gods!

While Wai-hinano was listening to these awful words of

(*a*), (*b*). Female deities of necromancy.
(*c*) *Akua,* literally, a god, or godlike, i.e., in an awe-inspiring manner.

Hiiaka she was dumbfounded by the tidings that Ka-ula-hea had waked from seemingly peaceful sleep in great perturbation, and that he had been seized with the most alarming and distressful symptoms. In her distraction and rage she still maintained a defiant attitude:

Aohe make ku'u alii ia oe!
Ke hoole mai nei na akua kane o ia nei,
O Ke-olo-ewa(b) nui a Kama-ua,(c)
He mana, he úi-úi, a-á,
He ana leo no ke Alii,
E ai ana i ka pua'a o Ulu-nui,(d)
I ka lalá Me-ha'i-kana,(e)
Hoole o Uli, akua o ia nei,
E hoole mai ana, aohe e make!

TRANSLATION

My lord shall succumb not to you!
The gods of the King affirm it —
Olo-ewa, son of the Rain-god,
Gifted with power and with counsel,
His voice rings out clear for the King:
He shall eat the fat of the swine,
Pluck the fruit of the bread-tree: Uli,
A god ever true to the king,
Declares that he shall not die.

(b) *Ke-olo-ewa,* an akua *ki'i,* i.e., a god of whom an image was fashioned. Some form of cloud was recognized as his body (Ke-ao-lewa(?)). One of his functions was rain-producing. Farmers prayed to him: "Send rain to my field; never mind the others." S. Percy Smith of New Zealand (in a letter to Professor W. D. Alexander) says that in Maori legend Te Orokewa, also called Poporokewa, was one of the male *apa,* guardians and messengers of Io, the supreme god who presided over the 8th heaven. According to Hawaiian tradition Ke-olo-ewa was, as Fornander has it, the second son of Kamauaua, a superior chief, or king of Moloka'i, and succeeded his father in the kingship of that island. His brother, Kaupe'e-pe'e-nui-kauila, it was who stole away Hina, the beautiful wife of Haka-lani-leo of Hilo, and secreted her on the famous promontory of Haupu on Moloka'i. For the story of this interesting tradition see Fornander's "The Polynesian Race," Vol. II, p. 31. After death he became deified and was prayed to as a rain god.

(c) *Kama-ua,* literally, the son of rain.

(d) *Ulu-nui,* meaning the crop-giver. This was the name of a king, or chief of Makawao, Maui, under whom agriculture greatly flourished.

(e) *Me-ha'i-kana,* the goddess of the bread-fruit tree; said to be one with Papa.

After each incantation that Hiiaka had uttered against Ka-ula-hea that king's disorder had flared up in more alarming proportions, and he cried out in agony and despair. But it was equally true that just as often as Wai-hinano had uttered her assurances that his trouble was but a trivial indisposition and that the male and female deities — above named — stood on his side and would not let him die, his courage had revived, he had felt a wave of healing influence pass through him and relief had come.

In explanation of this see-saw of hope and despair, sickness and relief, let it be stated that the two goddesses Ha-pu'u and Ka-lei-hau-ola and the two male deities Ke-olo-ewa and Kama-ua, to whom Wai-hinano had appealed by name as staunch friends of Ka-ula-hea, were, in fact, allies, or, more properly speaking, partizans of Pele and, therefore, subject to the call of Hiiaka. The kahuna Kaua-kahi-ma-hiku-lani who had charge of the case of Ka-ula-hea derived his power as a kahuna from these very same gods; but he well knew that if there was a conflict of interests the commands of Hiiaka would have to be carried out. As for the gods and goddesses above named, they, of course, knew their own position and that, as between Ka-ula-hea and Hiiaka, their service must be rendered to the latter. Willing enough they were, however, in return for the offerings laid on their altars, to feed the hopes of the sick man by temporary relief of his sharpest agonies.

As if this tangle of motives were not enough, the affair was yet further complicated by the appearance of Kapo — sister, or aunt of Hiiaka — on the scene, who came not only as an interested spectator but as a friend of king Ka-ula-hea. Her power to intervene was, of course, handicapped by the same limitations that touched the other gods and goddesses. She had the good sense to retire from the scene before things came to a critical pass.

Meanwhile messengers are flying about, seeking or bringing assurance of relief and restoration to health to the king. Hiiaka saw that the time had come for decisive action. She went close up to the great stone Paha-lele that still lies in the road near Wai-he'e and, before smiting against the rock the soul she held captive in her hand, she uttered the following kau:

E Kaua-kahi-ma-hiku-lani ma, e,
A pala ka hala haalei ma ke kaha o Maka-o-kú;

Haawi pauku oko'a me ko ha'i kini.
He aloha ole no o Kaua-kahi-ma-hiku-lani ma
I ka anaaná ia Ole-pau, e.
Lapu Ole-pau, e:
Ua akua ka ai a ka ilo!

She pauses for a moment, then continues:

Anu Wai-he'e i ka makani Kili-o'opu;
He i'a iki mai ke kele honua(*g*) *o* Wailuku,
Mai ke kila o Pa-ha'a-lele la, e.
Ha'alele ke ea o Ole-pau;
Ua pokaka'a ka uhane,
Ua kaalo ia Milu.

TRANSLATION

O Kau-akahi-ma-hiku-lani,
You cast away the wilted fruit,
And with it the fortunes of many:
'Twas an act of unlove, that of yours —
To hurl this prayer-shaft at Ole-pau:
He'll become but a houseless ghost;
The maggots shall batten like gods.
Waihe'e crouches in the cold blast
Of the raging Kili-o'opu.
This atom soul I plucked from the grave,
From a fastness desolate now:
The spirit flits from Ole-pau,
Goes down the steep to destruction,
To the somber caverns of Milu.

With this she dashed the captive soul against the rock, and that was the end of Ka-ula-hea.

There was something in the manner of Hiiaka as she called the name of the kahuna Kau-akahi that chilled the courage of the group of sorcery gods. They saw that their game was played out, and they sneaked away and hid themselves.

(*g*) *Kele honua*, an instance of a noun placed after its adjective. The meaning of *kele honua*, literally, the miry soil, a deep taro patch.

CHAPTER XVIII

HIIAKA EMPLOYS THE ART OF MAGIC AS A MEANS OF DISGUISING HERSELF—SHE VOYAGES TO MOLOKA'I—MEETS THE MO'O KIKI-PUA

"Let us make haste to leave this place," said Hiiaka. This was because she foresaw that she would be importuned to use her power to restore the dead king to life.

When these akuas, these spirits of necromancy, became convinced that they had been worsted in the fight and that the king was dead beyond all hope of recovery from them, they instructed the kahuna Kaua-kahi-ma-hiku-lani to desist from his useless incantations and to dispatch all his people in search of Hiiaka as the only one capable of reviving the king's life.

While toiling up the ascent of the hill Pulehu, the two women saw in the distance a great multitude of people pursuing them. Wahine-oma'o, in alarm, exclaimed "What in the world shall we do!" At once Hiiaka by the power of enchantment changed Wahine-oma'o into the shape of a little girl leading a dog, while she herself assumed the form of a bent old woman hobbling along with the aid of a stick; and as the multitude drew near they sat down by the wayside as if to rest.

The people in pursuit had seen and recognized Hiiaka and felt sure of soon overtaking her. But, on coming to the place, they found only a decrepit woman and a child leading a dog. They were taken aback and asked, "Where are the two young women who were traveling this way? Have you not seen them?"

"We have seen nothing of them," was the answer.

When the people reported to the kahuna that they had found only an old woman and a girl with a dog in tow, he saw through the trick at once and exclaimed, "Those are the very persons I want. Go and bring them."

The messengers of the kahuna next came up with Hiiaka and her companion at a place called Ka-lau-la'ola'o. There they found two girls of tender age busily employed in gathering lehua flowers and stringing them into wreaths; and, as before, they denied all sight and knowledge of the persons inquired for. The kahuna recognized that his people had again been victim-

ized and, upbräiding them for their lack of detective insight,
ordered them to renew the pursuit.

Once more, at Kapua, in Ka-ana-pali, did Hiiaka find it necessary to resort to the arts of magic in order to escape from her
pursuers. When the scouts of the kahuna arrived at the place
they found a household of busy women — a wrinkled matronly
figure was braiding a mat, while her companion, just returned
from the ocean, was laying a fire to broil a fish for the evening
meal. Not until they had gone some distance from the place
did it occur to their sharpening wits that the house had looked
spick-and-span new, and that they had seen no *man* about the
place. Yes—they had been fooled again by the wonderful art
of the girl Hiiaka.

Hiiaka was rejoiced to find a canoe on the point of sailing to
Moloka'i and the sailors gladly consented to give her a passage.
The people of Kapua were greatly taken with the beauty and
charm of Hiiaka and proposed, in all seriousness, that she should
remain and become one of them. When they found that she
was insistent to continue her journey at once, they one and all
warned her not to attempt the windward side of Molokai, declaring its coast to be precipitous and impassable, besides being
infested by a band of man-killing mo'o.

Hiiaka had no sooner set foot on Molokai's beach than her
ears were assailed with complaints against those lawless beings,
the mo'o. Two women, pallid and wasted with starvation, sat
in the open field moaning and bewailing their estate. At sight
of Hiiaka, as if recognizing their knight errant, they broke out
into loud lamentations. The mo'o had robbed them of their
husbands, and with them had gone their means of support and
their very desire for food. Hiiaka, as if recognizing their claim
upon her knight-errantry, with heartfelt sympathy for their
miserable condition, opened her mouth in song:

> Kui na ohi'a hele i ke kaha, e;
> Lei hele i ke kaha o Ka-pala-ili-ahi —
> Mau akua noho i ka la'i, e-e;
> Ua hele wale a lei-ó-a ke kino, e-e!

TRANSLATION

> Provide you wreaths of ohi'a
> To gladden the heart of travel:

You'll bring joy to these barren wastes
Of Ka-pala-ili-ahi. —
These creatures, sublime in their misery,
Sit shelterless, wasted, forlorn.

At this the women spoke up and said: "Our bodies are wasted only from our passionate love for our husbands. When they were taken from us we refused food."

Hiiaka was indignant at such folly and left them to their fate. Their way still continued for some distance through a barren region and Hiiaka again alluded in song to the barrenness of the land and the misery of the women who suffered their bodies to waste away:

Kui na apiki lei hele
O Ka-maló, e:
Akua heahea i ke kaha o Iloli.
He iloli aloha;
He wi ka ke kino, e-e!

TRANSLATION

Provide you a bundle of wreaths,
When the heart is ashes within.
The witches were ready with babble
In the barren land of Iloli: —
Their's merely a passion hysteric,
That shrivels the body like famine.

The good people of Halawa valley, where Hiiaka found herself well received, made earnest protest against the madness of her determination to make her way along the precipitous coast wall that formed Molokai's windward rampart. The route, they said, was impassable. Its overhanging cliffs, where nested the tropic-bird and the uaʻu, dropped the plummet straight into the boiling ocean. Equally to be dreaded was a nest of demonlike creatures, mo'o, that infested the region and had their headquarters at Kiki-pua, which gave name to the chief mo'o. Kiki-pua, being of the female sex, generally chose the form of a woman as a disguise to her character which combined the fierceness and blood-thirstiness of the serpent with the shifty resources of witchcraft, thus enabling her to assume a great variety of physical shapes, as suited her purpose. This last fact, had it stood by itself, would have decided Hiiaka's choice; for her journey, considered as a pilgrimage, had as an important side-purpose the extermination root-and-branch, of the whole cursed tribe of mo'o from one end of the land to the other.

(This Kiki-pua band of mo'o had included Haka-a'ano, the husband of Kiki-pua, also Papala-ua and her husband Olo-ku'i.(a) Kiki-pua had stolen away and taken to herself Olo-ku'i, the husband of Papala-ua, thus creating a bitter feud which broke up the solidarity of the band.)

The way chosen by Hiiaka led along the precipitous face of the mountain by a trail that offered at the best only a precarious foothold or clutch for the hand. At one place a clean break opened sheer and straight into the boiling sea. As they contemplated this *impasse,* a plank, narrow and tenuous, seemed to bridge the abyss. Wahine-oma'o, rejoicing at the way thus offered, promptly essayed to set foot upon it, thinking thus to make the passage. Hiiaka held her back, and on the instant the bridgelike structure vanished. It was the tongue of the mo'o thrust out in imitation of a plank, a device to lure Hiiaka and her companion to their destruction.

Hiiaka, not to be outdone as a wonder-worker, spanned the abyss by stretching across it her own magical pa-ú, and over this, as on a bridge, she and Wahine-oma'o passed in security.

The mo'o, Kiki-pua, took flight and hid among the cavernous rocks. But that did not avail for safety. Hiiaka gave chase and, having caught her, put an end to the life of the miserable creature. Thus did Hiiaka take another step towards ridding the land of the mo'o.

(a) *Oloku'i,* a high bluff that overlooks Pele-kunu and Wailau, valleys on Moloka'i.

CHAPTER XIX

HIIAKA FINDS A RELATIVE IN MAKA-PU'U — KO'O-LAU WEATHER — MALEI

Hiiaka's adventurous tour of Moloka'i ended at Kauna-ka-kai, from which place she found no difficulty in obtaining the offer of transportation to Oahu. The real embarrassment lay in the super-gallantry of the two sailors who manned the canoe. When the two men looked upon Hiiaka and Wahine-oma'o, they were so taken with admiration for their beauty and attractiveness, that they sneaked out of a previous engagement to take their own wives along with them, trumping up some shuffling excuse about the canoe being overladen.

Arriving at the desolate landing near the wild promontory of Maka-pu'u, it was only by a piece of well-timed duplicity that Hiiaka and her companion managed to shake off the sailors and relieve themselves from their excessive attentions.

While in mid channel, in sight of Ulu-ma-wao, a promontory whose name was the same as a near relative of the Pele family, Hiiaka poured out this reminiscence in song:

> Ku'u kane i ka pali kauhuhu,
> Kahi o Maka-pu'u(a) huki i ka lani
> Ka Lae o Ka-laau,(b)
> Kela pali makua-ole(c) olaila:—
> Anu ka ua i ka pali o Ulu-ma-wao,(d) e;
> E mao wale ana i ka lani kela pali:
> Ku'i, ha-ina i ke kai.
> I ke kai ho'i ke Akua,
> A pololi a moe au, e-e!
> Ku'u la pololi, a ola i kou aloha:
> Ina'i pu me ka waimaka, e-e!
> A e u'wé kaua, e-e!

(a) *Maka-pu'u,* a headland at the eastern extremity of Oahu, on which a lighthouse of the first class has been established within three years.

(b) *Lae o Ka-laau,* the south-western cape of Moloka'i, on which is a lighthouse of the first class.

(c) *Makua-ole,* literally, fatherless or parentless; seemingly a reference to the lonely inhospitable character of the place.

(d) *Ulu-ma-wao,* a hill in the same region as Maka-pu'u point. The name is said to mean a place having a very thin soil.

TRANSLATION

O fellow mine on the stair-like cliff,
Where Maka-pu'u climbs to the sky,
Companioned by Cape-of-the-woods,
That fatherless bluff over yonder:
Cold cheer the rain on Ulu-ma-wao;
That lone steep faints away in the sky,
While Ocean pounds and breaks at its base —
The sea is the home of the gods.
I lay in a swoon from hunger
What time I awoke from love's dream,
Love, salt with the brine of our tears.
Let us mingle our tears.

It was a question with Hiiaka whether to follow the Koolau or the Kona side of the island. The consideration that turned the scale in favor of the Koolau route was that thus she would have sight of a large number of aunts and uncles, members of the Pele family, whose ghosts still clung to the dead volcanic cones and headlands which stood as relics of their bygone activities, and where they eked out a miserable existence. The region was thickly strewn with these skeleton forms. Hiiaka first addressed herself to Maka-pu'u:

Noho ana Maka-pu'u i ka lae,
He wahine a ke Akua Pololi: —
Pololi, ai-ole, make i ka pololi, e-e!

TRANSLATION

Maka-pu'u dwells at the Cape,
Wife to the god of Starvation —
Hunger and death from starvation.

To this Maka-pu'u answered: "We love the place, the watch-tower, from which we can see the canoes, with their jibing triangular sails, sailing back and forth between here and Molo-ka'i." To this she added a little chanty:

E Maka-pu'u nui, kua ke au e!
Na mauü moe o Malei, e-e,
I ai na maua, i ai na maua, e-e!

TRANSLATION

Oh Maka-pu'u, the famous,
Back pelted by wind and by tide!
Oh the withered herbs of Malei!
Oh give us some food for us both.

To Malei Hiiaka addressed the following condolence:

Owau e hele i na lae ino o Koolau,
I na lae maka-kai o Moe-au;
E hele ka wahine au-hula ana o ka pali,
Naná uhu ka'i o Maka-pu'u —
He i'a ai na Malei, na ka wahine
E noho ana i ka ulu o ka makani.
I Koolau ke ola, i ka huaka'i malihini,
Kanaenae i ka we-uwe'u,
Ola i ka pua o ka mauu.
E Malei e, e uwé kaua;
A e Malei e, aloha-ino no, e.

TRANSLATION

I walk your stormy capes, Koolau,
The wave-beaten capes of Moe-au,
Watch-towers, where the women who brave the sea
May see the uhu coursing by —
Meat for the woman who faces the gale,
Sea-food for the woman Malei;
For her living comes from Koolau,
From the pilgrim bands that pass her way;
Yet we bless the herbs of the field,
Whose bud and flower is meat for Malei:
We pity and weep for Malei.

NOTE.—Malei was, I am told, a female kupua who assumed various bodily forms. Offerings were necessary, not for her physical but for her spiritual sustenance. The burnt offering was not merely pleasing for its sweet smelling savour, it was an aliment necessary to the creature's continued existence. For the same or a parallel reason, songs of praise and adulation (kanaenae) were equally acceptable and equally efficacious. Cut off the flowers of speech as well as the offerings of its worshippers, and a kupua would soon dwindle into nothingness.

"You are quite right," answered Malei: "the only food to be had in this desolate spot is the herbage that grows hereabouts; and for clothing we have to put up with such clouts as are tossed us by travelers. When the wind blows one has but to open his mouth to get his belly full. That has been our plight since your sister left us two old people here. Cultivate this plain, you say; plant it with sweet potatoes; see the leaves cover the hills; then make an oven and so relieve your hunger. Impossible."

As they traveled on Maka-pu'u and its neighbor hills passed out of sight. Arriving at Ka-ala-pueo, they caught view of the desolate hill Pohaku-loa, faint, famished, forlorn. The sight of it drew from Hiiaka this chanting utterance:

> Puanaiea ke kanáka,
> Ke hele i ka li'u-la,
> I Koholá-pehu, i ke kaha o Hawí, e.
> Wi, ai ole, make i ka i'a ole, e.

TRANSLATION

> Man faints if he travels till night-fall
> In the outer wilds of Kohala,
> In the barren lands of Hawi —
> It's famine, privation of bread, of meat!

"It is indeed a barren land. Fish is the only food it produces. Our vegetables come from Wai-manalo. When the people of that district bring down bundles of food we barter for it our fish. When we have guests, however, we try to set vegetable food before them."

To speak again of the kupua Malei, a few years ago, as I am told, a Hawaiian woman on entering a certain cave in the region of Wai-manalo, found herself confronted with a stone figure, from which glowed like burning coals a group of eight flaming eyes, being set in deep sockets in the stone. This rare object was soon recognized as the bodily dwelling of the kupua Malei. This little monolith at a later time came into the possession of Mr. John Cummins of Waimanalo.

CHAPTER XX

HIIAKA EXPERIENCES KOOLAU WEATHER

Hiiaka found many things to try her patience and ruffle her temper in Pali-Koolau: Squalls, heavy with rain-drops picked up by the wind in its passage across the broad Pacific, slatted against her and mired the path; but worse than any freak of the weather were her encounters with that outlaw thing, the mo'o; not the bold robber creature of Hawaii which took to the wilds, as if in recognition of its own outlawry, but that meaner skulk, whose degenerate spirit had parted with its last atom of virtuous courage and clung to human society only as a vampire, unwilling to forego its parasitic hold on humanity. It was in the mood and spirit begotten of such experiences that she sang:

Ino Koolau, e, ino Koolau!
Ai kena i ka ua o Koolau:
Ke ua mai la i Ma-elieli,
Ke hoowa'awa'a mai la i Heeia,
Ke kupá la ka ua i ke kai.
Ha'a hula le'a ka ua
I Ahui-manu, ka ua hooni,
Hoonaue i ka pu'u ko'a,
Ka ua poai-hale(a) o Kaha-lu'u.
Lu'u-lu'u e, lu'u-lu'u iho nei au
I ka puolo waimaka o ka onohi —
Ke kulu iho nei, e.

TRANSLATION

Vile, vile is this Koolau weather:
One soaks in the rain till he's full.
The rain, it pours at Ma-eli-eli;
It gutters the land at He-eia;
It lashes the sea with a whip.
The rain, it dances in glee
At Ahui-manu, moving

(a) *Ua poai-hale,* a rain that whisked about on all sides of a house. house.

·And piling the coral in heaps,
Shifting from side to side of the house,
This whisking rain of Kaha-lu'u.
Heavy and sad, alas, am I,
Mine eyes, a bundle of tears,
Are full to o'erflowing.

As they approached Kua-loa, the huge mo'o-dragon, Moko-li'i, reared himself up and, pluming and vaunting himself, sought to terrify them and prevent their passage. Hiiaka did not flinch in her attack. When she had killed the monster, she set up his flukes as a landmark which now forms the rock known to this day as Moko-li'i. The body of the dragon she disposed in such a way that it helped form the road-bed of the traveled highway. After this achievement she vented her feelings in an exultant song:

> Ki'e-ki'e Kane-hoa-lani
> Au Moko-li'i(b) i ke kai,
> I keiki, i Makahiapo na Koolau:
> Lau Koolau, kena wale i ka ino;
> He ino loa no, e!

TRANSLATION

> Kane-hoa lifts to the sky;
> Moko-li'i swims in the ocean —
> The first-born child of Koolau —
> A legion of fiends is Koolau,
> Eager for mischief, subtle of trick.

Coming to where the deep and narrow gorge of Ka-liu-wa'a valley opens out, Hiiaka discerned the nature-carved lineaments of her ancestor Kauhi ke-i-maka-o-ka-lani, as he was epitheted, a rocky form set in the pali, but veiled to ordinary sight by a fringe of ti and kukui. Its eye-sockets, moist with the dripping dew of heaven, gleamed upon her with a wondrous longing, which she answered in song:

(a) *Moko-li'i* (little snake), compound of *moko*, archaic form of *mo'o*, and *li'i*.

O Kauhi ke i-maka(*a*) o ka lani,
O ka pali keke'e o halawa-lawa,(*b*)
O kuahiwi mauna pali poko, ke he'e ia,
E like la me Ka-liu-wa'a,
Ka pali ololo-é(*c*) o Puna i Hilo;
O ka hala o Manu'u-ke-eu,(*d*)
E kui, e lei au:
O Kauhi, ka halu'a-pua,(*e*) maka á-lani —
O ka maka o ke akua,
I ka maka o Pe'ape'a.(*f*)
Uluulu ka manu i kona hulu;
Ke lele kaha ia lupe la;
Lawe ka ua, lawe ka makani,
A lawe ke ka-úpu(*g*) hulu manu,
Kele-kele i o akua la, e ke Akua.
He akua ia la, aohe ike mai:
O kana luahi(*h*) nui no ka maka,
Ke ala nei; — E ala;
E ala, e ala mai ana, e!
E ala e, Hi-ka'a-lani!(*i*)
E ala, e, ka Hooilo ua i ka lani!
E ala e, Maú,(*j*) wahine a Maka-li'i;
E ala, e!

(*a*) *I-maka*, a watch-tower. (This is a new word, not in the dictionary.)

(*b*) *Ha-lawa-lawa*, zigzag.

(*c*) *Ololo-e*, out of line; out of order; irregular. See *ololo*, in Andrews' Hawaiian Dictionary. Keke'e, halawalawa and ololo-e have the same generic meaning.

(*d*) *Manu'u-ke-eu*, the name of a mythical hala tree that once grew in Puna. The seed was brought from Kahiki by Ka-moho-alii, when he came from that land with Pele and others. They ate the drupe of it with salt and sugar-cane, and then Ka-moho-alii planted the seed. The tree that grew up was, of course, a kupua.

(*e*) *Halu'a-pua*, flower-bedecked; compound of *halu'a* (covered), and *pua* (a flower).

(*f*) *Pe'ape'a*, a bat; a creature regarded as a kupua.

(*g*) *Ka-upu*, some sort of a sea-gull.

(*h*) *Lu-ahi*, the object of a person's wrath or indignation.

(*i*) *Hika'a-lani*, facing heaven; looking up to heaven. This was the name given later to a beautiful princess on Oahu.

(*j*) *Ma-u*, literally, damp; the name of the wife of Maka-li'i, as here indicated. Maka-li'i, here used as the name of a deity, is also, 1. the name of the Pleiades; 2. the name of the month in which that constellation rises at the time of sunset; 3. the name sometimes applied to the six summer months collectively. The visible sign of Makali'i, as a deity or kupua, was a rain-cloud.

TRANSLATION

Kauhi, thou watch-tower of heaven,
Ensconced in the zigzag fluted wall —
Slipp'ry to climb as Ka-liu-wa'a,
Or the straggling Puna-Hilo hills. —
Ah, the drupes of Manu'u-ke-eu !
Let me string, let me wear them !
Thy body lies smothered in ferns ;
Thine eye shines on high like a star,
Or jeweled eye of bat, Pe'a-pe'a.
As a bird, now ruffle your plumage —
How sways the kite in the wind !
On balanced wing, then swing and float,
Warding off rain, warding off wind,
Like a sea-gull, clad in feathery mail,
Course about on the wings of a god.
He's surely a god ; yet hears he not ;
Fierceness gleams from his eye.
Now he looks, now turns — and to me !
Awake, thou explorer of heaven !
Awake, thou sender of Winter's rain !
The spouse, Ma-ú, of Winter is night ;
The time of arising has come !

This kupua, Kauhi, termed the watch-tower of heaven, having come from Kahiki in the train of Pele's followers, and having been stationed in this cliff, had got no further in his travels than Oahu. He bemoaned his fate as that of a malihini god, a stranger to the rest of the group. On being roused by this prayer-song of Hiiaka, as he gazed upon the beautiful goddess, a divine ambition stirred within him — to journey with her, enjoy her society, and make acquaintance with the land to which he was still a stranger. With this purpose in mind, at the conclusion of her address, he chanted this response :

O Pele la ko'u akua :
Miha ka lani, miha ka honua :

Awa i-ku,(a) awa i-lani,(b) keia awa,
Ka awa nei o Hiiaka,
I ku ai, ku i Mauli-ola;(c)
I Mauli-ola he awa kaulu-ola,(d) e,
No na Wahine, — e kapu-kapu-kai(e) ka awa,
E Pele honua-mea!
E kala, e Haumea(f) wahine;
O ka Wahine i Kilauea,
Nana i ai(g) a hohonu ka Lua;
O Ma-ú,(h) wahine a Maka-li'i;
O Lua-wahine(i) ka lani;
O Kukuena;(j) o na wahine
I ka inu hana awa;
Kanaenae a ke akua malihini,(k) e!

(a, b) *Awa i-ku, awa i-lani.* A clear understanding of these words calls for a reference to the customs, that had almost the dignity of a rite, that were observed in the handling of awa for purposes of worship, or as an offering to the gods. This began with the very digging of the awa root. He who did this had first to purify himself by a bath in the ocean, followed by an ablution in fresh water and completing the lustration with an aspersion of water containing turmeric, administered by a priest. Then, having arrayed himself in a clean malo, he knelt with both knees upon the ground and tore the root from its bed. Now, rising to his feet, he lifted the awa root to heaven, and by this act the awa was dignified and was called *awa i-ku.* The utterance (by the priest?) of the kanaenae, or prayer of consecration and eulogy, still further enhanced this dignity and set it apart as a special sacrifice to some god, or to the gods of some class. Awa thus consecrated was known as *awa i-lani.*

(c) *Mauli-ola,* the God of Health; also the name of a place. The same name was applied also to the breath of life, and to the kahuna's power of healing. In the Maori tongue the word *mauri* means life, the seat of life. In Samoan *mauli* means heart; in Hawaiian it means to faint. "Sneeze, living heart" ("*Tihe, mauri ora*"), says the New Zealand mother to her infant when it utters a sneeze. The Hawaiian mother makes the same ejaculation.

(d) *Ka-ulu-ola.* I can throw no light on this phrase further than is to be obtained in the above note.

(e) *Kapu-kapu-kai.* Awa was forbidden to women. Under certain circumstances, however, it was set before them. In such a case the tabu was first removed by sprinkling the root with sea water (*kapu-kai*).

(f) *Haumea,* the mother of Pele.

(g) *Ai.* In another version, instead of *ai,* I find *eli* or *elieli* used.

(h) *Ma-u,* the sister of Haumea, therefore aunt to Pele, also the wife of Maka-li'i.

(i) *Lua-wahine,* (lua-hine?), said to be an incarnation, or more properly, perhaps, a spiritual form (*kino-lau*) of Haumea.

(j) *Kukuena,* the goddess, *au-makua,* who presided over the ceremony of preparing awa for drinking; said to be an elder sister of Pele.

(k) *Akua malihini,* an epithet applied to himself by Kauhi, because, as previously stated, he had since his arrival from Kahiki been obliged to remain fixed in his station in the cliff and had thus been denied acquaintance with the other islands, especially the big island of Hawaii.

Hele ho'i ke ala mauka o Ka-ú
Hele ho'i ke ala makai o Puna,
I Ka-ma'a-ma'a,(*l*) i ka puale'i,(*m*)
E loa'a ka awa i Apua;(*n*)
Ka pi'i'na i Ku-ka-la-ula;(*o*)
Hoopuka aku la i kai o Pu'u-lena —(*p*)
Aina a ke Akua(*q*) i noho ai. —
Kanaenae a ke 'kua malihini.

TRANSLATION

Pele, indeed, is my god.
Calm be the heavens, peaceful the earth:
Here's awa fresh-torn from the ground,
Awa that's been lifted to heaven,
An off'ring for goddess Hiiaka,
A growth of the kingdom Mauli-ola,
Awa that makes for health and peace;
Its woman-ban cleared by aspersion.
Pele, O Pele of the sacred land,
And thou, O Mother Haumea;
Thou Woman of Kilauea,
Fire-goddess who dug the Pit deep;
Niece to Ma-ú, Maka-li'i's wife;
Own child of heavenly Hau-mea;
And thou Kukuena, that rules
In the rite of toothing the awa —
A brew that is fit for the gods —
Love-offering this of the stranger god,
Denied, alas, the road through upland
Ka-ú and the lowlands of Puna,

(*l*) *Ka-ma'a-ma'a*, a land in Puna.

(*m*) *Pua-le'i.* Bird-hunters often stripped off the lower branches from a selected lehua tree that was in full flower and then limed it to ensnare the birds that were attracted to its rich clusters. Such a tree was termed *pua-le'i.*

(*n*) *Apua*, a place in Puna.

(*o*) *Ku-ka-la-ula*, a place on the road that ascends from Puna to Kilauea. The same term was applied to the ruddy glow that appears on a mountain horizon just before sunrise.

(*p*) *Pu'u-lena*, said to be the name of a hill near Kilauea-iki. It is now commonly employed as the name of a wind, as in the old saying: *"Ua hala ka Pu'u-lena, aia i Hilo."*

(*q*) *Akua.* That was Pele herself. *"Aina a ke Akua i noho ai"* has passed into a saying.

To Ka-ma'a and the bird-limed tree —
Sure route to the potent root of Apua —
The up-road to Ku-ka-la-ula,
Thence leading to Sulphur-hill:
Land where the gods did once dwell!
A laud this, voiced by the stranger god.

At the conclusion of this kanaenae Kauhi said to Hiiaka, "If you are the woman that consumes the forests of Puna, when you travel I will go with you." (*"Ina ooe ka wahine ai laau o Puna, ooe hele, oau hele."*)

Hiiaka did not wish to offend the aggrieved deity; at the same time she could not consent to his proposition. In this dilemma she did her best to soothe his feelings and reconcile him to his lot:

Ku'u Akua i ka hale hau,
Hale kanáka ole,
E noho i ke kai o Ma'a-kua,
Alae ia e ke ki ohuohu, e!
Pene'i wale no ka iki Akua.
Auwe, ku'u Akua, e!

TRANSLATION

My god of the chilly mansion, —
A house without human tenant, —
Abide yet the blasts of the sea,
The slap of the broad leafy ti.
Such the advice of a lesser god:
My tender farewell this to Thee.

Kauhi was indignant at this evasive dismissal of his entreaty. The thought that Hiiaka should countenance his perpetual imprisonment in the bleak cliff filled him with rage. With a mighty effort he lifted himself and tore away the covering of tree-roots, earth and rocks that embraced him until he came to a crouching position. That was the limit of his power: he could do no more. A stony form in the mountain wall of Kahana, resembling the shape of a man on all-fours, remains to vouch for the truth of this legend.

Halemaʻumaʻu Crater, Kilauea, Hawaiʻi.

CHAPTER XXI(x)

HIIAKA DESCRIBES THE SCENE BEFORE HER

Hiiaka constantly showed a lively interest in the important features of the landscape, often addressing them as if they had been sentient beings. At Kai-papa'u, looking out upon cape Lani-loa, she greeted it as if it had been an old friend of the family:

> Lele Lani-loa; ua malie;
> Ke hoe a'e la ka Moa'e,
> Ahu kai i na pali;
> Kaiko'o lalo, e.
> Ua pi'i kai i uka, e.

TRANSLATION

> Fly Lani-loa, fly in the calm.
> At the moaning of Moa'e,(a)
> Mist veils the mountain walls.
> The breakers roll ever below,
> While Ocean climbs to the hills.

They passed through the lands of Laie, Malae-kahana and Keana and at Kahipa they saw the crouching figures of Puna-he'e-lapa and Pahi-pahi-alua, who stole away into the shelter of the pandanus groves without deigning to give them any salutation. At this show of disrespect, Hiiaka called out:

> Komo i ka nahele ulu hinalo,
> Nahele hala o Po'o-kaha-lulu;
> Oia nahele hala makai o Kahuku.
> Heaha la ho'i ka hala(y)
> I kapu ai o ka leo, e?
> I Hookuli ai oe i ka uwalo, e?
> E uwalo aku ana au;
> Maloko mai oe, e!

(x) I have purposely weeded out from the narrative, as popularly told, several incidents that have but little interest and no seeming pertinence to the real purpose of the story.

(a) *Moa'e,* the trade wind.

(y) There seems to lurk a play in this word *hala.* It stood not only for the pandanus tree; it also meant a fault, a sin.

We enter the fragrant groves,
Hala groves whose heads make a calm,
Wild growths by the sea of Kahuku,
But what, indeed, are your halas?
Shall their murmur forbid you speech?
Make you dumb to my salutation?
I make this kindly entreaty
To you who sit in the grove.

They crossed the Waimea stream on the sand-bar, which in ordinary weather dams its mouth and, climbing the rocky bluff Kehu-o-hapu'u, had a fine view of the ocean surges tossing up their white spray as they ceaselessly beat against the near-by elevated reef-fringe that parapets this coast, as well as of the Ka-ala mountains, blue in the distance.

(This bluff of Kehu-o-hapu'u until within a few years was the site of a little heiau, the resort of fishermen; and in it stood a rude stone figure of the fish-god Ku-ula. From the non-mention of this interesting object, we have to argue either that the discovery and worship of this idol was of later date than the times of Hiiaka or that she ignored it.)

Hiiaka, casting her eye about for objects of interest, was attracted by the odd appearance of the lily-like water-plant uki, the detached floating clumps of which looked as if they had been fire-smitten:

Ke ai'na mai la e ka wai
Ka maha uki o Ihu-koko;
Ke puhi ia la e ka makani.
Hako'i ka ua, ka wai iluna:
Ke kina'i ia ho'i ka iwi o ka wai a éha.
E há i ka leo — he leo wale no.

The lily tufts of Ihu-koko
Are gnawed away by the water
And thrashed about by the wind.

Beat down by the rain from heaven,
The wave-ribs are flattened out.
Hushed be the voice — merely the voice.

From the same vantage-ground — that of Kehu-o-hapu'u —
Hiiaka not only saw the dash of the ocean against the buttresses
of the near-by coast, her ears also were filled with a murmurous
ocean-roar that gave to the air a tremor like that of a deep
organ-tone:

> O Wai-alua, kai leo nui:
> Ua lono ka uka o Lihu'e;
> Ke wa la Wahi-awá, e.
> Kuli wale, kuli wale i ka leo;
> He leo no ke kai, e.

TRANSLATION

> Wai-alua, land of the sounding sea,
> With audience in upland Lihu'e —
> A voice that reaches Wahi-awá:
> Our ears are stunned by this voice —
> The voice, I say, of old Ocean!

The landscape still held her, and she continued:

> O Wai-alua, la'i ehá, e!
> Ehá ka malino lalo o Wai-alua.

TRANSLATION

> Wai-alua has a fourfold calm,
> That enfolds and broods o'er the land.

"Let us move on," said Hiiaka to her companion, "there's a
pang next my heart. Had I meat in my hand, we'd trudge to a
water-spring and so be refreshed until we came to the house of
a friend. Let us move."

From the plain near Lau-hulu Hiiaka took a fresh view of
Mount Ka-ala and, in a tone of bantering apology, said, "Forget
me not, O Ka-ala. Perhaps you complain that I have not
chanted your praises:"

O Ka-ala, kuahiwi mauna kehau,
Ke opú mai la, la, i Ka-maóha;
Poluea(a) iho la ilalo o Hale-auau;
Ke kini ke kehau anu o Ka-lena.
Akahi no ka nele o ka la pomaikai:
Aohe moe-wa'a(b) o ka po nei —
Ka moe-wa'a, e!

TRANSLATION

Ka-ala, dewy and forest-clad,
Bellies the plain at Ma-óha,
As it slopes to the land below.
The cool dew-fall comforts Ka-lena:
First pinch this of want mid good luck —
No dream of canoe-voyage last night,.
No dream of disaster at sea.

The story of Cape Ka-ena, that finger-like thrusts itself out into the ocean from the western extremity of Oahu, touches Hawaiian mythology at many points: Its mountain eminence was a *leina uhane,* jumping-off place, where the spirits of the deceased took their flying leap into ghost-land. Here it was that the demigod Maui had his *pou sto* when he made the supreme effort of his life to align and unite the scattered group of islands; and here can still be seen Pohaku o Kauai, the one fragment of *terra firma* his hook could wrench from its base. Here, too, it was that Pele stood when she chaffed the old demigod for having lured her on, as she supposed, with drum and fife to the pursuit of Lohiau; and now her sister Hiiaka stands in the same place. The subject was well worthy Hiiaka's muse:

Lele ana o Ka-ena
Me he manu la i ka malie;

(a) *Poluea,* ordinary meaning, to be nauseated; here it means to slope down.

(b) *Moe-wa'a,* literally, a canoe-dream. To dream of a canoe-voyage was considered an omen of very bad luck.

Me he kaha na ka uwa'u(*a*) la
Na pali o Nene-le'a;(*b*)
Me he upa'i na ke koa'e (*c*) la
Ka ale iwaho o Ka-ieie;(*d*)
Me he kanáka hoonu'u la i ka malie
Ka papa kea i ke alo o ka alá;
Ua ku'i 'a e ke kai,
A uli, a nono, a ula
Ka maka o ka alá,
E no-noho ana i ke kai o Ka-peku.(*e*)
Ka-peku ka leo o ke kai —
O Hoo-ilo(*f*) ka malama. —
Ke ku mai la ka pauli i kai,
Ka hoailona kai o ka aina:
A'e kai o Ka-hulu-manu;(*g*)
Kai a moana ka aina.
Ahu wale ka pae ki'i,
Ka pae newe-newe,
Ka pae ma nu'u a Kana-loa: —
A he hoa, a oia.
Hoohaehae(*h*) ana ka Lae-o-ka-laau, (*i*)
I kihe(*j*) ia e ke kai o Wawalu,(*k*)
Na owaewae(*l*) pali o Unu-lau
Inu aku i ka wai o Kohe-iki i ka pali —

(*a*) *Uwa'u,* a sea-bird, a gull.

(*b*) *Nene-le'a,* a place near Ka-ena point, close to Pohaku o Kaua'i.

(*c*) *Koa'e,* the tropic-bird, or bosen-bird.

(*d*) *Ka-ieie,* the channel between Oahu and Kauai.

(*e*) *Ka-peku.* The word kapeku, at the beginning of verse 13, means, I am told, querulous.

(*f*) *Ho'o-ilo,* or *Ho-ilo,* the cool or rainy season of the year, covering six months according to the Hawaiians. There was no such month (*mahina*) as *Ho'o-ilo,* or *Ho-ilo.*

(*g*) *Ka-hulu-manu.* The kai o Ka-hulu-manu is, as reported to me by a well-informed Hawaiian, a flood that submerged the land in mythological times, distinct from *Kai-a-ka-hina-alii.*

(*h*) *Hoohaehae,* to chase, to irritate, to tease.

(*i*) *Lae-o-ka-laau,* (literally, Cape of the Trees), the south-western cape of Moloka'i, on which the United States have established a first-class lighthouse.

(*j*) *Kihe,* to sneeze; to spatter; to wet with spray.

(*k*) *Wawalu,* a cove.

(*l*) *Owaewae,* gullied. This is an instance of the adjective being placed before its noun.

I ka pali ka wai,
Kau pu me ka laau.
Hoole ke kupa, huná i ka wai.(*m*)
Ehá ka muli-wai, wai(*n*) o Ka-ena.
Ena iho la e ka la o ka Maka-li'i;
O-i'o mai ana ke a me he kanaka koa la,
Maalo ana i ku'u maka;
Me he hauka'i la o ia kalana pali,
Kuamo'o loa, pali o Lei-honua.
Hiki iho nei no ka hauoli
I ka hiki'na mai a nei makani.
Heaha la ka'u makana i ku'u hilahila?
O ka'u wale iho la no ia, o ka leo, e!

TRANSLATION

Ka-ena Point flies on its way
Like a sea-bird in fair weather;
Like the wings of a swooping gull
Are the cliffs of Nene-le'a;
Like the lash of the bosen's wings
Is the curl of the breaking wave
In the channel of Iĕ-iĕ.
The gray sand that borders the lava
Drinks the waves like a thirsting man;
And purple and pink and red
Are the eye-spots of the bazalt
That gleam in the sea of Ka-peku.
The sea gives a querulous tone —
The season is that of Ho-ilo.
A cloud-pall shadows the ocean,
Sure sign of a turbulent sea,
Of a tide that will deluge the land,
Like the Flood of Ka-hulu-manu.
The god-forms stand in due order,
Forms that are swollen to bursting,
The group on Kana-loa's altar: —

(*m*) *Huna i ka wai.* The people of the region concealed the holes where water dripped, as it was very scarce.

(*n*) *Muli-wai,* literally a river, a poetical exaggeration.

Friends, allies, I reckon them all.
Cape-of-the-Woods entices us on,
Besprayed by the sea of Wawalu,
Forefront Unulau's gullied cliffs.
I drink of the water distilled
By the dripping pali walls,
Led forth in a hollowed log.
The rustic denies it and hides it:
Four water-streams has Ka-ena;
And the summer sun is ardent.
The blocks of stone, like warriors,
Move in procession before me —
Pilgrims that march along the crest
Of the steep ridge Lei-honua.
Ah, a new joy now do I find:
It comes with the breath of this wind!
And what is my gift in return?
To my shame, it's only my voice.

The rocks and huge bowlders that dotted the barren waste of
Ka-ena seemed to the travelers to glow and vibrate as if they
were about to melt under the heat of the sun, a phenomenon that
stirred the imagination of Hiiaka to song:

Liu'a ke kaha o Ka-ena, wela i ka La;
Ai'na iho la ka pohaku a mo'a wela;
Kahuli oni'o, holo ana i ka malie;
Ha'aha'a' ka puka one, ki'eki'e ke ko'a,
I ka hapai ia e ka makani, ka Malua:
O'u hoa ia i ke Koolau, e.
A pa Koolau, hoolale kula hulu;
Kahea ke keiki i ka wa'a,
'E holo, oi malie ke kaha o Nene-le'a;
Aohe halawai me ka ino i ka makani;
Ka pipi lua o ka ale i ka ihu o ka wa'a.
He wa'awa'a(a) ka makani, he naaupo;
Ke kai ku'i-ké, koke nalo ka pohaku!

(a) *Wa'a-wa'a,* simple-minded; unsophisticated; "green;" the name of
two youths mentioned in tradition, one of whom committed blunder after
blunder from his soft-hearted stupidity.

Ke kupa hoolono kai, o Pohaku-o-Kaua'i.(*b*) e,
A noho ana o Pohaku o Kaua'i i kai, e!

TRANSLATION

Ka-ena, salty and barren,
Now throbs with the blaze of the sun;
The rocks are consumed by the heat,
Dappled and changed in their color:
The sand-holes sink, the coral forms heaps,
Urged by the breath of Malua —
That fellow of mine from Koolau:
When blows Koolau, then bristles the plain.
Then calls the lad to the sailor,
Speed on while calm is Nene-le'a ;
Such time you'll meet with good weather;
The lap of the sea 'gainst the bow —
A most thoughtless, good-natured, wind, that.
When choppy the sea, hid are the rocks!
A man of the sea art thou, well versed
In its signs of storm and of calm,
O Rock, thou Rock of Kaua'i!

(*b*) *Pohaku o Kaua'i.* The most audacious terrestrial undertaking of the demigod Mawi was his attempt to rearrange the islands of the group and assemble them into one solid mass. Having chosen his station at Kaena Point, the western extremity of Oahu, from which the island of Kaua'i is clearly visible on a bright day, he cast his wonderful hook, Mana-ia-ka-lani, far out into the ocean that it might engage itself in the foundations of Kaua'i. When he felt that it had taken a good hold, he gave a mighty tug at the line. A huge bowlder, the Pohaku o Kaua'i, fell at his feet. The mystic hook, having freed itself from its entanglement, dropped into Palolo Valley and hollowed out the crater, that is its grave. This failure to move the whole mass of the island argues no engineering mis-calculation on Mawi's part. It was due to the underhand working of spiritual forces. Had Mawi been more politic, more observant of spiritual etiquette, more diplomatic in his dealings with the heavenly powers, his ambitious plans would, no doubt, have met with better success.

CHAPTER XXII

HIIAKA ADDRESSES POHAKU-O-KAUA'I — THE TWO WOMEN RIG UP A CANOE — SHE SALUTES KAENA — SALUTE TO HAUPU — SEES LOHIAU'S SPIRIT FORM

Hiiaka had large acquaintance with the natural features of every landscape, and if those features were of volcanic origin she might claim them as kindred through her own relationship with Pele. It was hers to find friendship, if not sermons, in stones. This Pohaku-o-Kaua'i, to whom Hiiaka now addressed herself, though in outward form an unshapen bowlder, as we see it today, — the very one that Mawi drew from its ocean-bed with his magic hook Mana-ia-ka-lani — was in truth a sentient being, alive to all the honor-claims of kinship. To him, in her need, Hiiaka addressed herself:

> E Pohaku o Kaua'i i kai, e,
> A po Ka-ena i na pali,
> I wa'a no maua
> E ike aku ai i ka maka o ke hoa,
> O Lohiau ipo, e!

TRANSLATION

> O sea-planted Rock of Kaua'i,
> Night shadows the cliffs of Ka-ena:
> A canoe for me and my fellow;
> We would look on the face of our friend,
> Lohiau the dearly beloved.

"I have no canoe," said Pohaku o Kaua'i. "The one I had was wrecked in a storm while on a fishing trip. One huge wave came aboard and split her from end to end. We had to swim for it. But surely, such a beautiful woman as you will have no trouble in finding a canoe. There must be no lack of canoes making the trip to Kaua'i."

"In the lack of a canoe, let us have a plank, such as I see you are there using for a shelf."

"If that will serve you, you are welcome," said the old man.

"We shall also need an outrigger-float for our craft," Hiiaka remarked.

"An ama (outrigger-float) is a thing I lack," he answered.

"You must have some block of wili-wili —such as that one, for instance, wihch you use to hold your fishhooks," Hiaaka urged.

The old man was able to meet their demands. The two women then set their wits to work and finally succeeded in lashing the parts together in such fashion as to make something that would serve as a canoe.

Hiiaka, as the one in command, sat astern and Wahine-oma'o in the bow. As they sailed away Hiaaka saluted Cape Ka-ena in these words:

> Holo Ka-ena, la,
> Me he wa'a kaukahi la i ka malie; —
> Ka lau hoe, lau hoe o Kua-o-ka-la;(a)
> Ke kowelowelo(b) la o Lehua, e;
> O Lehua ho'i, e!

TRANSLATION

> Ka-ena speeds along
> A single canoe in the calm;
> The four hundred rays that dart from
> The Back of the Sun sink down
> In the sea at Lehua,
> The western waves of Lehua.

When well out in the channel of Kaieie the sight of the famous Hill of Haupu, that now appeared to lift its head like a water-fowl stemming the tide, was an inspiration to song. Mingled with the pleasure, however, was the chagrin and indignation that came from knowing that at that very moment her own lehua preserves in Kona were suffering ravage from fire by the act of Pele:

(a) *Kua-o-ka-La* (the back of the sun), a personification and deification of that orb.

(b) *Kowelowelo*, to sink into; to be submerged.

O Haupu,(*a*) mauna ki'e-ki'e,
Huki a'e la, pa i ka lani;
Waha(*b*) keiki ma ke kua;
Hi'i Ke-olewa(*c*) ma ke alo;
Au ana Ni'ihau i ke kai.
Pau a'u lehua i ka manu, e,
Pau, e, o a'u lehua, ho'i, e!

TRANSLATION

Famed Haupu, the mighty hill,
Lifts head till she touches heaven;
On her back strapped a suckling child,
While she fondles a fleecy cloud,
And Niihau swims the ocean tide.
Oh, my lehuas! spoiled by the birds!
Alas, my lehuas, alas!

"What a notion!" Wahine-oma'o exclaimed. "Who in the
world is meddling with your lehuas?"

While they were sailing along the precipitous coast of Ka-
lalau, set in the windward wall of the island, Hiiaka saw standing at the mouth of a cave high up on the precipice, the spirit
form of one who was no other than Lohiau, and again she was
moved to song:

A Ka-lalau, a Ke-é,
A ka pali au i Haena,
E peahi mai ana ka lawakua(*a*) ia'u la;
Peahi, e peahi mai ana ka lawakua ia'u.
Owau keia, o ka maka o ke aloha, la,
O ke aloha, ho'i, e!

TRANSLATION

Off the coast of Lalau, off Ke-é,
When nigh the cliffs of Haena,

(*a*) *Haupu,* a famous hill on Kauai, visible from Oahu. When it was
capped with a cloud, Hawaiians said, *"Ua kau mai ka pua'a i Haupu; e ua
ana."* If that occurred in the rainy season, they said it was about to clear.

(*b*) *Waha,* the same as *haawe,* i.e., a load for the back. In this case it
was a bank of mist or clouds.

(*c*) *Ke-olewa,* a hill, smaller than Haupu, on the side towards Kipu-kai.
The word also applied to the floating clouds about the mountain.

The loved one beckons, he beckons,
The loved one beckons to me.
I am the one — the eye-scout of love:
Love, indeed, is my errand, aye love!

The ghost-form of Lohiau still continued to show itself as they sailed; and when it signalled a recognition of Hiiaka by beckoning to her, she could but answer it:

Ua pu'e ia e ke one ka lehua o uka;
Ua ho-á iki ka ula i ka papa;
Ua huná i ke kino i ka pohaku;
O ka pua na'e, ke ahu nei i ke ala —
Alanui hele o Ka-unu-kupukupu;(b)
Hele li'u-lá(c) o ka poha-kau,(d) e ;
Kaulia(e) a ka poha-kau he kilohana(f) ia;
He maka'ika'i ia no Ka-hua-nui;(g)
He kahiko ia no ka wai o kaunu,(h) e.
A kaunu anei, o ke aloha ia ?
A ia'u la, éha oe!

TRANSLATION

The upland lehua is clinker-heaped;
Wee flame-buds crop up on the plain ;
The tree-trunk is hidden with rocks,
Yet its flowers encarpet the path:
The road this that leads to desire —
One's travel stays not at twilight,

(a) *Lawa-kua*, a precious object bound to the back; applied, therefore, to a child, a dear friend and the like; the local name applied to a wind at Ka-lalau.

(b) *Ka-unu-kupukupu*, a land in Puna. The intrinsic meaning of the phrase is an increasing, overmastering, passion *ka-unu*, a passion; *kupukupu*, to grow up, to increase.

(c) *Li'u-la*, twilight.

(d) *Poha-kau*, a resting place where the burden-carrier leaned back and relieved his shoulders of their burden for a time.

(e) *Kaulia*, old form of *kauia* (*kau ia*). It connotes the removing from the back the *haawe*, preliminary to a long rest.

(f) *Kilohana*, here means a comfort, a relief.

(g) *Ka-hua-nui*, the elder sister of Lohiau.

(h) *Kau-nu*, desire, passion. *Wai o kau-nu*, lit., the water of love— "the warm effects."

Nor to ease one's back of its load.
My journey's to Ka-hua-nui;
She is the goal of my passion.
If love be the targe of thy aim,
And I that targe, ruin awaits thee !

CHAPTER XXIII

THE LAME FISHERMAN — HIS EPIC RECITAL
CELEBRATING PELE

On arriving at Haena, Hiiaka did not go at once to Lohiau's place but to the house of Malae-ha'a-koa, a man of chiefish rank, and one who had the reputation of being a seer. He was lame and unable to walk. For this reason his wife, Wailua-nui-a-hoano, had carried him down to the seashore and, leaving him there to his fishing, had gone home to her work of tapa-making. She was busily wielding the tapa club in the *hale kuku kapa* while Hiiaka stood outside the enclosure and sang:

> Kunihi ka mauna i ka la'i, e,
> O Wai-aleale, la, i Wai-lua;
> Huki iluna ka popo ua o Ka-wai-kini;
> Alai ia a'e la e Nounou,
> Nalo ka Ipu-ha'a,
> Ka laula ma uka o Ka-pa'a, e.
> I pa'a i ka leo, he ole e hea mai.
> E hea mai ka leo, e !

TRANSLATION

> The mountain turns the cold shoulder,
> Facing away from Wai-lua,
> Albeit in time of fair weather.
> Wai-kini flaunts, toplofty, its rain-cap;
> And the view is cut off by Nounou,
> Thus Humility Hill is not seen,
> Nor Ka-pa'a's broad upland plain.
> You seal your lips and are voiceless:
> Best to open your mouth and speak.

The woman Wai-lua-nui-a-hoano received in silence this sharp reproof of her haughty and inhospitable conduct, couched, though it was, in the veiled language of symbol. Her eyes left the work in hand and followed Hiiaka and Wahine-oma'o as they turned and faced the path that climbed the pali wall.

Malae-ha'a-koa, lame, guileless, innocent of all transgression, meanwhile, sat and fished. He had cast afresh his triple-hooked line, blown from his mouth into the water the comminuted fragments of the shrimps whose bodies baited his hooks and, as he waited for a bite he chanted a song (to the god of good luck) that reached Hiiaka's ear:

> Pa mai ka makani o ka lele wa'a, e:
> Makani kai ehu lalo o ka pali o Ki-pú.
> I malenalena i Wai-niha i ka'u makau:
> He i'a, he i'a na ka lawaia, na Malae-ha'a-koa, e!

TRANSLATION

> A wind-squall drives the canoes in flight,
> Dashing the spray 'gainst the cliff of Kipú.
> Peace, waves, for my hook at Wai-niha:
> Come, fish, to the hook of the fisher,
> The hook of Malae-ha'a-koa!

Hiiaka's answer to this was a song:

> O Malae-ha'a-koa, lawaia o ka pali,
> Keiki lawaia oe a Wai-niha,
> Mo'opuna oe a Ka-nea-lani,
> Lawaia ku pali o Haena;
> Au umauma o ke ala haki;
> He i'a na ka lawaia,
> Na Malae-ha'a-koa, e.

TRANSLATION

> I hail thee, Malae-ha'a-koa,
> Thou fisherman of the cliffs.
> As a youth you fished at Wai-niha;
> Grandson thou to Ka-noa-lani,
> Fishing now 'neath the bluffs of Haena,

Sometime breasting the steep mountain ladder.
Send fish, O Heaven, to this fisherman;
Send fish to Malae-ha'a-koa.

As if obedient to the charm of Hiiaka's incantation, the breeze
sank to a whisper and the ruffled surface of the ocean took on a
calm that brought fish to the fisherman's hooks.

Malae-ha'a-koa looked up from his work and, though he did
not recognize Hiiaka, he had an intuitive sense that it was her
power that had quieted the elements and, with a shrewd insight,
he divined that she was of the Pele family. "It is you then that
has made this day one of calm;" and he continued his address
in song:

> Ooe ia, e ka wahine ai laau o Puna,
> E ka lalá i ka ulu(a) o Wahine-kapu, e;
> He i'a, he i'a na ka lawaia,
> Na na Akua wahine o Puna, e.

TRANSLATION

> Thou art she, O tree-eater of Puna,
> O branch of Wahine-kapu's bread- tree.
> Swarm, fish, to the fisherman's hook —
> Fish for the godlike woman of Puna.

Malae-ha'a-koa felt a genial thrill pervading his system; new
vigor came to him; he found himself able to stand on his feet
and walk. Some new and wonderful power had come into his
life. In the first flush of his ecstacy, he gathered up his fishing
tackle, thrust the hooks and lines into his basket and walked
triumphantly home on his own feet. Without a word to his
wife, he began to tear down a portion of the fence that enclosed
the house-lot.

"What are you about?" exclaimed his wife; "tearing down
our fence! . . But what has happened to you? Here you are
for the first time in many years able to walk on your feet!"

The man made no immediate reply, but kept on with his work.
When she repeated her questionings and expressions of wonder,

---

(a) *Ulu o Wahine-Kapu.* Wahine-kapu was the name given to the plateau over which Kaneohoalii presided, a very tabu place. As to the bread-
fruit tree *Ulu,* I have been able to learn nothing; this is the first mention of
it I have met with.

he quietly asked, "Have you not seen two women about the place?"

"There were two women who came this way," she answered thoughtfully.

"Would you think it! They were divine beings," he exclaimed in a tone of conviction. "We must spread for them a feast. You had better prepare some luau."

Malae-ha'a-koa himself, alii as he was, with his own hands set about dressing and preparing a dog for the oven. This was his own token of service. At his command his people brought the material for an abundant feast.

Hiiaka saw from a distance the smoke of Malae-ha'a-koa's imu and recognized the bustle preparatory to a feast, she exclaimed to her companion, "The lame man has saved the day."

When the repast was nearing its end and the people had well eaten, Malae-ha'a-koa and his wife stood forth and led in the performance of a sacred dance, accompanying their rhythmic motions with a long mele that recited the deeds, the events, the mysteries that had marked Pele's reign since the establishment of her dominion in Hawaii:

> O kaua a Pele i haká i Kahiki,
> I hakaká ai me Na-maka-o-ka-ha'i. [1]
> Mahuka mai Pele i Hawaii;
> Mahuka Pele i ona onohi,
> I na lapa uwila,
> E lapa i na mahina, la!
>   Elieli, kau mai! [2]

> He kai moe nei no Pele,
> No ke Akua;
> He kai hoolale i na moku.
> Ha'i aku kai i Hana-kahi, [3]

---

(1) *Na-maka-o-ka-ha'i*, an elder sister of Pele, with whom she had trouble over the question of tabus, rights and privileges, involving the right to dominion over the volcanic fires. Pele was not only a stickler for her own rights and privileges but ambitious for their extension. The result was she had to flee for her life. (For the story of this trouble see p. V of the introduction.)

(2) *Elieli, kau mai!* A solemn expression often found at the end of a prayer. Hawaiians are unable to give an exact account of its meaning. The phrase *kau mai* by itself means overshadow me, sit upon me, possess me.

(3) *Hana-kahi*, an appelation applied to Hilo derived from the name of an ancient king.

I ke one o Wai-olama[4] iluna.

Ako ia ka hale[5] a ke Akua;

Ke amo 'a la ke ko'i[6]

Ke Akua la i uka.

Haki nu'anu'a mai ka nalu mai Kahiki;

Popo'i aku i ke alo o Kilauea,

Ke kai huli i ke alo o Papa-lau-ahi.

Kanáka hea i ke ála —

Kou pua'a-kanu,[7] Wahine kui lehua

Ka uka i Ola'a, ku'u moku lehua

I ke alo o Heeia, o Kukuena[8] wahine.

Komo i ka lauwili[9] na hoalii

I ka nahele o Puna —

A'e, a'e a noho.

Eia makou, kou lau kaula, la!

Elieli, kau mai!

---

(4) *Wai-o-lama,* the name applied to the eastern section of Hilo town, including the sand-beach and the river there located.

(5) *Ako ia ka hale.* The hands elevated and the fingers brought together in the form of an inverted V were, I am informed, an accepted symbol that might be used in place of a heiau at a time when distress or emergency made impossible the erection of such a structure. David Malo narrates a similar incident as occurring in the mythical story of Wakea at a time when he was in peril and beset by his enemies.

(6) *Ko'i ke Akua.* There is a division of opinion as to the meaning of this passage. Some, including J. W. P., think it may be the shortened, poetical form of ko'iko'i, heavy, referring to the timber used in building a temple for the deity. Others take the view that the word *ko'i* should be given its face-value. I see in it a possible reference to pahoehoe, the plates of which, in their hot and nascent state, are capable of felling a forest as effectively as a *ko'i*. One expounder (Pelei-oho-lani) finds in this word *ko'i* a reference to a symbolical lifting of the thumb of the left hand as a sign of prayer. The arguments on the one side and on the other are not quite convincing.

(7) *Kou pua'a kanu.* Pua'a-kanu is the name of a place in Puna, said to be the spot where Pele had her sexual encounter with Kama-pua'a, the swine-god. I look upon it as meaning the encounter itself.

(8) *Kukuena wahine,* an elder sister of Pele. (Some one says the first born of the Pele family. This assertion is not verified by other authorities). She had charge of the making and distribution of the leis and of the ceremonies connected with formal awa-drinking. She was, in short, a sort of lady of the bedchamber to Pele.

(9) *Lauwili,* literally, an entanglement. It refers to the lustful attack made by Kama-pua'a on Pele, an attack to which she gave seeming acquiescence.

He kai ehu ko Kohala-loa,
Kai apa'apa'a [10] ko ka pali i uka;
He kai kiei pali ko Kupehau,
Kai pi'i hala o ka aina:
Ke popo'i aku la i kai o Maui
Ke kai a ka Wahine ali'i,
O ke kai kui lehua a Pele,
A ko'u akua la, e!
    Elieli, kau mai!

Hiiaka was so greatly impressed with this mele that she commanded Wahine-oma'o to restrain herself and observe the dignity of the occasion by eating more quietly. The young woman, thereupon, moderated her gusto and concluded her repast with less smacking of the lips; and the singers proceeded:

E oe mauna i ka ohu ka pali,
Kahá ka leo o ka ohi'a, uwé:
Ike au i ke ahi ai alá,
Ka luahine [11] moe naná
A pápa enaena, wai hau, a wa'a kauhí. [12]
Ilaila Pepe mua, Pepe waena, [13]
O Pepe ka muimui —[14]
O kihele ia ulu, [15] ka maka hakaikea
O Niheu [16] Kalohe, ka maka kahá la.
    Elieli, kau mai!

---

(10) *Apa'apa'a,* the name of a violent wind, here used adjectively.

(11) *Luahine moe nana,* Pele, who is depicted as an old woman huddled up on a lava plate. The snoring must refer to the sounds made by the lava while in action.

(12) *Wa'a kauhi,* an unrigged canoe, without *iako* or *ama.*

(13) *Pepe mua, Pepe waena.* This a detail in the development of the figure in which flowing lava is compared to a canoe. The *pepe* is a chock such as is put under the canoe when it is at rest on land. *Mua, waena* and *muimui* mean respectively at the bow, amidships and astern.

(14) *Muimui,* an elided form of mulimuli, the hindmost.

(15) *Kihele ia ulu.* Kihele, to bail out; ulu—the belly of the canote, its swell amidships, the place where the bilge would settle. The implication is that, if the water is not bailed out, the incrusted salt will form a spot like the staring eye of Niheu.

(16) *Nïheu,* a mythological hero who is always spoken of as kalohe, mischievous, because of his restlessness and stirring energy. His mother, Hina, had been abducted by a pirate chief who lived on the high bluff of Haupu, on Moloka'i. Niheu and his brother Kana, whose body was a rope of immense length, went to their mother's rescue, in which they succeeded, after many adventures. The eyes of Niheu were a marked feature in his appearance, being described as large and searching.

A Moloka'i nui a Hina,[17]
A Kaunu-ohua[18] he pali,
A kukui o Haupu.[19]
Haupu ke akua li'ili'i;
Puka mai Pele, ke Akua nui,
Me Haumea, me Hiiaka,
Me Kukuena, me Okaoka:[20]
O ke a ke ahi iki, e a!
He onohi no Pele,
Ka oaka o ka lani la, e!
    Elieli, kau mai!

A Nana'i[21] Ka-ula-hea,[22]
A Mauna-lei kui ka lei.
Lei Pele i ka i-e-i-e, la;
Wai hinu po'o o Hiiaka;
Holapu ili o Haumea.
Ua ono o Pele i kana i'a,
O ka honu o Poli-hua —[23]
Honu iki, a-ī no'uno'u,
Kua papa'i o ka moana;
Ka eä nui, kua wawaka.
Hoolike i ka ai na Pele,
I na oaoaka oaka i ka lani, la!
    Elieli, kau mai!

A Kaua'i, i ke olewa iluna,
A ka pua lana i kai o Wai-lua,
Naná mai Pele ilaila:
E waiho aku ana o Ahu.

---

(17) *Hina*, the goddess with whom Wakea consorted after he had divorced his wife Papa by spitting in her face. Hina became the mother of the island of Moloka'i From such a distinguished parentage arose the proverbial saying "Moloka'i nui a Hina."

(18) *Kaunu-ohua*, a hill on Moloka'i between Halawa valley and Puko'o, where is said to repose the body of Pele.

(19) *Haupu*, a hill on Moloka'i.

(20) *Okaoka*, said to be the flame-body of Pele, or the small stones, *iliili*, that entered into the composition of her body.

(21) *Nana'i*, an archaic form of Lana'i.

(22) *Ka-ula-hea*, a goddess with whom Wakea consorted after his divorce of Papa. The name also of a historic king of Lana'i, as well as of a *kaula*—prophet—attached to the disreputable set of gods that infested Lana'i at one time.

(23) *Poli-hua*, a sandy cape on Lana'i famous for its sea-turtles.

Aloha i ka wai li'u[24] o ka aina:
E ála mai ana Mokihana,
Wai auau o Hiiaka.
Hoopa'apa'a[25] Pele ilaila;
Aohe kahu e ulu[26] ai.
Keehi aku Pele i ka ale kua loloa:
He onohi no Pele,
Ka oaka o ka Lani, la.
    Elieli, kau mai!

Holo mai Pele mai ka Hikina,
A kau ka wa'a i Mo'o-kini;[27]
Noho ka ua i Kumalae;
Ho'okú Pele ma i ke ki'i;
Noho i ke ki'i a Pele ma,
A ka puá o Ko'i.[28]
Kanaenae Pele ma ilaila;
Ka'i a huaka'i mai Pele
A ka lae i Lele-iwi;[29]
Honi i ke ala o ka hala,
O ka lehua o Mokau-lele;[30]
Oia ka Pele a kui la.
He kunana hale ka Pu'u-lena,
He hale moe o Papa-lau-ahi,
He halau no Kilauea.
    Elieli, kau mai!

---

(24) *Wai-li'u,* full form, *wai-li'u-la,* mirage.

(25) *Hoopa'apa'a Pele ilaila.* Pele had planted a spring at this place, near Wai-lua, Kaua'i. Kama-pua'a, in company with two dragon-goddesses, Ka-la-mai-nu'u and Kilioe, who will find mention later in the story, took possession and moved the spring to another spot. When Pele came that way again, after a wordy contention with the two dragons, she slew them.

(26) *Ulu,* to guard, to farm, to protect. The kahu was the one who offered the sacrifices and prayers that were necessary to the maintenance of power and life in an artificial divinity, such as many of the Hawaiian deities were.

(27) *Mo'o-kini,* literally, the multitude (40,000) of dragons; the name of a heiau in Puna. There is also a heiau in Kohala called by the same name.

(28) *Ko'i,* said to be a kupua who had to do with carving and finishing the canoe. Pua seems to be epithet applied to the group of workmen who assisted him.

(29) *Lele-iwi,* a cape on the Puna side of Hilo bay.

(30) *Mokau-lele,* the name of a little land in Hilo situated near the point where the eruption of 1881-1882 came to a stand-still.

Haule mai Pele mai Kahiki mai;
O ka hekili, o ke ola'i, o ka ua loku,
O ka ua páka o Ha'i-ha'i-lau-mea-iku
O na wahine i ka wao o Mau-kele, la.
Ho mai ana Pele li'u la, e;
Au miki, au huki ka ale kua loloa;
Nu'anu'a ka moana i ka lili[31] o Pele:
O ke 'Kua nui ke ku'i la iluna o ka lani;
Wahi'a ka papa ku, ka papa i ao'a,
Ka papa a Kane ma i he'e ai i Maui. —
Ka Haili-opua,[32] ke 'Kua o ka La.
A Wai-a-kahala-loa[33] i akea.
  Elieli, kau mai!
O Wa'a[34] ka i naná i ka auwa'a lawaia
Ku kapa kai, e Kohala,
O ke 'Kua lapu, e Pu'u-loa,
Ke uwalo la i ka mea hele;
Ke Akua kui lehua o Kua-o-ka-la,
Kui mai ana i Maka-noni;
Ka la pu'u, la helu o pua* la'a;
Ka la aku ho'i, e Kahuoi, i ka uka anu.
E olohe Ko'e-ula,[35] e mauna mai ana
Ka hikina o ka La o Kumu-kahi ma.
E haliko a'e ana ka a'ama,[36] lele hihe'e;
O Kohala ke kaula'i 'na la,
E ka la pumehana ole o ka po;

---

(31) *Lili.* This word, accented on the final syllable, means to rush,' to move with one fixed purpose in view. It is to be distinguished from *lili,* having the accent on the penult, and meaning to be angry, jealous, alienated. (My authority is J. M. Poepoe). The word is not given by Andrews in his Dictionary.

(32) *Haili-opua,* the name of a deity. It means the piling-up of cloud-portents.

(33) *Wai-a-kahala-lea,* the Green lake, in Puna. This was, no doubt, much larger and of more importance in ancient times than it is now.

(34) *Wa'a,* the name of a *kaula,* soothsayer, who observed the omens in the heavens and instructed the fishermen. He had his station on or near the hill Maka-noni, in Puna.

(35) *Ko'e-ula,* a family of *Kupua,* superhuman creatures, who had power over men's lives. They were, in truth, some kind of mud-worms, or glow-worms. They came out from their subterranean retreats to see Pele.

(36) *A'ama,* an edible black crab whose shell has a highly decorative pattern. It is said to have been used as a special, or sacred food by certain priests.

---

* In one text this is *Pu-ala'a,* said to be a place in Puna. I have amended it to make better sense.

O ka la pe'[37] ai, o ke ao kau aku iluna
I ka malama, la.
    Elieli, kau mai!

He make no Aua'a-hea, i kalua ia
I ka pua'a aohe ihi[38] ka lau ahea —
Ka ipu kaumaha a ke Akua,
Ka mamala kapu a na hoali'i.
Ku'i i ka lani ka hekili;
O ka ua loku o Ka-ula-hea;[39]
O ka oka'i nu'u o ke ao,
O Ka-o-mea-lani[40] e ua la:
Aha o ka hala ia.
Líli ke Akua:
Akahi Pele a hokahoka;[41]
Akahi Pele la a ne'ene'e;[42]
Akahi Pele la a ai pau;[43]
I pau i kou hoa, i oni i ke a;
I pahoehoe,[44] ai oe i ka mauna.
Auhea pahoehoe la?
Noho iho la ka lau kaula
E ka pau[45] hale o ke Akua —

---

(37) *Pe'ai*, a contracted form from *pe'e*, to hide. In this case, the meaning seems to be to hang low in the heavens.

(38) *Ihi*, another form for *uhi*, to cover, or covered. The *ahea*, or *aheahea* is a common plant that was cooked and eaten like luau. It was also used as a poultice, after heating.

(39) *Ka-ula-hea*. See note 22.

(40) *Ka-o-mea-lani*, a god of rain. He indicated his presence by piling up volumes of white clouds.

(41) *Hokahoka*, disappointed, fooled, deceived; said of Pele in view of her painful experience with Kama-pua'a.

(42) *Ne'ene'e*, to shift about, as Pele had to do because her back was pierced to the bone by the sharp points of a-a on which she lay during her affair with Kama-pua'a. The point of the irony is to be found in the fact that she was as a rule indifferent to the roughness of the bed on which she lay. Yet she was accustomed—so the story goes—to choose pahoehoe as a bed.

(43) *Ai pau*, literally, to eat the whole; and for the first time.

(44) *Pahoehoe*. The mention of pahoehoe in this and in the following line has reference to a saying, or belief, which asserted that Pele was covered with an armor of pahoehoe. It is as if the poet sought to banter her on this popular notion.

(45) *Pau hale*, literally, the destruction of the house, meaning, of course, the deflowering of Pele.

E Kane-ula-a-Pele,[46] o Ku-ihi-malanai-akea,[47]
He hoalii na Pele, he noho ana ai[48] laau,
Na wahine pule mana, nána i papawalu.[49]
    Elieli, kau mai!

Kiope,[50] kiope mai ana ke ahi a kánaka
Ilalo o Kilauea, a i ku mau-mau wá;[51]
A ikuwá mai ana ka pihe a ke akua
Iluna, i ka pali o Mauli;[52]

---

(46) *Kane-ula-a-Pele,* literally, the red man of Pele, meaning Ka-moho-
alii, a brother of Pele. He is described as having a ruddy complexion and
reddish hair. He presided over the council of the Pele gods.

(47) *Ku-ihi-malanai-akea,* one of the forms or attributes of god Ku, the
Trade-wind. The word Malanai by itself is often used in modern Hawaiian
poetry to signify the same thing.

N.B.—The occurrence of the preposition *e* in verse 147 illustrates the
somewhat vague and, at times illogical, use of prepositions in Hawaiian
poetry. If I read this passage correctly, Kane-ula-a-Pele and Ku-ihi-malanai-
akea are in apposition with *hoalii,* the subject of the verb *noho;* and, that
being the case, instead of the preposition *e* we should have the particle *o*
standing before Kane- . . . as we find it before Ku- . . . . The explanation of this anomaly, it seems to me, is to be found in the demand of the
*H*awaiian ear for tone-color, at any cost, even at the expense of grammar.

(48) *He noho ana ai laau,* a session of the gods in which they partook
in common of some *laau,* medicine, or spiritual corrective, as a sign of
mutual amity, even as the North American Indians smoked the peace-pipe
in token of friendly relation between the participants. This *laau* is said
to have been none other than the tender buds of the *a'ali'i,* which was
chewed by the members of the assembly and was deemed to be not merely
a symbol but an active agent in the production of amity and a good understanding.

(49) *Papa-walu,* literally, eightfold. The *wahine* are the Hiiaka sisters,
seven in number. The inclusion of Kukuena fills the number to eight.

N.B.—It should be noted that during the time of Pele's disqualification,
or retirement, or disgrace, Hiiaka-i-ka-poli-o-Pele would be the one to
control the affairs of the Pele family.

(50) *Kiope,* to scatter, said of a fire, in order to extinguish it.

(51) *Ku mau-mau wa.* The literal meaning is, stand in order, or, as I
have put it, stand shoulder to shoulder. It corresponded to and served the
purpose of a sailor's chantey, and was employed in the ancient times to Hawaiian history to give spirit and precision to the work of the men straining
at the hauling line of a canoe-log. The koa tree has been felled and rudely
fashioned; a strong line is made fast to one end of it, and the men, having
ranged themselves along, rope in hand, their chief, sometimes standing on
the log itself, gives the signal for them to be ready for a start by uttering
the inspiring cry "I ku mau-mau wa!" "I ku mau wa," answer the men,
and with a mighty pull the huge log starts on its way to its ocean-home.

(52) *Mauli,* contracted form of *Mauli-ola;* the name of a *kupua,* a deity,
who had to do with health, after some ideal fashion, a sort of Hygeia;
also the name of that kupua's mystical abode. The name Mauli, or Mauli-
ola, was also given, as I learn, to the site of the present Kilauea Volcano
House.

O ka huawai maka[53] i ane'i,
O kánaka nana i huli-pueo[54] ka wai.
Pu oe i kau laau me kou makaainana;[55]
Hopu au i ka'u laau, hahau[56] i ke Akua.
Ku'u'a[57] a'e Pele lapu'u'na[58 Pele;
Waiho ana ilalo, lapu'u ka moe,
A kau la ilalo la pahoehoe ai oe.
Auwe! pahoehoe la, e holo e ka wa'a;
E ka'a ka mauna.
Ola Hiiaka i ka poli o Pele.
Ho'i aku e, ho'i aku iluna i ka maláma.
A'ama pi'i a'e iluna i Kauwiki;[59]
Iho mai a'ama i ke aka o kánaka;
Ho'oili[60] a'ama, ku i ka laau;
Lawe'a a'ama, hao'na i ka eke;
Kaohi paiea[61] i ka pola o ka malo;
Ku ana paiea ilo' ka unuunu;
Lei ana paiea i ka hua limu-kala;
Kau ana paiea iluna i ka alá;
Maunu[62] paiea, ha'alele i ka eke.

---

(53) *Hua-wai maka,* literally, an unripe water-gourd. In this place it means a small collection of dew or rain-water, a water-hole. (54) a thing much sought after by men, even as the owl—as remarks the poet in the next verse—searches after it. Whether the poet is correct in his assertion about the owl, is more than I can say.

(55) *Pu oe i kau laau me kou makaainana.* Kou makaainana is, undoubtedly, Pele. The reference is to the practice spoken of in note 48.

(56) *Hahau i ke Akua,* offer to the god.

(57) *Ku'u ia a'e Pele.* (In the text the *ia* is shortened to *a*). The meaning seems to be that Pele is exonerated from blame. That would not, however, alter the facts and render back to Pele the sacredness that belonged to her uncontaminated body.

(58) *Lapu'u 'na Pele.* This seems to have a double meaning, referring at once to the dismissal of hard feelings against Pele and to her rising up from her customary attitude in repose, that with her head crouched forward and her legs drawn up towards the body.

(59) *Kauwiki,* a hill in Hana, Maui, famous in history.

(60) *Ho'oili,* to come together in a bunch, said of fish. This is an unusual use of the word, though an old Hawaiian (J. T. P.) tells me his mother used it in this way. It refers not to the swarming of fish, but their bunching together when driven.

(61) *Paiea,* a species of crab that resembles the a'ama. The background color of the paiea is black; this is strewn with spots and markings of dark red, producing a highly artistic effect. The specimen I examined was found in the Honolulu fish market and came from Kona, Hawaii. In spite of mutilation, it still retained a formidable claw.

(62) *Maunu paiea.* The Hawaiian fisherman often prepared his bait by chewing it fine, after which he blew it into the water to attract the fish. The poet finds a parallel between this action of the fisherman and the discharge of venomous words by an angered person.

Nie[63] au, Moala, ehia inu awa?
Ehá: o Eä,[64] o Honu,[65] o Kukuau,[66] o
    Hinalea,[67]
O ka apu-hihi,[68] o ka hihi-wai;[69]
Ei' a'e loli-pua,[70] ei' a'e loli-koko;
Ei' a'e loli-ka'e, ei' a'e Leleä.[71]
O Leleä makua, makua o Kahi-kona,[72]
Nána i hanu, kaha ka ua koko:
Ha'i'na a'e ana ka mana
O ke Akua iwaho la, i lili.
    Elieli, kau mai!

Pelei-oho-lani informs me that the following verses are found
in another version of this mele immediately following verse [183]:

O kukulu ka pahu a ka leo hokiki(v) kanawai,
He kua(w) a, he kai(x) oki'a, he ala(y) muku

TRANSLATION

Let the drum, tho torn, snarl out the law
Of the burning back, deep ocean's gulf,
And God's short bridge to heaven by the bow.

----

(63) *Nie,* an elided form of niele, to question.
(64) *Ea,* the sea-turtle.
(65) *Honu,* the land-turtle.
(66) *Kukuau,* a hairy, spotted crab, said to be poisonous.
(67) *Hinalea,* a name applied to fish of several different species, among
which one that is rare is the Hinalea akilolo (Macropharyngodon, geoffrey,
Quoy and Gaimard). Another less rare, though beautiful, species is the
Hinalea i'iwi (Gomphosus tricolor, Quoy and Gaimard).
(68) *Apuhihi.*
(69) *Hihi-wai,* a bivalve shell that is found clinging to rocks or reeds
in fresh or brackish water streams. Its dorsum is jetty black, its front
white, shading into yellow.
(70) *Loli-pua, loli-koko* and *loli-ka'e,* different species of holothuriae,
or sea-slugs, some of which are esteemed as food by the Hawaiians. They
were, nevertheless, looked upon as kupua.
(71) *Lelea,* a marine creature that is said to be slimy and adheres to
the rocks.
(72) *Kahi-kona,* said to be a god of the fishermen.

(v) *Leo hokiki,* an imperfect tone caused by a torn drumhead.
(w) *Kua a.* The penalty of approaching Pele from behind was death:
she is said to have had a consuming back.
(x) *Kai oki'a,* an engulfing abyss.
(y) *Ala muku,* the rainbow. (For further comments on these difficult
passages, see notes 11, 12, and 13, on page 114.)

Ua lilí ka lani me ka ua;
Ua o'oki ka lani, poele ka honua
I ka hanau ana o na hoali'i:
Hanau ke kaikamahine ho'onou[73] o ka lani;
Hemo mai he keiki kane;
Oili ka ua koko iluna.
Hanau o Kuwalu[74] me kana kane,
O Ku-ihi-malanai-akea;
A ai, e Pele, i kou aina —
Ai'na ka ohi'a, ka ulu hala i kai o Lele-iwi.
He moku Pana-ewa, he oka wale Ka-ú;
He pu'u o Pele nui.
Kahi, e Pele, i kou aina, hoolewa ke au.
    Elieli, kau mai!

Ku i Wai-lua ka pou hale a ka ipo;
Hoolono i ka uwalo, ka wawa nui
O Ulupo[75] ma oli nei; aohe uwalo mai, e.
Aloha ino o Ikuwá[76] ma oli nei.
Ke lele la ka eká[77] mua,
Ka ino a ka makani.
Ukiuki, kolo e, Kau-lana,
Ka ua lele aku a lele mai:
Lele a Puhi-lala, lele a kau-lana —
Ka hoaka,[78] e Hiiaka, e!
Nowai ke kanaenae?
No ka ohana a Haumea ke kanaenae.
Ku'u 'a e Kane ke ko'a:
I ka ia nei manawa ia.
No Pele, no Hiiaka no ka honua,
Ka honua ne'i, ka honua lewa,
Ka lani iluna.

---

(73) *Ho'o-nou o ka lani.* This must be Pele. The word ho-onou is used of a person striving to accomplish some physical task, as of a woman straining in labor.

(74) *Ku-walu,* literally, eighth in order of succession.

(75) *Ulu-po,* said to be the name of a heiau at Kailua, Oahu.

(76) *Iku-wa,* the name of a month in the Hawaiian year, corresponding, according to one account, pretty closely to October; according to another nomenclature it corresponds pretty nearly to our April. The name etymologically connoted thunder and reverberations.

(77) *Eka mua,* literally, the first blast of a storm; here used figuratively to mean the first sexual ecstacy.

(78) *Hoaka,* a setting forth in figures. (Hoakaka).

O Ána-ku,[79] ku ka aha iloko:
O Haamo[80] he ala i hei a'e ia,
He pahu[81] i kula'i 'na, he pa i a'e ia;
He kahua i hele ia, he luana mau'u;
He kaunana ko, okana piko;
He hola moena, he lawe'na ipukai;
He ukuhi'na wai, he kaumaha ai:
He hainá no ka hale, e.
Noa, noa ia hale — ua a'e 'a,
Ua komohia no wai-honua.
Ku ana o halau[82] ololo,
Ka hale o Pele i noho ai.
Maka'ika'i mai Kini o ke Akua.
Ho'i aku e, ho'i aku iwaho 'na!
He kahuna pule ole, he li'i pule ole!
Mai komo wale mai i ka hale o Pele,
O ko'u Akua, la!
    Elieli, kau mai!

E kau ana kiko[83] i ke alia kiko;
Hele a mo'a[84] kiko akahi nei au;
Kaele pu'epu'e,[85] ne'ine'i;[86]
Ka-ele pa-kiko-kiko.[87]

---

(79) *Ana-ku,* the name of a cave situated somewhere in the caldera of Kilauea, a place of assembly for the gods. Its use here is evidently for a highly figurative purpose, and has, of course, to do with Pele and her affair with Kama-pua'a.

(80) *Ha-amo,* the name of the road to Ana-ku. (Peleioholani).

(81) *Pahu.* It is doubtful whether this means a drum or a post. In either case, in the smash-up of the one or the overthrow of the other, the figure evidently is designed to set forth the confusion caused by the catastrophe—Pele's debauchment. The other figures that follow have the same purpose.

(82) *Halau ololo,* literally, a long shed or canoe-house, meaning a place of common assembly for people. The figure is applied to Pele and is intended to declare that, through her affair with Kama-pua'a she had degraded herself and robbed her body of its tabu, its sanctity.

(83) *Kiko,* a mark to indicate a tabu. Two *ti* leaves placed crosswise, and held in place by a pebble, would constitute a kiko.

(84) *Mo'a,* literally, cooked; meaning that the tabu has expired, been abrogated.

(85) *Pu'e-pu'e,* the hills of taro. *Kaele* means the division or apportioning of them.

(86) *Ne'ine'i,* the more scattered, smaller, hills of taro, those that are nearer the bank.

(87) *Pakikokiko,* the scattered taro plants that grow in the watercourse.

Ua noa ka aina; e kapu keiki;
E kapu ke nui; e kahe na wai;
E ka haki ana, ku ka opeope;
O Kulipe'e noho i ka Lua;
A lele, e, na hoalii o Ku-wawá;
O Ku-haili-moe, o ka naele o Hawaii.
Akahi nei au a ho'i aku nei mai ou aku la,
A lele pakohana mai.
    Elieli, kau mai!

TRANSLATION

Of Pele, her warfare in Kahiki
With her sister Na-maka-o-ka-ha'i;
Of her flight to the land of Hawaii,
A flight like the eye-shot of dawn,
A flight like the lightning's flash,
That rivals the full of the moon!
    Wonder and awe possess me!

For Pele the ocean sleeps afar,
For Pele the godlike one!
A surge now cradles the islands
And breaks on the land Hana-kahi,
O'erflooding the sands of Wai-o-lama.

God's temple is roofed with the fingers,
And the thumb is lifted in earnest prayer
By the concourse met in the uplands.
High piles the surf that sweeps from Kahiki;
It breaks at the foot of Kilauea;
Is driven back by the hot lava plates.
Now calls from the wayside a human voice;
Your suitor, Goddess who rifled the bloom
From my Ola'an park of lehua
That smile in the lap of Heeia
And the wreath-goddess Kukuena.

What a bestial and nondescript mix-up
Embroiled our chief in the thickets of Puna!
What a passionate mounting! what a stay!
Small show of regard for your fellow peers!
    Wonder and awe possess me!

Wild the sea-mist at Kohala-loa,
Sea roughed by the breeze from the upper hills,
Sea that peeps o'er the cliffs of Kupehau,
Invading the groves of pandamus;
It reaches the lowlands of Maui —
The sea of this Goddess, this Queen.
The lehuas are twisted like garlands
At the touch of this sea of god Pele;
For Pele, indeed, is my god.
   Wonder and awe possess me!

Thou mountain wall all swathed in mist,
Now groans the mountain-apple tree;
I see a fire of blazing rocks;
I see an aged dame, who snores
On lava plate, now hot, now cold;
Now 'tis canoe in shape, well propped,
A chock 'neath bow, midships, astern;
Needs bail the waist where drains the bilge,
Else salt will crust like staring eye —
Gray roving eye of lawless Niheu.
   Wonder and awe possess me!

On famed Moloka'i of Hina,
At the pali of Unu-ohua,
Where burn the lamps of Haupu,
Assemble the throng of little gods.
Then comes forth Pele, a great god,
Haumea and Hiiaka,
And Kukuena and Okaoka:
If the small fire burns, let it burn!
'Tis the beaming of Pele's eye,
The flashing of heavenly fire.
   Wonder and awe possess me!

Now to Nana'i of Ka-ula-hea;
At Mauna-lei Pele plaits her a wreath;
She plaits it of í-e-íe;
Hiiaka pelts head with ginger cone;
Haumea anoints her body;
And Pele eats with zest the flesh
From the turtle of Poli-hua —

A young thing, short in the neck,
Backed like a crab from the sea,
Like a sea-turtle plated and patterned —
Turned into meat for Pele,
Food for the heavenly flame.
    Wonder and awe possess me!

From the ether above Kaua'i
To the blossoms afloat at Wailua
Ranges the flight of Pele's gaze.
She sees Oahu floating afar;
Feels thirst for the wat'ry mirage;
Inhales the scent of mokihana —
The bath-water of Hiiaka.
She once had a contest there;
She had no tenant to guard the place.
Pele spurns with her feet the long waves;
They give back a flash like her eye,
A flash that's repeated on high.
    Wonder and awe possess me!

When Pele came voyaging from the east
And landed at Mo'o-kini —
The rain poured down at Ku-malae —
Her people set up an image,
And there they made their abode,
With the workmen who carve the canoe;
And they offered prayers and gave thanks.
Then Pele led them in journey
To the cape of Lele-iwi,
Where they breathed the incense of hala.
With Mokau-lele's rich lehua
Goddess Pele weaved her a wreath.
They built a village at Pu'u-lena,
Her bedroom at Papa-lau-ahi,
A mighty hall at Kilauea.
    Wonder and awe possess me!

When Pele fell through from Kahiki
Bitter the rain, lightning and quaking —
The big-dropped rain that shatters the leaves
Of the women folk in Mau-kele's wilds.

Pele came in the dusk of the night,
With toss and sway of the long-backed waves.
The ocean heaved at Pele's rush;
The great god thundered in heaven;
The strata of earth were uptorn;
The reef-plates broken, crushed; and rent
Was the surf-plank of Kane at Maui.
What a piling of portents by the Sun-god
Over the Green Lake Ka-hala-loa!
    Wonder and awe possess me!

It was Wa'a gazed on the fishing fleet,
His watch-tower the cliffs of Kohala;
While the witch-ruler, O Pu'u-loa,
Entreated the wayfaring one,
And the goddess who gilds the lehua
Set aglow Maka-noni's sunlit verge.
One day for gath'ring and choosing
The flowers devoted to worship,
The next day in upland frosty Huoï.
The earth-creatures glimmer and glow
While the eastern sun tops Kumu-kahi.
Sidewise the black crab springs from his hole
And Kohala spreads out 'neath the orb
That fails to give warmth to the night,
And the Sun hangs low in the sky,
And the clouds, they canopy heaven.
    Wonder and awe possess me!

Aua'a-hea meets death, spite of
Steam-bath, — a boar unpurged of bristles —
And poultice hot of aheahea,
An herb that serves as a dish for the gods,
A tidbit for the king's table.
Thunder resounds in the heavens; rain falls,
Bitter as tears of Ka-ula-hea;
Clouds, torn and ragged, fill the sky,
A piled-up ominous cloud-pillar,
A fabric reared by heaven's rain-god —
A collect of evils was that.

The gods were aghast at the scandal:
For once Pele found herself duped;
For once Pele shifted in bed;
For once Pele drank to the dregs —
The cup was the brew of her consort;
Her bed the spikes of a-ä.
Stone-armored, passion had slaked.
Where then was her armor of stone?
The prophets, in congress assembled,
Consult on the rape of the goddess —
Red-headed Kane, Ku of the Trade-wind,
Compeers of Pele, consumers of trees,
The women of eight-fold incantations.
   Wonder and awe possess me!

They stamp out the fire in the Pit;
"Stand shoulder to shoulder," their cry;
"Shoulder to shoulder," echoes the throng
On the heights of Mauli-ola, —
Where the green leaf distills the water ,
Men search for like hov'ring owls.
Chew thou the herb with thy friend,
I will offer mine to my god.
The fault of Pele's condoned;
She lifts herself from her huddle in bed —
A couch far down in the Pit —
It now becomes plates of smooth lava,
How like the flight of a swift canoe
Is the flow of the pahoehoe,
As the mountain melts and rolls away!
Hiiaka, the darling of Pele,
Then soars aloft to the realms of light,
As the crab climbs up Kau-wiki —
The crab retreats from man's shadow —
And when these black ones huddle together
They are easily clubbed with a stick;
Their bodies then are thrust in the bag.
As the gray crab tugs at the malo's fold;
As he stands mid the heaped-up coral,
While round him wave the pods of rough moss,
Or he rests on the flat coral plate;
As, ta'en from the bag, he's chewed into bait,

Lava fields of Kīlauea, Hawai'i.

So men spit forth their bitter words.
How many guests at awa, Sir Crab?
Four gods, is the answer returned,
Tortoise, and Turtle, and Kukuau,
And Hinalea, and with them are
Apu-hihi and Hihi-wai, along with
Loli-pua and Loli-koko,
And Loli-ka'e and Lele-á.
Lele-a-makua fathered
The fisherman's god, Kahi-kona.
When he breathed, red as blood poured the rain,
A sign of the power and wrath of the god.
    Wonder and awe possess me!

The heavens were turmoiled with rain clouds,
The firmament sealed, earth black as midnight,
At the birth of the princely ones:
The heaven-urging princess was born;
Then came forth a man-child, a prince,
And the blood-red rain poured down.
Then was born Ku-walu and her lord,
Mala-nai, the far-breathing Trade-wind;
And thou, O Pele, then ate of thy land,
Consuming the groves of ohi'a
And Lele-iwi's palms by the sea.
Pana-ewa still was a park;
Ka-ú was made a cinder-patch;
By her might Pele threw up a mountain.
Overwhelm your lands, O Pele;
Let your fire-streams flow!
    Wonder and awe possess me!

Her lover's house-post stands in Wai-lua;
There Pele hears a call that appeals;
'Tis a song voiced by Ulu-pó.
She utters no word to answer
This pleading babel of voices,
Now comes the first thrill to virgin flesh;
Impatient, the princeling crawls on his knees;
There's plenteous downfall of tears, as when
Rain-columns fall, or men leap and dive,
Head-first, feet-first, into the flood.

These symbols will tell the tale, Hiiaka.
For whom do I make this offering of song?
For the ancient stock of Haumea.
God Kane planted the coral reefs;
A work that done in Pele's time;
For Pele, for Hiiaka the land —
This solid ground that swings and floats
Beneath the o'erhanging arch of heaven.

At Ana-kú once met the gods; the road
Thither lay through Ha-ámo; — but now,
Its drum is dismantled, its fence o'erleaped;
The terrace trampled, a litter of straw,
Champed sugar-cane, heaped odds and ends;
A spread for mats; a clutter of dishes;
There's dipping of water, serving of food. —
What a desecration of the house!
The house is degraded and trodden;   .
Its tabu place entered, deflowered —
Now stands a hall of common resort
Where once stood the house of Pele.
Now come the Pigmy Gods on a visit.
Be off! be gone from the place!
A prayerless priest, a prayerless king is yours:
Enter not prayerless the house of Pele.
For Pele, I swear it, is my god!
    Wonder and awe possess me!

The tabu flags fluttered in place, just now;
And now, the flags are removed by you.
Men parcel the hills in the taro patch;
They parcel the clumps in the taro ditch:
The land goes free, the children secure;
Unvexed be the people; the waters run free;
Food-bundles shall bulk in the patch;
Kuli-pe'e shall keep to the Pit;
The princes of clamor shall fly away.
Give place to Ku, the smoother of lands,
The planter of forest and field.
I go in peace from your presence forth;
I came to you in my nakedness.
    Wonder and awe possess me!

CHAPTER XXIV

HIIAKA LEARNS OF THE DEATH OF LOHIAU

With a nice feeling of etiquette, Hiaaka's hosts allowed the day of her arrival to pass with no inquiry as to the purpose of her visit. But on the morning of the morrow Malae-ha'a-koa asked the question that put himself in sympathetic touch with his guests.

"I have come to escort Lohiau as a lover to the bed of Pele," said Hiiaka.

"Lohiau has been dead many days," they both exclaimed. "He took his own life out of a passionate infatuation for one of the the Hono-pú(a) women."

"Let that be as it may," Hiiaka answered; "I will go and see for myself."

Now Kahua-nui, the sister of Lohiau, had laid his body to rest in a sepulcher close to her own residence; but on examination the place was found to be empty. It was evident that the body had been spirited away. Hiiaka, turning her gaze to the mountain, discerned a ghostly form standing at the mouth of a cave. It was the ghost of Lohiau. In an effort to soothe and attract him, Hiiaka, with arms extended and face uplifted, in passionate utterance gave vent to her emotions:

> Ku'u kane i ka pali o Ha-ena,
> Mai na aina pali a pau loa,
> Mai Hoolulu no a Poli-hale la;
> Ku'u kane ho'i, e-e!

TRANSLATION

> At last, my dear man, at last,
> On this rugged cliff of Haena!
> I have searched the whole mountain side,
> From Ho'o-lulu's booming fall
> To Poli-hale's buttressed flank.
> I have found thee at last, my man!

(a) These Honopu women, two in number, were mo'o, witches, related to Kilioe, a famous witch-mo'o of Hawaii, and their names were Kili-oe-i-ka-pua and Ka-lana-mai-nu'u.

Again she scanned the lineaments of the shadowy form if she might find there the picture her mind had imaged. At second view, the ghostly unreality of the tenuous image so greatly shocked her imagination by its contrast to her ideal of a true flesh-and-blood lover, that she amended her first utterance:

Aole a'e nei ke kane,
He hoa pili no ke ahiahi,
He hoa kaunu no ke aumoe,
No ka waena po loloa
O ke hooilo, la:
Ku'u kane ho'i, e-e!

TRANSLATION

This, surely, is not the lover
To cling to one in the twilight,
To fondle in the midnight watch
Of a long, long, wint'ry night.
Where, oh where art thou, my man?

A creepy thrill came over Hiiaka as she saw the bloodless lips open and heard these answering words from the mouth of the weird object that stood on the pali wall:

Ku'u wahine, e-e !
Hoohewahewa oe ia'u, la.
Eia au la i Ka-lalau, e-e;
I ka pali au o Hoo-lulu, la;
Ku'u wahine ho'i, e-e !

TRANSLATION

Alas, my woman, alas !
You wail in soul-recognition.
I was yonder at Ka-lalau,
Or some time perched at Ho'o-lulu.
Surely thou art the woman, thou !

With the desire to soothe the bewildered soul Hiiaka again spoke:

Ku'u kane i ka makani Kilihau,(a) Kili-opu,(b)
Ke pu'e(c) ka wai o ka mauna;
He mauna pali no Ka-lalau
A maua e hele ai —

Me oe, me ke kane la, ku'u kane,
Ku'u kane o ka wa po wale,
O ku'u wa iluna o ke alo la —
Ku'u kane ho-i, e !

TRANSLATION

My man of the wind-driven mist,
Or rain that plunges clean as a diver,
What time the mountain stream runs cold
Adown the steps at Ka-lalau —
Where we shall ere long climb together,
With you, my friend, with you,
Companion of the pitchy night,
When heavenward turns my face —
Thou art, indeed, my man.

A moment's pause and she resumed:

E ku'u kane, e-e,
He leo e wale ho'i kou,
He leo no ka hanehane,(d)
No ka pololei(e) kani kau mauna o uka la;
Ku'u kane ho'i, e-e!

TRANSLATION

Alas, my man, alas!
How altered is your voice,
Changed to the trilling note

(a) *Kili-hau,* the name given to a local wind accompanied by a fine rain.
(b) *Kili-opu,* a name descriptive of a wind and rain-shafts that, plunging into the water, made as little splash as a skillful diver.
(c) *Pu'e* This word is here used in an unusual sense to mean cold.
(d) *Hanehane,* the shrill, seemingly far-off, wailing of a ghost; ghostly.
(e) *Pololei,* an archaic name applied to the land shell, now known as *pupu-kanioi.* This was supposed to utter a delicate trilling cry similar to that of the cricket.

Of the plaintive Pololei
That trills on the mountain ridge:
Yet thou art, indeed, my man!

Kahua-nui was greatly moved when she heard the words of
Hiiaka and said, with emotion, "It is evident you loved my
brother, that handsome fellow — dead ! If only the woman
had been like you! What a pity that he should have wasted
himself on such a good-for-nothing !"

"Tell me, pray, where did you lay your brother's body ?"
asked Hiiaka.

"Yonder," said she, pointing to a grass house. "Lima-loa,
who hails from Kauna-lewa, in Mana, bound on the thatch.
That job completed, he went away with all the men of the place
to bewail him. We two women alone remain to keep watch
over him. There he lies and we stand guard over his sepulcher."

Then Hiiaka, girding herself with her divine attributes as a
goddess of Kilauea — the power which, on occasion, availed to
flood the plains of Puna with sounding plates of pahoehoe, or
to heap up the rugged aä at Maukele — reached into the sepulcher in search of Lohiau's body. But it was not there. It had
been stolen away by the two mo'o-witches (Kilioe and Ka-
lana-mai-nu'u) and lodged in a cave high up in the inaccessible
mountain side.

The emotions of Hiiaka at this turn of events found expression in song:

A Lima-loa(a) i ke kaha
O Kauna-lewa ho'i e-e:
Ako Mana i ka hale ohai —
Aina ko hele la, e-e, —
Hoopunipuni i ka malihini:
Puni ho'i au, e-e!

TRANSLATION

The deed this of Lima-loa,
That wonder-monger who works
In the barren land of Maná;
Who roofs Maná with ohai —

(a) *Lima-loa,* the god Mirage.

One there munches cane as he plods.
His to deceive the stranger;
I'm the victim of his deceit!

Hiiaka, at the mention of Lima-loa and the part he had taken
in constructing the house that served as a sepulcher for Lohiau,
jumped to the conclusion that he had been the body-snatcher of
Lohiau. Kahuanui strongly dissented from this view. "There
can be no doubt," said she, "that my brother's body lies in that
sepulcher at this very moment. That is the reason for my keeping guard over the place. But why stand we here? Let us go to
my home."

As Hiiaka went with her she again had sight of the ghost-
form of Lohiau standing in the door of the cavern, and she addressed to him this mele:

Ako nanani maka i Wawae-nohu,(a) e-e;
Me he nanai hale la Ka-ula i ke kai;
Ke amo a'e la i ka lima o Kaunu-lau, e-e;
Ke hoa la i ke kua o Lei-no-ai —
He ai aloha na olua, e-e!

TRANSLATION

His airy phantoms queer the eye
At Wawae-nohu, and yon islet
Ka-ula, like a lanai, looms at sea;
While lifts the hand of Kauna-la'a
To smite the back of Lei-no-ai:
The sight enchants you twain.

Hiiaka paused for a moment and then continued in a reflective
mood:

O Ka-ula nui ka i akaka,
Ua po Ka-halau-a-ola(b) i ka noe;

(a) *Wawae-nohu*, the name given to a red cloud seen at sunset in the
west from Mana, Kauai.
(b) *Ka-halau-a-ola*, literally, the hall of health. The more commonly
used appellation Mauli-ola, was both the name of a deity and of a mystical
place. One may infer from their use that Halau-a-ola meant rather a sort
of house-of-refuge, a place of security from the attack of an enemy, while
Mauli-ola had in view a mystical, beatific, condition. The former is illustrated in the line describing Kama-pua'a's escape from Pele's onslaught:
    Noho ana Kama-pua'a i ka Halau-a-ola.
    Kama-pua'a finds refuge in the hall of life.

O ka manu na'e ke lele nei
Kai luna o Wa'a-hila, la;
Ke noho la i Lei-no-ai:
He ai aloha keia ia oe la, e-e!

TRANSLATION

Famous Ka-ula looms crystal clear;
Misty and dark the Temple of Health:
Yet the birds keep flying around
And about the hill Wa'a-hila.
They settle at Lei-no-ai,
A sight most pleasing to you.

Hiiaka now perceived two female figures squatted at the entrance of the cavern, which they had carefully blocked and were guarding. These were the creatures that had stolen away the body of Lohiau. She at once raised her voice and addressed them with this threatening language:

E Aka, e Kilioe-i-ka-pua, e-e!
Na wahine kapa ole e nene'e wale nei
I ka hapapa ku'i opihi,
O ka luna i Hala-aniani,(a) la;
Na wahine kapa ole.

TRANSLATION

Ah!— Aka, and you Kilioë,
Dowered with flowerlike beauty,
You women with naked bodies,
Who sometime flit o'er the reef-plates,
Now squat over Hala-aniani!
You shameless, you naked ones!

The magic of these words worked their death-purpose. The way to the sepulchral cave was now unobstructed. As they came, however, to the base of the cliff, they found that the ladder had been removed — the mischievous work of the witches.

(a) *Hala-aniani*, a small lake of fresh water in a cave at Haena, in which the writer has bathed.

Wahine-oma'o was aghast. "There is no ladder for us to climb up by," said the woman.

"Turn your face to the cliff," was Hiiaka's answer.

The girl did so and used her best efforts to climb the mountain wall. The day was far spent and darkness would soon come on. Thereupon Hiiaka invoked the Sun, bidding it stand still at the mouth of the river Hea:

> E Kini, e hiki i Kauai, i kou aina;
> O koa maka-iwa(a) o Halawa,(b)
> Paia Kona i ou kino,
> Akua nui o Hiiaka, la.
> Hiki e, pi'i e, iho e!
> E kau i ka muli o Hea;(c)
> Kau malie oe, e ka La!

TRANSLATION

> Come to your land to Kauai, ye hosts!
> Ye warrior-gods, keen eyes of pearl!
> Put forth your strength, O Kona —
> The mighty goddess Hiiaka!
> I bid you rise, climb, and descend!
> Now stay your flight, O Day!
> Stand still, O Sun, o'er Hea's water !

(a) *Koa maka-iwa*, idols with eyes of mother o' pearl. To this class belonged Ku-kaili,-moku, the famous war god of Kamehameha.

(b) *Halawa*, the largest valley on Molokai, a stronghold of priestcraft and sorcery. "Ua o'o na pule o Moloka'i," the incantations of Moloka'i are ripe, became a proverbial expression.

(c) *Hea*, a stream near Haena.

CHAPTER XXV

HIIAKA UTTERS MANY PRAYERS TO RESTORE LOHIAU TO LIFE

Before proceeding to her task Hiiaka instructed Malae ha'a-koa to call in the guards stationed at Lohiau's sepulcher and to keep the hula going for the next ten days as an attraction to draw off the people from playing the spy on her performances.

Hiiaka and her companion conquered the impossible and scaled the mountain wall as if their feet had the clinging property of the fly. Lohiau's ghost would have escaped, but with birdlike quickness she caught it. At her command Wahine-oma'o gathered certain aromatic and fragrant herbs of the wilderness, and having made a fire, they bruised and warmed the simples and spread them upon a sheet of leaves.

While Wahine-oma'o kept fast hold of the feet, Hiiaka forced the soul-particle to pass in through one of the eye-sockets. It went as far as the cavity of the chest, then turned back and strove to escape. Hiiaka guarded the ways of exit and with skillful manipulations compelled it to go on. Reaching the loins, it balked again; but Hiiaka's art conquered its resistance and the human particle extended its journey to the feet. There was a twitching of these parts; the hands began to move, the eye-lids to quiver; breath once more entered the body. They lifted and laid it on the blanket of aromatics and restoratives, swathing it from head to foot.

Hiiaka set a calabash of water before her and, addressing Wahine-oma'o, said, "Listen to my prayer. If it is correct and faultless, our man will live; but if it is wrong or imperfect, he will die."

"He will not survive," replied Wahine-oma'o gloomily.

> Kuli ke kahuna i-mua
> Ia ku'i, nei, anapu, iluna, ilalo
> O Hana-ia-ka-malama,(*a*) *o* Mai-u'u,(*b*) *o* Ma-a'a,(*b*)

(*a*) *Hana-ia-ka-malama,* a benevolent goddess who presided over the tabus that were the birthright of certain chiefs. The rules and observances that etiquette prescribed in the life and conduct of such a chief were intricate and burdensome to the last degree. It was, for instance, required that an infant who inherited this sort of a tabu must not be placed in such a position that the sun's rays could shine on its vertex.

(*b*) *Mai-u'u, Ma-a'a,* two goddesses (of the wilderness) whose function it was to string or twine *leis* and wreaths for the decoration of the superior gods. All the gods here mentioned were sometimes grouped under the appellation *Akua o ka wa po*—gods of the night-time—the fact being, however, that they worked as much by day as by night.

O Nahinahi-ana,(c) awihi, kau Kanaloa —
He akua, ua lele i ka lani,
Me Kuhulu ma(d)— o ka hanau a Kane,(e)
A na Wahine:(f)— o na Wahine i ka pa'i-pa'i:(g)
O Pa'i-kua,(h) o Pa'i-alo,(i) o Pa'i-kau-hale;(j)
O loiele ka aha,(k) o lele wale(l) ka pule,
A pa ia'u, pa ia oe;(m)
Halulu i ka manawa, he upe,
He waimaka — he waimaka aloha, e-e!
I e-e, holo ho'i, e-e!

TRANSLATION

Stand to the fore, O Priest; shrink not
Tho thunder's growl and lightning's flash
Fill heaven's vault above, below.
Come Mistress of tabus; come ye who string leis,
And the Goddess who mixes the dyes.
Kanaloa, alert, soars aloft,

(c) *Nahinahi-ana*, another name for the goddess *Hina-ulu-ohi'a*, **under** which appellation her function was to make the dyes used in coloring and printing the tapas.

(d) *Kuhulu ma.* The particle-affix *ma* indicates that this name, or cognomen rather, comprises a group—in this case a family group—of deities. Under the family cognomen *Ku* were ranged a large and important group of deities, to whom were given individual appelations appropriate to their functions. Thus, *Ku-huluhulu* and *Ku-ka-ohi'a-laka* were deities worshipped by the canoe-makers. *Ku-hulu* and his set (*ma*) exercised a function akin to that of the water-carrier. They had charge of the fabled, life-giving water of Kane, *Wai a Kane*, and served it out according to the needs of men.

(e) *Hanau a Kane*, offspring of Kane. This appellation is intended, apparently, to cover the whole list of names already mentioned and, perhaps, some to be mentioned later in the mele.

(f) *Wahine.* Who these women, goddesses, were is brought out in what follows.

(g) *Na Wahine i ka pa'ipa'i*, literally, the women who clapped, or applauded; but more closely specified as:

(h) *Pa'i-kua*, the goddess who slapped the back, as was done in the hula.

(i) *Pa'i-alo*, the goddess who slapped the chest, as was also done in the hula.

(j) *Pa'i-kauhale*, she who knocked at the doors of the village, i.e., who roused the people generally.

(k) *Aha*, the charm of a pule, its ceremonial correctness, its power as an incantation.

(l) *Lele wale*, to get off the track; to go astray; to fail to hit the point.

(m) *A pa ia'u, pa ia oe*, with results disastrous to me and to you.

With hairy Ku, — the offspring of Kane —
And the Women who cheer with a touch,
On the back, the chest, or knock at the door;
Lest the charm depart, the prayer go wrong,
With damage to me and damage to you —
A pain in the head, a drooling nose,
A shedding of tears — of love and regret.
Now let the prayer speed on its way!

"How was my prayer?" asked Hiiaka, turning to Wahine-oma'o.

"It was a good prayer," she replied. "Its only fault was that it sped on too quickly and came to an end too soon."

"In its haste to obtain recovery, no doubt," said Hiiaka.

"Perhaps so," the woman replied.

"Listen now to this prayer," Hiiaka said. "If it is a good prayer our man will recover:"

A luna i Wahine-kapu,(a)
A Kilauea i ka Lua;
A lele, e, na Hoalii,(b)
O Ku-wa'a,(c) o Ku-haili-moe,(d)
O ka naele(e) o Hawaii.
E hi'i kapu o Kanaloa,
O Kui-kui,(f) o Koli-koli,(g)
O Kaha-ula,(h) o ka oaka kapa ulaula,

(a) *Wahine-kapu*, a bluff in the north-western wall that surrounds the caldera of Kilauea, the tabu residence of god Ka-moho-alii, a brother of Pele.

(b) *Hoali'i*, (*Hoa*, companion and *alii*, chief); a fellow chief.

(c) *Ku-wa'a*, a god who presided at the hauling of a canoe-log. The shout raised on such an occasion, though it sounds almost like a repetition of this god's name, being "ku maumau wa," had a different origin.

(d) *Ku-haili-moe*, one of the Ku gods, whose function it was to induce or preside over dreams at night.

(e) *Naele o Hawaii*, probably meaning the whole broad area of Hawaii. One view would make it refer specially to the swampy lands.

(f) *Kui-kui*, an archaic form of the word *kukui;* here meaning both the candle made from the kukui nut and the god who had the same under his special charge.

(g) *Koli-koli*, the god who presided over the snuffing of the kukuinut candles. These were made by stringing the roasted nuts on a coconut leaf-rib.

(h) *Kaha-ula*, the goddess who presided over erotic dreams.

Kapa eleele, o Kapa-ahu, o Lono-makua,(*i*)
O ke oahi maka a ka Ua la, e-e!
I e, holo e-e!

Ho, comrades from the sacred plateau!
Ho, comrades from the burning gulf!
Hither fly with art and cunning:
Ku, who fells and guides the war-boat;
Ku, who pilots us through dream-land;
All ye Gods of broad Hawaii;
Kanaloa, guard well your tabus;
Candle-maker, Candle-snuffer;
Goddess, too, of passion's visions;
Lightning red all heaven filling —
Pitchy darkness turned to brightness —
Lono, come, thou god of all fire;
Come, too, thou piercing Eye of Rain:
Speed, speed my prayer upon its quest!

"How is my prayer?" said Hiiaka, turning to her companion.
The answer was the same as before.

Hiiaka devotes herself to gentle ministrations of healing; but
without intermitting the chanting of prayer-songs, the burden
of whose petition is that the Spirit of Health shall prevail in
Lohiau and restore him completely. After again sprinkling the
body with water from the calabash, she breaks forth:

Ia ho'uluulu ia mai au,
E Kane-kapolei(*a*) imua e-e;
Ia ulu Kini o ke Akua, la;
Ulu mai o Kane, o Kanaloa —
O Hiiaka, kaula mana ia, e-e,

(*i*)   *Lono-makua*, a god one of whose functions was to act as guardian
of fire. When Pele and Kama-pua'a fought together and Kama-pua'a had
succeeded in extinguishing the fires of Kilauea, Pele, in dismay, appealed
to Lono-makua, saying, "There is no fire left." Lono-makua calmly pointed
to his armpit and said, "Here is the fire, in these fire-sticks," (*aunaki* and
aulima). The armpit was his place for carrying these sticks. When the
Hawaiians first saw a White man with a lighted pipe in his mouth, smoke
issuing therefrom, they said, "Surely, this is the great god Lono-makua;
he breathes out fire."

(*a*)   *Kane-kapolei*, god of flowers and shrubs.

Nana i ho'uluulu i na ma'i —
A a'e, a ulu, a noho i kou kuahu.
Eia ka wai la, he Wai Ola, e-e!
　E ola, ho'i, e-e!

TRANSLATION

Come, enter, possess and inspire me;
Thou first, God of the flowery wild;
Ye roving sprites of the wildwood;
And master gods, Kane and Loa; —
Hiiaka, who calls you, lacks not
In power to heal and inspire —
Pray enter, and heal, and abide
In this one, your patron and guard.
Here is water, the Water of Life.
　Give us this Life!

As in archery the character of the arrow, the skill of the archer, and the caprice of the air-currents that blow athwart the course of the arrow's flight may severally or collectively make or mar success, so likewise with the kahuna and his praying, success or failure were spelled by the quality of his prayer-shaft, by the manner of his utterance of it, and lastly, by the physical and moral state of the atmosphere as to the existence or absence of noise and disturbance.

It was not, then, through a mere silly curiosity or pride of utterance that Hiiaka appealed to her attendant to learn what she thought of her prayer. Nor was it a vain and meaningless compliment when the latter declared the prayer to be good, the conditions favorable. At the same time she could not repress the criticism that from her emotional stand-point of view, the prayer seemed short.

Again Hiiaka sprinkled the body with water from the calabash while she uttered this prayer-song:

Eia ana au, e Laká,(a)

(a) *Laka,* a god, or demi-god of various functions, such as fishing, agriculture, and house-building. Malo mentions Ku-ka-ohi'a-Laka as a god invoked by canoe-makers. Laka is evidently derived from the name *Rata,* which in Tahiti, Raro-tonga and New Zealand is the name of the ohi'a tree. Laka is to be distinguished from Laka, the goddess of the hula.

Kane a Ha'i-wahine(b)—
Ha'i pua o ka nahelehele,
Haki hana maile o ka wao,
Houluulu lei, ho'i, o Laká;
O Hiiaka, kaula mana ia, e-e,
Nana i ho'ouluulu na ma'i.
A a'e, a ulu, a noho i kou kahu:
Eia ka Wai la; he Wai Ola, e-e!
E ola, ho'i, e-e!

TRANSLATION

Here stand I in stress, Laká,
Thou husband of Haina-kolo.
What flowers have I plucked in the wild,
What maile stripped in the forest,
To twine into wreaths for Laká:
Thus toiled the seer Hiiaka;
And her's was the magic of cure.
But come thou, mount, enter, possess;
Give life to thy servant and priest.
Here's water, the Water of Life!
    Grant life!

The work of completely restoring Lohiau by the necromancies of the kahuna, like a process of nature, required the ripening hand of time. The utterance of prayer must be unremitting.

(b) *Haina-kolo*, the same as *Ha'i-wahine*, the name used in the Hawaiian text. Ha'ina-kolo is a name that spells tragedy. She was a princess of Hawaii who married a mythical being, Ke-anini-ula-o-ka-lani and went with him to his home in the South. Being deserted by her husband, after the birth of her child,   , she started to swim home to Hawaii. Arriving in a famished condition in Kohala, she ate of some ulei berries without first making an offering to the gods. For this offense she was afflicted with insanity, and being distraught, she wandered in the wilderness until her repentant husband sent for her and restored her by his returning love.

CHAPTER XXVI

HIIAKA CONTINUES HER PRAYERS

While Hiiaka in her ministrations did not omit anything that might aid and expedite Lohiau's physical recovery, her chief reliance was in the spiritual aid of the gods; for which purpose prayer followed prayer like the pictures in a moving show:

HE MELE KUNIKUNI NO LOHIAU

Kulia, e Uli,(a)
Ka pule kanana ola i mua o ke kahuna:
Kaulia i ke Alohi-lani;(b)
Kulia i Kupukupu o-luna nei.
Owai Kupukupu?(c)
O Ilio uli,(d) o Ilio mea,(e)
O Ku-ke-ao-iki;(f)
O Ku-ke-ao-loa;(g)
O Ku-ke-ao-poko;(h)
O Ku-ke-ao-apihapiha(i) o ka lani;
O ke Kanáka(j) o ka mauna;
O na hoa o ka ulu(k) laau;

(a) *Uli*, the chief aumakua of sorcery, but at the same time having power as a healer if she would but exercise it.

(b) *Alohi-lani* (literally, the shining heavenly ones); the notions that prevail as to its precise meaning in this place are vague.

(c) *Kupukupu*, a benevolent deity who healed diseases and who caused vegetation to flourish.

(d) *Uli*. In this connection the word means black. *Ilio* is a cloud.

(e) *Mea*, yellow. *Ilio mea*, a yellow cloud.

(f) *Ku-ke-ao-iki*, a form of the god Ku, a small cloud—hand-size— that grew and grew until it became ominous and seemed to fill the heavens.

(g) *Ku-ke-ao-loa*, a cloud-omen grown to full size.

(h) *Ku-ke-ao-poko*, said to be a cloud that quickly dissolved itself in rain.

(i) *Ku-ke-ao-apihapiha*, a sky full of small clouds, probably the same as our "mackerel sky." All these different kinds of clouds are forms in which Ku showed himself.

(j) *Kanaka o ka mauna*. This undoubtedly means Ku-pulupulu, a god of the canoe-makers. He seems to have had much influence over the lawless *Kini Akua*. He it was who contracted for the building of a canoe for the hero Laka.

(k) *Uhu laau*, another form of ulu; a shady place.

E ku ai, e hina(*l*) ka omaka(*m*) e pule.
Ua kana:(*n*) kahe ka wai,(*o*) e Ka-hoalii;(*p*)
Moku i ka piko,(*q*) e.
O imi, imi, o nalowale, i loa'a e —
Loa'a kau hala, uku i ka oiwi.
No ke aloha i kono, haele maua;
I ike aku au i ka uwé ana iho, e.
Eli-eli kapu, eli-eli noa. Ua noa-a!

TRANSLATION

Attend, o Uli: a prayer this for life,
Poured forth in the house of the priest.
Let it touch the hearts of the shining band,
The princes who rule in the heavenly courts.
Who is this healer named Kupukupu?
His are the soot-black swine, the yellow dog;
The tiny cloud-bud and the cloud full-blown;
The cloud quick with rain, and the sky
That is mottled and checkered with clouds;
The tall Man, the Lord of the Mountain;
His fellows who rest in the tree-shade —
Bent-kneed, they pray in their forest-temple.
Suffice it: here's flowing bowl, Hoalii.
Seek the God; stay not till you find him.
If at fault, an offering this for your flesh.
The twain of us came at the call of love,
That my tears might pour with the others.
Profound the tabu; profound be the peace!
It is peace!

Prayer followed on the heels of prayer:

(*l*)   *Hina,* to sit or kneel for prayer.

(*m*)   *Omaka,* a quiet, silent, place in the wilderness suitable for prayer.

(*n*)   *Kana,* another form of *kena,* enough.

(*o*)   *Wai,* the awa cup.

(*p*)   *Ka-hoalii,* one of the gods who came with Pele from Kahiki.

(*q*)   *Piko.* The operation of trimming the thatch over the door of a house was a ceremonious operation and was termed *oki ka piko.* No one would think of sitting in the doorway or of standing on the door sill; it was sacred to Ka-hoalii (mentioned in the 14th line.)

Kulia, e Uli,(a) ka pule kanaenae ola;
Kulia i ke Alohi-lani.
Uī 'a kupua o luna nei:
Owai kupua o luna nei?
O Ilio-uli(c) o ka lani;
O Ilio-mea,(d) o Ilio-ehu;(e)
O Ku-ke-ao-iki;(f)
O Ku-ke-ao-loa;(g)
O Ku-ke-ao-poko;(h)
O Ku-ke-ao-awihiwihi-ula(i) o ka lani;
O Kánaka(j) o ka mauna,
Na Hoa(k) hele o ka ulu-laau;
Na Keo-lani,(l) i ku ai, e Laka;
O Maka'a-pule.(m)
Kahe ka wai o na Hoalii;
Nei wale ka pili moku;
Wawa, kupina'i, kuwawa o Ku-haili-moe;(n)
O Ha'iha'i-lau-ahea;(o)
O na Wahine(p) i kapa ku, i kapa eleele —

(a) *Uli*, the arch-goddess of sorcery and *anaana* (praying to death). It seems to be implied that she has healing power as well as power to kill. Or, it may be, she is invoked, retained, to keep her from enlisting on the side of the opposition.

(c) *Ilio-uli o ka lani*, the slaty-blue clouds, here appealed to as *kupua*, beings possessed of power for good or ill.

(d) *Ilio-mea*, a white cloud (cumulus).

(e) *Ilio-ehu*, a cloud having a ruddy tint from the light of the sun.

(f) *Ku-ke-ao-iki*, clouds broken up into small fragments, like our mackerel sky.

(g) *Ku-ke-ao-loa*, the long stratus clouds, here represented as an embodiment of Ku.

(h) *Ku-ke-ao-poko*, a small compact cloud standing detached from its fellows.

(i) *Ku-ke-ao-awihiwihi-ula*, a ruddy cloud, ragged at its border.

(j) *Kanaka o ka mauna*, probably the Kini Akua, the host of elfins, kobolds and brownies—godlings—that peopled the wilderness.

(k) *Hoa hele o ka ulu-laau*, an apposition clause that explains the previous appellations.

(l) *Na Keo-lani*, goddesses of healing.

(m) *Maka'a-pule*, a term applied to an ohi'a fruit (mountain apple) when so ripe that its seed rattled within the drupe. It was then in the finest condition for eating.

(n) *Ku-haili-moe*, the same god as *Ku-haili-moku*, who bedecked the land with greenery, a god also worshipped by the canoe-makers.

(o) *Ha'iha'i-lau-ahea*, said to be the same as *Ha'ina-kolo*.

(p) *Wahine i kapa ku*, the woman who stood in the outskirts of the assembly.

Na ke aloha i kono e hele;
Hele mai la au, o Hiiaka,
I ke aloha a ka hanau:
Hanau ke ola;
A ola, a ola, e-e!

This mele-pule, though closely resembling, in many parts identical with, that on page 144 seems worth reproducing here.

TRANSLATION

Speed, O Uli, this prayer for health;
Give it wings to the heavenly courts.
The question is asked the shining band:
Who are the spirits of power up here?
The azure Cloud-god that floats on high;
God Ku of the Cumulus cloud-bank;
Ku of the Mackerel-patchéd sky;
Ku of the Cloud that roofs the horizon;
Ku, the Cloud-god sailing apart;
And Ku, the Cloud-god, ruddy and ragged;
The Heroes, too, who dwell in the mountains,
Our Comrades they, who range the forest;
Women-gods of the ether who heal —
Powers that hold with thee, God Laká:
He gives men the rich-ripe mountain-apple.
The Gods pour out their healing water;
The bunchy thatch-grass waves in awe;
God Echo whose voices rumble afar;
And the Landscapist Ku and the Princess
Who plucked and ate the fateful ulei.
The women who sit in the outskirts,
All clad in robes of funeral black —
Great love has prompted their coming.
I Hi'iaka, the shadow, have come,
From love to my birth-mate, my sister.
Be this, then, the birth-place of life!
Oh for life! for life! give us life!

"How is it with you, O Lohiau?" inquired Hiiaka.

"Continue to kneel at the shrine. Prostrate yourself at the lake of our mistress," answered Lohiau.

Thereupon, Hiiaka, greatly encouraged, resumed her praying and chanted in a clear tone:

A ka luna i Kilauea,
A Wahine-kapu i ka Lua;
Kapu na papa elima o ka Lua;
Kapu Kilauea i ke ahi a ka Wahine —
Kapu ia Ka-moho-alii, he alii hanau kapu.
E ho'i au e ike me ku'u haku.
Ke haku'iku'i mai nei ka lani;
Owaowá ka honua;
Ua moe kánaka kai o ka honua;
Ua ala kukui a Kane.
Kane-po, hooulu mai;
He hiamoe kapu kou hoala ana.
E ala e, Kahiki-ku;
E ala e, Kahiki-moe;
E ala ho'i au, ua hiki mai oe;
Ua ala ka lani, ua ala ka honua;
Ua ala ka uka, ua ala ke kai.
Akahi la o ke aloha i hiki mai ai; .
Ke ho'onaue nei, naue ku'u houpo.
I ka houpo ka lele hewa a Kane;
Ilaila ke kia'i ho'iho'i aina.
Ala a moe i ke ka'i o ko haku;
Ala mai no, e!
Eia au o Hiiaka.
Ala mai, ho'i!
(I e! Holo e!)

TRANSLATION

On the heights about Kilauea;
With the sacred dame in the Pit —
Five tabu strata has Kilauea;
Tabu's the Pit through the Goddess' fire;
Tabu hedges round Moho-alii —
A tabu god was he from his birth.
To these will I go with my lord.
The heavens above are in turmoil;
The earth beneath is riven;
The Sea-powers of earth are sleeping;
The Torch of Kane has risen:

O God of the Night, inspire me!
Thy sleep needs a sacred waking.
Awake, O Kahiki-ku!
Awake, O Kahiki-moe!
I, too, will awake at thy coming.
The heavens are awake, and the earth
Is astir from mountain to sea.
To-day comes the first pang of love;
My heart, my heart, how wildly it moves!
My breast is torn, torn by God Kane.
In the breast lurks the mischief of Kane —
The heart is the fortress of Honor's guard.
Awake! repose in thy sovereign's care.
I pray thee awake!
Here am I, Hiiaka.
Awake, I beg and entreat thee!
Let my prayer speed its way!

To the grist of prayers which Hiiaka, with chanting tone, had already brought to the prayer-mill of the gods, she now added, or — following the figure employed by the Hawaiian narrator — laid on the altar of the gods(a) (*uhau*) the following; her mental attitude being that of one who was angling — again to borrow the Hawaiian figure — literally, fishing (*paeaea*)(b) for a favor, a benefit:

Ke hooulu au, e Kane-kapolei, i mua,
I o ulu Kini o ke Akua;
Ulu mai o Kane, o Kanaloa.
O Hiiaka au la, o ke kaula, a ke kahuna,
Nana i hana, nana i hooulu;
A hooulu au i ke ola, a he ola no;
He ola ho'i kou, e Lohiau-ipo i Haena;
A ola ho'i, he ola;
He ola nui, he ola iki;
He ola a kulia i ka nu'u;
A ola oe, e Lohiau-ipo.
　　I e! holo e!

(a)　*Uhau*, to lay down or offer a prayer, as, e.g., *uhau i ka pule*. The offering of the prayer is considered as a physical act, the same as laying down a pig or a fish on the altar of the god.

(b)　*Paeaea*, a fishing rod; the act of fishing. Hiiaka is represented as fishing for a favor.

To the temple, its healing rite,
I summon you, Kane-kapoléi;
Pray gather, ye Wilderness Host;
Come Kane, and come Kanaloa;
Hiiaka, prophet and priest, am I:
It is mine to inspire, to perform:
I have striven for life and life came —
Your life, Lohiau of Haena —
Aye, life, life indeed;
Life in its fullness, life in detail;
Life to stand at the temple shrine:
Such life be yours, beloved Lohiau!
Urge on; let the cure work!

Hiiaka chanted also another prayer:

E Lono, e Lono, e Lono-ku-lani,
E Lono noho i ka wai,
O houlu oe, o inana oe;
Hoinana i ke ola;
Ho'opu'epu'e ana oe i ka wai,
I ka Wai, ka Wai Ola a Kane,
Ka Wai Ola a Kanaloa,
I ka Hikina, i ke Komohana —
I wai hua, i wai lani!
I e, holo e!

O Lono, Lono, God Lono on high,
Lono, whose realm is the watery vast —
Inspirer, promoter, art thou;
Give aid to this work of perfect cure;
Thou givest life's magic to water,
The living water, Water of Kane,
The living Water of Kanaloa,
Which flows in the east, flows in the west,
In the bubbling fount, in heaven's rain.
Speed now, urge on the cure!

Prayer quickly ‑followed prayer, like the moving pictures in a shifting scene:

> Eia ana au, e Laká,(a)
> Kane a Ha'i-wahine;
> Ha'i pua o ka nahelehele,
> Ha'i hana maile o ka wao,
> Houluulu lei ho'i o Laká;
> O Hiiaka kaula mana ia, e;
> Nana i ho'uluulu na ma'i;
> A a'e, a ulu, a noho i kou kahu.
> Eia ka wai la, he Wai ola, e!
> E ola, ho'i, e-e!

TRANSLATION

> Here stand I in stress, Laká,
> Thou husband of Ha'inakolo;
> What flowers have I plucked in the wild,
> What maile stripped in the forest,
> To twine into wreaths for Laká!
> Thus toiled the seer Hiiaka;
> For hers was the magic of cure.
> But come thou, mount, enter, possess;
> Give life to thy servant and priest.
> Here's water, the Water of Life!
> Grant life in abundance, life!

The conclusion of this prayer saw Lohiau quite restored to consciousness, but in a state of utter bewilderment as to his surroundings. He found himself most unaccountably in a small rocky chamber with two women who were utter strangers in attendance on him. Before him, as he looked out, hung the apron of a mountain precipice, while in the distance and far below tossed the ocean, a familiar sight that called him back to earth at once, stirring pleasant fancies in his mind and waking in him a yearning for the sea.

(a) *Laka,* a god, or demi-god, of various functions, including fishing, agriculture and a participation in house-building. He was also one of the gods invoked by canoe-builders. The name is evidently the same as *Rata,* the appellation, in Tahiti, Raro-tonga and New Zealand, of the lehua (Metrosideros lutea). N. B. This Laka is to be carefully distinguished from the female Laka, the goddess and patron of the hula as well as necromancy.

CHAPTER XXVII

THEY DESCEND FROM THE CLIFF BY RAINBOW BRIDGES — LOHIAU, RESTORED, GOES A-SURFING

Hiiaka's work of healing was now accomplished. She had seen the cold and withered form gain fullness, warmth and color; been cheered by the oö-a-moa, the crowing sigh that came with the inrush of air to the lungs — and now he stood before her in physical perfection.

The question — asked by Wahine-oma'o — how they were to climb down from their inaccessible position was answered by the sudden appearance of three rainbows that arched themselves conveniently at their feet, and on these, as on ladders, they climbed from the dizzy height to the sleeping village below. Under the priestly guidance of Hiiaka, they all now resorted to the ocean and with the aid of its waters performed the rite of cleansing from the ceremonial defilement that came from the touch of a corpse. With this cleansing each one of them seemed to have a new birth of physical perfection. As they came up out of the water their bodies seemed actually to glow with a fresh and radiant beauty.

The touch of salt water woke in Lohiau a longing he could not resist. He took his surf-board and, with face to the incoming rollers, made for the open sea. The place was one where he had often sported before, prescriptive custom having in fact set it apart for the exclusive use of the chiefs.

The "fish"— as the Hawaiians called the Milky way — was already declining in the west and beginning to pale at the approach of a new day, and Lohiau still rode the waves.

That same night Kahua-nui, Lohiau's sister, woke from her sleep with a start. She went out of doors and, lifting her eyes to the mountain wall, saw a light gleaming in the cave where lay her brother's body. She rubbed her eyes to remove the cobwebs of sleep — yes, there it was, a quivering light, set like an eye in the socket of the mountain wall, and figures moving about. She rushed back into the house where slept her husband and stirred him with her foot.

"What are you about!" demanded the man. "Do you want to kill me?"

"Get up; there's a fire burning in the cave, up the mountain. Come!"

"What crazy fit possesses you," muttered the man as he went out. "To knock my wind out with such a kick! — and there's no fire up there, merely a star sinking in the west. That's all there was to it. Go to bed!"

The woman was silenced but not convinced. Her sleep continued to be broken. She fancied that she heard a human voice calling to her; yet, on listening, she could distinguish only the moaning of the surf. In her restlessness she wandered forth again and stood in the cool vault of night. The endless monotone of the ocean filled her ears, but it told her nothing new. She sought her bed again and turned her face to the mat in a resolute effort to sleep. She dozed, but the subtle goddess evaded her. Thoughts of her brother floated through her mind, and the booming of the surf now seemed to assume a more intimate tone and by some witchery of the imagination led her out under the winking stars, closer to old Ocean's moan, and made her think: how Lohiau did delight in the surf; what pleasure he took in riding the billows! Thus she murmured to herself. At that moment her straining vision detected an object moving with the waves. "Some man surfing in our tabu waters — yet how can that be? Have not all the men of the village gone over to Niihau? Paoa urged them to go." She moved along the beach. By this time it was dawn.

"There comes a woman," said Wahine-oma'o.

"His sister, Kahua-nui," Hiiaka remarked quietly.

Wahine-oma'o called to her by name and went forward to meet her.

"Ah, it is you two women," Kahua-nui exclaimed.

"Where's your husband?" Wahine-oma'o asked.

"Asleep in the house."

"Go and call him; tell him to take his canoe and go over to Niihau and bring Paoa," said Wahine-oma'o. "Lohiau is alive and well. Look, there he comes on the surf-board."

In a tumult of joy the woman ran to the house and shouted the tidings to her husband. Nakoa-ola, girding his malo about him as he came out of the door, made all speed for the halau; shoved the canoe down the slope of the beach; looked to the lashings of the outrigger; saw that the paddles, bailer and what not were in place; stepped the mast; arranged the sail and the sheet; then, with a final push, he leaped in astern and set his course for Niihau.

The story of Lohiau's miraculous return to life spread like wild fire until the whole population of the little island of Niihau was buzzing with the wonder. Paoa, in his haste and excitement, neglected the ordinary civilities and failed to invite his visitor to "come in and eat." They took canoe on the instant and were the first to arrive at Haena.

At sight of Lohiau, whom they found quiet and thoughtful, surrounded by a houseful of people, in conversation with his sister and two women who were strangers, they set up a wailing cry of joy that was chorused by the whole company.

The great raft of attendants, men and women, round-eyed with wonder, reached Haena in successive arrivals later in the day. First came those who eagerly credited the report of Lohiau's resurrection; scattering along after them, strangers and those who were in any degree skeptical of this great mystery. Each hour saw a bunch of new arrivals, not from Niihau alone but from all parts of Kauai.

When Kahua-nui and her husband had first wept over Lohiau, embracing and kissing him, uttering their welcome in joyous cries of wailing, they turned to the two women, the strangers, for Lohiau bade them extend their welcome to "these two women who have brought me to life again."

"Where are they from?" Kahua-nui asked.

"I know not; I only know they have given me life."

"It was worth while for my brother to have died to secure two such beautiful women as you," said Kahua-nui as she faced Hiiaka.

"The other one is more beautiful than we are," Hiiaka answered.

"Where is she?"

"Toward the Sunrise," Hiiaka answered.

"What is the name of the country?" queried Kahua-nui.

"Hawaii."

"Who is the woman," persisted Kahua-nui.

"Her name is Pele."

"I know her." Kahua-nui spoke with lower tone.

"She it was who sent us to fetch Lohiau. We found him dead. 1 worked according to my ability — you see, our man is alive again."

CHAPTER XXVIII

THE GODS COME TO LOHIAU'S FEAST

Under the direction of Kahua-nui — the woman to whom belonged the executive mind — proclamation was made throughout the land, in the name of Lohiau, commanding all the people to collect the necessary food and material in preparation for a great feast, that they might celebrate properly Lohiau's return to life.

It was to be an occasion of unparalled interest and importance: a chief, famed for his manly beauty and popular talents, rescued from the grave; the magician who had accomplished this marvel, a woman of surpassing beauty; an old-time feast, with its lavish profusion; the hula, with its lyric and epic thrills: a combination of attractions that appealed to every taste, whether of sage, epicure, frivolous dilettante or dull-witted peasant, it was sure to be the event of a lifetime. All were invited and all came.

The halau in which the people assembled was a temple of Flora, or rather of her Polynesian sister Láka. At the request of Hiiaka, whose every wish was law, one half of the hall was screened off by a rustic partition as a special feasting hall for the gods. "My relatives," said Hiiaka, "are numerous."

In this part of the halau were laid the sacrificial viands for the supply of an immense host. Having commanded silence, Hiaaka, after the manner of prayer, invited the attendance of the gods. A hush fell upon the assembly; the air was stirred by the fanning of many wings. No speech, no human voice, only the gentle clash of wooden dishes, the rustle of leaves, the gurgle of deep potations and the subdued sounds of gustation came from the place into which no human foot or eye dared intrude. At the conclusion of the affair, when Hiiaka, in priestly fashion, had pronounced the absolving word *noa* and the stewards were again at liberty to enter the precinct where the immortals had just now celebrated their symposium, it seemed, at first glance, as if nothing had been touched. The leafy bundles of fish and fowl and meat remained unopened, but they proved to be empty; the coconuts, unbroken, were yet devoid of meat; the bananas were found to be but hollow skins. The substance, the essence, had been filched away by some inscrutable power. This was the *ai inoino* — consumption to the last morsel — practiced by the gods.

It was a solemn affair, after all, this parting feast, at which, in spite of the babel of voices, weighty affairs had to be settled. Malae-ha'a-koa published the fact that the beautiful woman who sat in their mist was Hiiaka, the sister of Pele; that her art had captured the unhappy flitting ghost of Lohiau, restored it to its renovated and matchless form and that, in fulfillment of her errand, she was about to lead him away with her to be the bed-mate of the goddess who ruled the volcano.

Paoa — he whose tempestuous nature had not long ago sworn vengeance against the author of Lohiau's taking-off — now spoke up and declared his purpose to go with his master on this his new and strange adventure. Lohiau restrained him.

"I go with these two women. If I die — so be it — 'twere a glorious end, — with these two who rescued me from the grave and brought me back to the delights of your society. If I live and make my abode on Hawaii, it will be for you to come and share the blessings of my new home." Then, addressing himself specially to Paoa, "You will remain here, as my deputy, ruling over the land. If my adventure fares well, I will come and fetch you — if . . . ill, your coming would not advantage. . . . You shall stay here."

CHAPTER XXIX

HIIAKA'S ADDRESS TO CAPE KAENA

The mountains were still in shadow, but the star of morning was on high and rosy fingers in the east heralded the approach of day, taming the flare of the torches and making them almost a superfluity as the canoe — with Hiiaka occupying the pola, Lohiau in the stern holding the steersman's paddle and Wahine-oma'o ensconced in the bow — curvetted to the waves and shot out into the blue sea. One paddle-stroke and the craft had cleared the land, another and it had traversed the heaving chan-nel of Iē-iē-waena, another and it was beached on the sands of Mokuleia. At this point Hiiaka parted from her two companions, directing them to call for her with the canoe at a designated place.

Hiiaka's first care was to pay her respects to the aged one, her ancestor, Pohaku-o-Kaua'i; after that to her ancestral divinity

Kaena,(a) a name in modern times bestowed on the western cape of Oahu. She turned this point and passed into the sweltering lea where the sun poured its merciless heat and, as she climbed the slope of the Waianae mountain, looking back on the route just accomplished, according to her custom, she uttered her comments in song:

> Kunihi Kaena, holo i ka malie;
> Wela i ka La ke alo o ka pali;
> Auamo mai i ka La o Kilauea;
> Ikiiki i ka La na Ke-awa-ula,
> Ola i ka makani Kai-a-ulu Koholá-lele —
> He makani ia no lalo.
> Haöa ka La i na Makua;
> Lili ka La i Ohiki-lolo;
> Ha'a-hula le'a ke La i ke kula,
> Ka Ha'a ana o ka La i Makáha;
> Oï ka niho o ka La i Ku-manomano;
> Ola Ka-maile i ka huná na niho;
> Mo'a wela ke kula o Walió;
> Ola Kua-iwa i ka malama po;
> Ola Waianae i ka makani Kai-a-ulu,(a)
> Ke hoá aku la i ka lau o ka niu.
> Uwé o Kane-pu-niu(b) i ka wela o ka La;
> Alaila ku'u ka luhi, ka malo'elo'e,
> Auau aku i ka wai i Lua-lua-lei.
> Aheahe Kona,(c) Aheahe Koolau-wahine,(d)
> Ahe no i ka lau o ka ilima.
> Wela, wela i ka La ka pili i ka umauma,
> I Pu'u-li'ili'i, i Kalawalawa, i Pahe-lona,
> A ka pi'i'na i Wai-ko-ne-né-ne;
> Hoomaha aku i Ka-moa-ula;
> A ka luna i Poha-kea
> Ku au, nana i kai o Hilo:

(a) *Kai-a-ulu,* a sea-breeze that comforted Waianae.

(b) *Kane-pu-niu,* a form of god Kane, now an uncarved bowlder; here used in a tropical sense to mean the head. The Hawaiians, impelled by the same vein of humor as ourselves, often spoke of the human head as a coconut (pu-niu).

(c) *Kona,* here used as a local name for the sea-breeze.

(d) *Koolau-wahine,* a wind, stronger, but from the same direction as the Kona.

Ke ho'omoe a'e la i ke kehau
O a'u hale lehua i kai o Puna,
O a'u hale lehua i kai o Ku-ki'i.

TRANSLATION

Kaena's profile fleets through the calm,
With flanks ablaze in the sunlight —
A furnace-heat like Kilauea;
Ke-awa-ula swelters in heat;
Koholá-lele revives in the breeze,
That breath from the sea, Kai-a-ulu.
Fierce glows the sun of Makua;
How it quivers at Ohiki-lele —
'Tis the Sun-god's dance o'er the plain,
A riot of dance at Makaha.
The sun-tooth is sharp at Kumano;
Life comes again to Maile ridge,
When the Sun-god ensheaths his fang.
The plain Walió is sunburned and scorched;
Kua-iwa revives with the nightfall;
Waianae is consoled by the breeze
Kai-a-ulu and waves its coco fronds;
Kane-pu-niu's fearful of sunstroke;(e)
A truce, now, to toil and fatigue:
We plunge in the Lua-lei water
And feel the kind breeze of Kona,
The cooling breath of the goddess,
As it stirs the leaves of ilima.
The radiant heat scorches the breast
While I sidle and slip and climb
Up one steep hill then another;
Thus gain I at last Moa-ula,
The summit of Poha-kea.
There stand I and gaze oversea
To Hilo, where lie my dewy-cool
Forest preserves of lehua
That reach to the sea in Puna —
My lehuas that enroof Kuki'i.

According to another account, — less mythical — Hiiaka, on

(e) The author begs to remark that sunstroke is unknown in all Hawaii.

her departure from Haena, packed off Wahine-oma'o and Lohiau in the canoe, while she herself started on afoot.   Before
proceeding on her way she turned herself about and, as was her
wont, made a farewell address to the precipitous cliffs of Ka-
lalau and to the deity therein enshrined:

O Ka-lalau, pali a'ala ho'i, e,
Ke ako ia a'e la e ka wahine;
A'ala ka pali i ka laua'e(a) e
I Hono-pú, Wai-aloha.
Aloha oe la, e-e !

TRANSLATION

Your verdant mountain walls, Lalau —
Where the nymphs pluck harvest of wreaths —
Fragrant with breath of lau-a'e,
Fed by love's waters at Hono-pú;
My farewell love goes forth to you.

Hiiaka now left behind her the wild and precipitous region of
Kalalau and, passing through Miloli'i, came into Maná, a region
famous for its heat, its sand-hills, and its tantalizing mirage.
Maná was also the haunt of a swarm of little beings, elfs,
brownies and what not, to whom Hiiaka courteously offered her
salutations:

O Maná, aina a ke Akua,(b) e-e,
Aina a ke Akua i ka li'u;
O ka pa'a kolo hele i o, e-e !
E ho'i mai ana ka oe(c) i o'u nei, e-e.

TRANSLATION

Maná, thou land of the godling host,
Thou land of that wonder — mirage;
Swarming with creatures that creep and crawl !
.   .   .   .
But you're coming to take me hence !

(a) *Lau-a'e,* a fragrant plant that grows in the woods of Kauai.
(b) *Akua.* The word akua was used not alone to designate the gods,
it was also applied to any superhuman or supernatural being. The reference here is to the little creatures that swarmed in the land.
(c) *Oe.* This last line is evidently addressed to her traveling companion, Wahine-oma'o, whom she descried in the canoe in the offing.

According to this version of the narrative, which is the preferable one, Hiiaka now took passage in the canoe and from Maná the reunited party sailed away. for Oahu. By this happy reunion the otherwise dissevered narrative is brought into harmony and conflicting versions no longer pull away from each other like two ill-trained steers.

The voyage was not without enlivening incident. When the canoe had reached a point where the surges began to roll in the direction of Oahu Hiiaka saw two monster sharks disporting themselves in the waves whom she recognized as relatives on the side of her paternal grand-father, their names being Kua and Kahole-a-Kane. This was her second encounter with these sea-monsters; the first was on her recent voyage to Kauai, an encounter which had threatened serious results, if not disaster, to Hiiaka's expedition. As the story goes, when Kua and Kahole had become aware that Hiiaka's going was for the purpose of bringing Lohiau to the bed of Pele, they were moved to great disapproval of her enterprise: "A mere man," said they. "The idea of mating him with Pele is atrocious; and he is a dead man at that."

After taking counsel with the sea-goddess Moana-nui-ka-lehua, who had her boudoir in the deep waters of Iëïë-waena, with her aid they raised a commotion in the sea and Hiiaka barely escaped being swamped by a mighty water-spout. For her part Hiiaka was quite ready to overlook this rough play of her old kinsfolk and to do the agreeable with them and she accordingly addressed them kindly: "How lucky for me is this meeting again with you out here in the ocean ! It will enable me to relieve my hardships by a smack of real comfort."

The two sea-monsters felt unable to respond to Hiiaka's advances in a like spirit with her's. Their consciences plead guilty. "Look here," said Kua to his fellow, "this is our grandchild."

"Yes," his companion replied, "and she will put us to death. We'd better hide ourselves, you in your patch of surf, I in mine."

"That sort of a ruse won't avail us in the least," objected Kua.

"What then? Where shall we flee for safety?"

"To the mountains back of Waianae, to be sure," asserted Kua.

This suggestion meeting with the approval of his companion, they hastened to land and, having divested themselves of their shark-bodies and resumed human form, they made for the mountains and hid themselves in the palaá fern. Hiiaka was greatly disappointed that these two old people should have so utterly mis-

North coast of Moloka'i, from Kalawao.

conceived her attitude of mind toward them as to rob her of their interesting company. She expressed her observations in song:

A makani Kai-a-ulu lalo o Waianae,
E wehe aku ana i ka lau o ka niu.
Ha'i ka nalu o Kua a ala i ka po;
I hiki aku, i moe aku iuka ka luhi o ke kai:
Moe no a huli ke alo(*a*) i ka paia.
Hiki ka alele a kou ipo
A koena lau ka ula,(*b*) e:
He ula aloha, e !—
Makani pahele-hala(*c*) o Kamaile-húna,
Ke wahi mai la e nahá lalo o Malamalama-iki.
Ike'a Wai-lua(*d*) — ke kino o ka laau,(*e*)
Pau pu no me ke kino o ka Lehua(*f*) wehe'a:
Wehe'a iho nei loko o ka moe,
Malamalama oko'a no olalo me he ahi lele la !
He'e, e-e !

TRANSLATION

A cat'spaw ruffles the Waianae sea,
Lifting the fronds of the coco-palm;
The waves of Kua rise betime
And haste to repose neath the cliff,
To sleep secure with face to the wall.

(*a*) *Huli ke alo i ka paia.* To sleep with one's face turned to the wall was reckoned to indicate a high degree of confidence in one's safety.

(*b*) *Ula,* a tingling in the ears. Tinnitus aurium, a tingling in the ears, or any similar symptom in that organ was regarded as a sure sign that some person was making a communication from a distance. This superstition, or sentiment, in regard to tinnitus aurium was not peculiar to the Polynesian. In Der Trompeter von Saekkingen I find the following:
Laut das *Ohr klingt,* als ein Zeichen,
Dass die Heimath sein gedenket,—

(*c*) *Pahele-hala,* litterally, shaking the hala (pandanus tree). Hala also also meant fault or sin. The figure is to be taken to mean a shaking of sins, in other words, a casting of them away, a disregarding of them.

(*d*) *Wai-lua,* an abyss in the water. The reference is, of course, to the shark-gods.

(*e*) *Laau,* wooden. The reference is to the shark-bodies of the two monsters which became dead, wooden, when discarded by them on their coming out of the ocean and resuming ordinary human form.

(*f*) *Lehua.* The full name is Moana-nui-ka-lehua, a goddess (mermaid) whose domain was in the abyss of the Ieie-waena channel. For further details see remarks in the text.

Then comes my herald of peace, with
Its ear-tingling(*b*) message of love,
Offering bounty and pardon as free
As the wind that shakes the hala tree.
Drawn is the bolt and open the door
Of the secret chamber under the sea,
Revealing the tricks of the merfolk twain,
Their bodies dead as the corpse of King Log,
And with them that of the Mermaid Queen;
For a ray has pierced to their resting place,
As a lightning flash illumines the deep.
You're caught, my fellows, you're caught!

Neither Kua nor Kahole-a-Kane were relieved of their guilty fears by Hiiaka's soft words. They continued their flight along the same path which was soon afterwards followed by Hiiaka in her climb to Poha-kea. The only penalty inflicted by Hiiaka, when at last she came up with them and found them penitent, cowering in the brush, was their retirement from the ocean: not a light stroke, however, being almost the equivalent of taking away a mariner's commission, thus separating him from his chosen element, his native air.

CHAPTER XXX

WHAT HIIAKA SAW FROM THE HEIGHT OF POHAKEA

To return now to Hiiaka, who, after a hot climb, is standing on the summit of Pohakea; she is gazing with rapt and clear vision far away in the direction of her own home-land, her *moku lehua,* in Puna. Her eyes, under the inspiration of the moment, disregard the ocean foreground, on whose gently heaving bosom might be seen the canoe that holds Lohiau and Wahine-oma'o snailing along to its appointed rendezvous. Her mind is busy interpreting the unusual signs written in the heavens: a swelling mountainous mass of flame-shot clouds, boiling up from some hidden source. It spells ruin and desolation — her own forest-parks blasted and fire-smitten; but, saddest and most heart-rending of all is the thought that her own Hopoe, the beautiful, the accomplished, the generous, the darling of her heart — Hopoe has been swallowed up in the rack. Hopoe, whose accepted emblem and favorite poetical metamorphosis was a tall lehua tree in full blossom, is now a scarred rock teetotumed back and forth by the tides and waves of the ocean. This thought, however much she would put it aside, remained to fester in her heart.

(We omit at this point a considerable number of mele which are ascribed to Hiiaka and declared to have been sung by her while occupying this mountain perch at Poha-kea. Application to them of the rule that requires conformity to a reasonable standard of relevancy to the main purpose of the narrative results in their exclusion.)

The song next given — by some dubbed a *pule,* because of its serious purpose, no doubt — seems to be entitled to admission to the narrative:

> Aluna au a Poha-kea,
> Ku au, nana ia Puna:
> Po Puna i ka ua awaawa;
> Pohina Puna i ka ua noenoe;
> Hele ke a i kai o ka La-hiku o a'u lehua,
> O a'u lehua i aina(*a*) ka manu;
> I lahui(*b*) ai a kapu.
> Aia la, ke huki'a(*c*)la i kai o Nana-huki —
> Hula le'a wale i kai o Nana-huki, e !

TRANSLATION

> On the heights of Poha-kea
> I stand and look forth on Puna-
> Puna, pelted with bitter rain,
> Veiled with a downpour black as night !
> Gone, gone are my forests, lehuas
> Whose bloom once gave the birds nectar !
> Yet they were insured with a promise !
> Look, how the fire-fiends flit to and fro !
> A merry dance for them to the sea,
> Down to the sea at Nana-huki !

Hiiaka now pays attention to the doings of the people on the canoe in the offing. It is necessary to explain that, on landing

---

(*a*)　*Aina,* to furnish food.
(*b*)　*Lahui,* wholly, entirely.
(*c*)　*Huki,* to fetch a wide course; to deviate from a direct course.

at Mokuleia, she had ordered her two companions to continue
their voyage and meet her on the other side of Cape Kaena
whose pointed beak lay close at hand. Lohiau, nothing loath —
a pretty woman was company enough for him — turned the
prow of the canoe seaward and resumed his paddle. After
passing the cape, the ocean calmed, making the work of steering
much less arduous. Now it was that Lohiau, feeling the warm
blood of young manhood swell the cockles of his heart and
finding opportunity at hand, made ardent love to his attractive
voyage-companion. He pressed nose and lip against her's and
used every argument to bring her to accept his point of view.

Wahine-oma'o had a mind of her own and thought not at
all averse to love and its doings and though very much drawn
to this lover in particular, she decidedly objected to compromis-
ing her relations with Hiiaka, but above all, with the dread
mistress of the Volcano, with whom she must ere long make
reckoning. Like Pele, Wahine-oma'o permitted the kisses of
Lohiau for a time, but, knowing that passion grows by what it
feeds on, she presently cut short his rations and told him to be-
have himself, enforcing her denial with the unanswerable argument that she was well persuaded that they would be seen by
Hiiaka. It was even so. It was worse. Hiiaka did not content herself with throwing temptation before Lohiau, as one
might place raw meat before a hungry dog; by some witchery
of psychologic power she stirred him up to do and dare, yet at
the same time she impelled Wahine-oma'o to accept, but only a
certain degree, for she carefully set bounds to their conduct.
And this, be it understood, is but the opening act of a campaign
in which Hiiaka resolves to avenge herself on Pele.

When at length Hiiaka centered her attention on the actions
of the people in the canoe, it needed but a glance to tell her
that the contagium planted in the soil of Lohiau's mind had
worked to a charm. Her own description — though in figures
that seem high-wrought and foreign to our imaginations — had
better tell the tale:

> Aluna au o Poha-kea,
> Wehe ka ilio(a) i kona kapa;

(a) *Ilio,* dog. It is explained that the meaning covered by this figure
is a storm-cloud and that the stripping off of its garment, *wehe....i kona
kapa,* meant its break up into the fleecy white clouds of fair weather. It
seems that if the head of this cloud-dog pointed to the west it meant rain,
if to the east, fair weather.

Hānai alualu(*b*) i ke kula o Miki-kala,(*c*)
I ke kula o Puha-malō(*d*)
Hakaká, kipikipi o Kai-a-ulu(*e*) me ke kanáka;
Ua ku'i-ku'i wale a ha'ina(*f*) na ihu;
Ua ka i ka u me ka waimaka,
I ke kula o Lualua-lei,(*g*) e !
Ku'u lei aloha no olua no, e !

TRANSLÁTION

I stand ahigh on Poha-kea;
The dog of storm strips off his robe;
A zephyr fans yon heated plain of
Miki-kala and Puha-malō : —
Wild strife 'tween the man and the Sea breeze:
I see noses flattened, broken,
Fountains become of water and tears!
This my garland of love to you two !

Hiiaka's voice had the precious quality of carrying her words and making them audible to a great distance, when she so willed. Her song, therefore, did not, on this occasion, waste itself in the wilderness of space. The caution it imposed had its effect. Lohiau and Wahine-oma'o calmed their passionate contentions and proceeded discreetly on their way   Having passed Kalae-loa,(*h*) their canoe swung into that inverted arc of Oahu's coast-line, in the middle of which glisten, like two parted rows of white teeth, the coral bluffs that were the only guard at the mouth of Pearl Lochs.

Before descending from her vantage ground on Pohakea, Hiiaka indulged her fancy in a song that was of a different strain. Looking towards Hilo, she describes the rivers, swollen by heavy rains, rushing impetuously along in bounding torrents,

---

(*b*) *Hanai alualu*, to fan with a gentle breeze. Alu-alu is another form for oluolu.

(*c*, *d*) *Miki-kala* and *Puha-malo*, names of places along the coast of Oahu in the region under observation.

(*e*) *Kai-a-ulu*, a wind felt on the leeward side of Oahu.

(*f*) *Ha'ina na ihu*. *Ha'i*, to break or be broken. The Hawaiian kiss was a flattening of nose against nose. The breaking of noses, as here, therefore, means excessive kissing.

(*g*) *Lualua-lei*, the name of a plain in this region.

(*h*) Barber's Point.

while men and women leap into the wild current and are lifted
on its billows as by the ocean waves:

> A makani Kua-mú(a) lehua ko uka;
> Ke ho'o-wa'a-wa'a a'e la
> E uä i Hana-kahi,(b) e-e:
> Ke uä la, uä mai la Hilo
> A moku kahawai, piha akú la
> Na hale Lehua(c) a ke kai, e-e!

TRANSLATION

> Kua-mú pays toll to the forests —
> Cloud-columns that veer and sway,
> Freighted with rain for Hilo,
> The Hilo of Hana-kahi.
> The channels are full to the brim —
> A tide that will flood ocean's caverns,
> The home of the mermaid Lehua.

After a moment's pause she resumed, though in quite a different strain:

> Aia no ke 'kua la i uka;
> Ke hoá la i ka papa a enaena,
> A pulelo(d) mai ka ohi'a o ka lua;
> Maewa(e) ke po'o, pu'u, newa i ka makani,
> I ka hoonaue ia e ka awaawa, e-e!

TRANSLATION

> The god is at work in the hills;
> She has fired the plain oven-hot;

(a) *Kua-mu,* said to be the name of a wind, the blowing of which caused
heavy rain in the woods back of Hilo.

(b) *Hana-kahi,* an ancient king of Hilo, frequently mentioned in poetry,
whose name is used to designate the district.

(c) *Hale Lehua,* an evident allusion to the goddess, or mermaid, Moana-
nui-ka-Lehua. She was a relative of Pele and had her habitation in the
ocean caverns of Ie-ie-waena, the channel between Oahu and Kauai. Her
story belongs to the time when the sun-hero Mawi was performing his wonderful exploits.

(d) *Pulelo,* a word descriptive of the tremor of the flames that wrapped
the trees.

(e) *Maewa,* to fork, or branch, said of the flames.

The forest-fringe of the pit is aflame; —
Fire-tongues, fire-globes, that sway in the wind—
The fierce bitter breath of the Goddess!

As the canoe drew near to the appointed rendezvous at Pu'u-
loa, Hiiaka lifted her voice in a chanting song addressed to
Lohiau and Wahine-oma'o:

Ku'u aikane i ke awa lau(c) o Pu'uloa,
Mai ke kula o Pe'e-kaua,(d) ke noho oe,
E noho kaua e kui, e lei i ka pua o ke kauno'a,(e)
I ka pua o ke akuli-kuli,(f) o ka wili-wili;(g)
O ka iho'na o Kau-pe'e i Kane-hili,(h)
Ua hili(i) au; akahi no ka hili o ka la pomaika'i;
Aohe mo-ewa'a(j) o ka po, e moe la nei.
E Lohiau ipo, e Wahine-oma'o,
Hoe 'a mai ka wa'a i a'e aku au.

TRANSLATION

We meet at Ewa's leaf-shaped lagoon, friends;
Let us sit, if you will, on this lea
And bedeck us with wreaths of Kauno'a,
Of akuli-kuli and wili-wili.
My soul went astray in this solitude;
It lost the track for once, in spite of luck,

(c) *Awa lau,* leaf-shaped lagoon; a highly appropriate epithet, when applied to that system of lochs, channels and estuaries that form the famous
"Pearl Lochs," as any one acquainted with the place will admit.

(d) *Pe'e-kaua,* the name applied to a portion of the plain west of Pu'u-
loa.

(e) *Kau-no'a,* a parasitic plant (Cassytha filiformis) consisting of wiry
stems that cling to other plants by means of small protuberances or
suckers.

(f) *Akuli-kuli,* a low, vine-like plant, said to have fleshy leaves and
minute flowers.

(g) *Wili-wili* (Erythrina monosperma), a tree having light, corky wood,
much used in making the outrigger floats for canoes. Its flowers, of a
ruddy flame-color, make a splendid decoration.

(h) *Kane-hili,* a name applied to a part of the plain west of Pu'u-loa.
Notice the repetition of the word hili in the next verse. Hili means astray,
or distressed.

(i) *Hili,* to go astray, to lose one's way. Assonance by word-repetition
was a favorite device of Hawaiian poetry. The Hawaiian poet did not use
rhyme.

(j) *Moe-wa'a,* literally a canoe-dream. To dream of a canoe was an
omen of ill luck. It was also unlucky to dream of having gained some
valued possession and then wake to the disappointing reality.

As I came down the road to Kau-pe'a.
No nightmare dream was that which tricked my soul.
This way, dear friends; turn the canoe this way;
Paddle hither and let me embark.

Hiiaka again in command, the tiger in Lohiau's nature slunk
away into its kennel, allowing his energies to spend themselves in
useful work.   Under his vigorous paddle the little craft once
more moved like a thing of life and long before night found
itself off the harbor of Kou, the name then applied to what we
now call Honolulu.

CHAPTER XXXI

HIIAKA VISITS PELE-ULA AT KOU — THE HULA KILU

At the entrance to this land-locked harbor of Kou a pretty
sight met their eyes: a moving picture of men and women in the
various attitudes of lying, kneeling or standing on boards, riding
the waves that chased each other toward the sandy beach.   The
scene made such an appeal to Hiiaka's imagination that she
opened her heart in song:

> Ke iho la ka makani
> Halihali pua o Nu'uanu, e-e;
> Aia i kai na lehua,
> Ke naná la o Hilo;
> Ke ka ia ho'i ka aukai, e-e;
> Na lehua i ka wai o Hilo,
> O Hilo ho'i, e-e!

TRANSLATION

> Down rushes the wind and sweeps along
> The blossoms of Nu'uanu:
> Afloat in the sea are the flowers —
> A scene that takes one to Hilo,
> Whose tide lines them up as a lei;
> For bloom of lehua to drift
> Far at sea is a Hilo mark.

When, after this battery of compliment, they came close up to where the princess Pele-ula — who, as will be seen, was a power in the land — having exchanged still further compliments, Hiiaka invited her to come aboard. Pele-ula, very naturally, declined this kind offer, but with a fine show of hospitality in her turn begged that they would honor her by being her guests during their stay in the place, assuring them of hospitable entertainment and such pleasures as her court could offer. Under her piloting, accordingly, they made their way by paddle across the beautiful land-locked harbor of Kou and, entering the Nu'uanu stream — in those days much broader, sweeter and deeper than now — turned into its eastern branch and erelong found themselves at the landing from which a path led up to Pele-ula's residence. Imagine the fairy scene, if you will; — a canoe-load of smiling nereids piloted by a mermaid princess swimming on ahead, with a merry convoy of mermaiden and mermen following in the wake.

A word in regard to this little land, now lying close to the heart of Honolulu itself, which still bears the same name as its old-time mistress, Pele-ula. To the kamaaina the sturdy samang tree, whose vigorous bole parts the traffic of Vineyard Street just before its junction with the highway of Nu'uanu has long been a familiar object. This fine tree has a history of its own and can claim the respectable age of not less than forty years. The land about it has borne the classic name of Pele-ula for a period of centuries that hark back to the antiquity of Hawaiian tradition. The sightseer of to-day who views the region from the macadamized roadway, some ten feet above the level of the surrounding land, must not judge of its former attractiveness and fitness as a place of residence by its present insalubrity — now shut in by embankments, overhung by dank and shadowy trees, its once-pure stream either diverted for economic purposes or cluttered and defiled with the debris of civilization. A study of the region, on the inner — *mauka* — border of which lies Pele-ula, will easily convince the observer that within a short geologic period the wash of silt and mud from higher levels has filled in and converted what must have been at one time a clear salt-water basin into the swampy flats that not long ago met the eye. Now, of course, this whole alluvial basin has been still further filled in and artificially overlaid with a more-or-less solid crust of earth and rock to meet the demands of Honolulu's ever expanding growth.

To return to our narrative: to this hamlet of Pele-ula, such as

it was in the days of Arcadian sweetness — if not of light —
Hiiaka and her select company now enter as the honored guests
of a woman distinguished alike for her beauty, her spiritual
subtility and insight — she was a *makaula* — and for her devotion to pleasure. One of her chief diversions, naturally enough,
was the hula, especially that form of the dance which was used
in connection with that *risqué* entertainment, the kilu,(*a*)

By evening, when the travelers had washed away the encrust-
ing salt, warmed and dried their apparel at an outdoor fire,
filled nature's vacuum at the generous table of their hostess,
while they were sitting in the short gloaming of the tropics, en-
joying the delicious content that waits on rest after toil, Pele-
ula interrupted the silence:

"The people will have assembled in the hall by this time. Shall
we move in that direction?" Her glance was first at Hiiaka
as the leader of the party; her gaze rested on Lohiau.

"Let the resident guests be the first. When they are settled in
their places it will be time enough for us to come in," was the
reply of Hiiaka.

"As you please," nodded Pele-ula.

Wahine-oma'o rose to her feet as Pele-ula was departing. At
this move Hiiaka said, "When you reach the hall go and take a
seat by your man friend." She meant Lohiau. Thereupon she
gave vent to this enigmatical utterance:

> Po Puna(*x*) i ka uwahi ku'i(*b*) maka lehua;
> Na wahine kihei-hei(*c*) paü heihei(*d*) o uka

(*a*) *Wa'a-hila* is said to have been the name of a favorite hula of Pele-
ula; so called after a princess who, with her brother Ka-manu-wai, ex-
celled in the performance of this dance. Her name has been perpetuated in
an old saying that has come down to us: *Ka ua Wa'a-hila o Nu'uanu*. This
is a gentle rain that extends only as far down Nu'uanu valley as to Wyllie
or Judd street.

(*x*) *Po Puna.* Puna, as the home-center of volcanic action, knew what
it was to be darkened by a volcanic eruption. Puna here stands for Hiiaka
and her companion whose home it was. The night that overshadows Puna
represents allegorically the intriguing designs of Pele-ula.

(*b*) *Maka lehua.* The lehua buds stand for the harmony, kindly affection and love that up to this time had existed between Lohiau and the two
women escorting him. Pele-ula is the smoke that blights the lehua buds.

(*c*) *Kihei-hei,* frequentative form of kihei, to wear.

(*d*) *Pau heihei.* The pau heihei was a fringe of vegetable ribbons strung
together and worn about the loins, thus serving as the conventional shield
of modesty among the people of the olden time. The modifying expression,
o uka, implies that the use of this particular form of pau was rather a sign
of rusticity.

E noho ana ka papa lohi o Mau-kele,(e)
Ha'a(f) ho'i ka papa e; ha'a ho'i ka papa,
Ke kahuli(g) nei, e-e!

TRANSLATION

Puna's day is turned into night;
Smoke blasts the buds of lehua;
The nymphs, in fringéd woodland paü,
Sit the glare lava-plates of Mau-kele:
Unstable, the lava-plates rock,
They tilt and upset.

She turns to Lohiau and says, "You had better be going to the
hall. When you go in take a seat by your friend." This advice
is puzzling: the friend must have been Wahine-oma'o and it was
customary for men and women to sit apart. Then she resumed
her song:

Mai Puna(h) au, e-e, mai Puna:
Ke ha'a la ka lau o ka lima,(i) e-e;
O ke oho o ka niu e loha(j) ana i kai, e-e!

TRANSLATION

I come from the land of Puna —
A partner I in a triple love.
Ah, look! his fingers are passion-clutched!
Like fronds of the palm, they shall wilt.

(e) *Papa lohi o Mau-kele,* glistening lava plates of Mau-kele. Mau-kele
was a land in Puna. The implication is that these women, Pele-ula, Waikiki and the rest of them are plotting to steal away the affections of
Lohiau.

(f) *Ha'a ho'i ka papa,* the lava plates rock: that is the plot is a shaky
fabrication and will. . . .

(g) *Kahuli,* topple over.

(h) *Puna.* There is a punning *double entendre* involved in the use of
this word here. A *puna-lua* was one who shared with another the sexual
favors of a third party. The implication is that Hiiaka and Wahine-oma'o
stood thus towards Lohiau. See also note (a).

(i) *Lau o ka lima,* leaves of the hand. The spasmodic working (*ha'a*)
of the fingers was deemed to be a sign of lustful passion. It is here attributed to Lohiau.

(j) *Loha,* to droop, to be fooled; here to be understood in the latter
sense of Pele-ula.

As she sauntered on her way to the dance-hall she concluded her song:

> Mai Puna au, e, mai Puna au,
> Mai uka au o Wahine-kapu;(*k*)
> Mai O'olu-eä,(*l*) i ke ahi(*m*) a Laka, la.
> Mai Puna au, e-e!

TRANSLATION

> Bethink you, I come from Puna —
> In the power of a triple love,
> Girt with the might of Wahine-kapu:
> Beware the baleful fires of Laka:
> Remember, I come from Puna.

The inner meaning and intent of this highly wrought figurative and allegorical language, which Hiiaka, according to her custom, utters at detached intervals in the form of song, does not lie on the surface, and is furthermore obscured by an untranslatable punning use of the word Puna.

To explain the motive of this song, Hiiaka perceives that Pele-ula and Lohiau, who had once upon a time been lovers, are mutually drawn to each other by a rekindling of the old flame. In the case of Pele-ula the motive of ambition to match her own spiritual power as a *makaula* — seer — with that of the young woman who comes to her as the plenipotential ambassador of Pele is even stronger than the physical passion. In the kilu now to be performed she sees her opportunity.

She will use it for all it is worth, not only that she may taste once more the delights offered by this coxcomb, but that she may pluck from the hand of this audacious creature of Pele's endowment a wreath for her own wearing.

As to Lohiau, that plastic thing, his character, is as clay in

---

(*k*) *Wahine-kapu,* one of the female deities of the Pele family who had her seat on an eminence at the brink of the caldera of Kilauea which was reverenced as a tabu place.

(*l*) *Mai O'olu-ea.* O'olu-ea, as a place-name calls for a preposition in mai. O'olu-ea, however, contains within it a verb, *olu,* to be easy, comfortable, and as a verb *olu decides* the mai to be an adverb of prohibition. In this meaning the caution is addressed to Lohiau.

(*m*) *Ahi-a-Laka,* a land in Puna. The double sense, in which it is here used, gives it a reference to the fires of passion.

the hands of the potter, under Pele-ula's manipulation. He is all for pleasure. Honor, constancy, ordinary prudence, are not in his purview. Hiiaka's immediate presence suffices to restrain and guide him; in her absence, his passion, a rudderless bark, is the sport of every wind that blows.

Hiiaka, on arriving at the halau, sat by herself. Lohiau, as she observed, was sitting with Wahine-oma'o and Waikiki. Pele-ula, who was sitting alone on her side of the hall, now showed her hand by sending one of her men, named A'ala, to invite Lohiau to come over and sit with her. At this Hiiaka spoke up: "I will sit by you."

"So be it, then," answered Pele-ula. At the same time she muttered to herself, "But she wasn't invited."

A'ala, who caught the aside of his mistress, also put in, "It's Lohiau whom she invites."

At this Hiiaka bravely laid down the rule, which was the accepted one, that the men and the women should sit on opposite sides of the halau; averring that any other disposition would be sure to breed trouble. Pele-ula could not but agree to this and accordingly, Wahine-oma'o and Waikiki, leaving their seats by Lohiau, came over and sat with Hiiaka and Pele-ula.

When the presiding officer of the game — the *la anoano(a)* — had called the assembly to order with the well known cry *"pu-heo-heo"* and it came to the placing of the *pahu kilu* — short pyramidal blocks of wood — before each one of the players, who sat in two rows facing each other and separated by a considerable interval, Hiiaka objected to the way in which they were placed. A sharp discussion then arose between Pele-ula and Hiiaka, but the younger woman carried the day and won her point.

Lohiau had a great and well-deserved reputation as a skilful champion in the game of kilu. When, therefore, it came his turn to hurl the kilu(*b*) and send it spinning across the mat with an aim that would make it strike the pahu, which was its targe, everybody looked for great things and it was openly predicted that he would win every point.

Lohiau preluded his play with a song:

(*a*)   *La anoano,* literally, quiet day.

(*b*)   The kilu, which gave name to the sport, was an egg-shaped dish made by cutting a coconut or small gourd from end to end and somewhat obliquely so that one end was a little higher than the other.

Ke hele la ka au-hula(a) ana o Ka-lalau;
Ke po'i la ke kai o Milo-li'i;
Ka laau(b) ku'i o Makua-iki:
Lawe i ka haka la, lilo!
Makua, keiki i ka poli e, i ka poli.
I ka poli no ka hoa a hele;
Kalakala i ke kua ka opeope aloha.
Auwe ho'i, e-e!

TRANSLATION

I venture the cliffs of Ka-lalau;
The wild waves dash at the base —
The breakers of Milo-li'i —
Scaling the ladder that climbs Makua.
The ladder, alas, the ladder is gone!
The child in my heart has grown a man.
My heart found room for this travel-mate;
But now! — I strip from my back
That emblem — that burden — of love!
Alas for emblem and love!

The "child in the heart that has grown to be a man" is Lohiau's old love for Pele-ula, which now wakes up into new life at the sight of his old flame. The old love has, however, in a sense become a burden. It stands in the way of the new-born affection that has sprung up in his heart for Hiiaka.

It was after the chanting of this mele that Lohiau threw his kilu. But, to the consternation of the audience and his own bewilderment, his play was a miss. His aim had been true, his hand steady, the whirling kilu had gone straight on its way as if sure of the mark, then, to the utter amazement of all experts, like the needle of the compass influenced by some hidden magnet, it had swerved and gone wild.

Hiiaka, from the other side of the hall, now took her turn at the kilu, with a prelude of song:

(a) *Au-hula-ana.* When the road along a steep coast is cut off by a precipice with the ocean tossing at its base, the traveler will often prefer to swim rather than make a wide inland detour. Such a place or such an adventure is called an *au-hula* or *au-hula-ana.*

(b) *Laau ku'i,* literally, spliced sticks; a ladder, or some contrivance of the sort to aid the traveler in climbing a pali.

A makani pua ia lalo,(*a*)
Moe ko'a ka huhu, aia iloko ho'i, e-e.
Ho'i a ka lili a ka pua o ka wao,
Noho ilaila ka hihi, ka pa'a
A ka manawa(*b*) ho'i e-e

TRANSLATION

A gust of wind from the west
Lays bare the jagged reef:
Pride makes its lair in the wilds,
Mid tangle of vine and tree:
So anger abides in the brain.

In this song Hiiaka exposes the unworthy plot that was simmering in Lohiau's mind, whom she typifies by a gust of wind blowing from the west, the general direction of Kauai.

At the first throw the kilu hit the wooden block and then, as if not content with its accomplishment, after caroming off, returned like a bee to its blossom, and this action it repeated until it had scored not one but three points. There was the thrill of triumph in Hiiaka's tone as she sang again:

O ku'u manawa na'e ka i hei i ka moe;
Ooë na'e ka'u e lawe la; lilo,
Lilo oe la e, auwe!

TRANSLATION

Aha, my will has snared the bird,
And you are my captive, yes you:
Your purpose is foiled, ah, foiled!

With another prelude of song, Lohiau offered himself for another trial, kilu in hand:

A makani pahele — hala kou Maile-húna;
Ke wáhi mai la Malama-iki;
Nohá Wai-lua,(*a*) pau ka pua.
Pau no me ke kino o Kalehua-wehe,(*b*) e-e.

(*a*) *Lalo*, below, to leeward; therefore to the west, meaning Lohiau, who came from the leeward island of Kauai.

(*b*) *Manawa*, the fontanelles; the heart and affections.

(*a*) *Wai-lua*, a river on Kauai.

(*b*) *Lehua-wehe*, a land in Honolulu; here meaning Pele-ula herself.

TRANSLATION

The volant breath of the maile
Has the strength of the fruiter's crook;
It opens a trail in the jungle.
Wai-lua breaks bar; the small fry are out,
The complots, too, of Lehua-wehe.

This attempt was a failure like those that had gone before.
Lohiau, thereupon, sought relief for his artistic disappointment
in song:

Wehe'a iho nei loko o ka moe;
Malamalama no me he ahi lele la,
No lalo, e; auwé ho'i au, e!

TRANSLATION

Failed, failed in my choicest ambition! —
Heralded, like a shooting star! —
Fallen, fallen, alas and alas!

The game has by this time resolved itself into a contest of wits
as well as of skill, and the two chief antagonists are — strange
to relate — Lohiau, the man who was called back from the grave
and the woman to whom he owes his life, Hiiaka.

As a prelude to her next play Hiiaka gave this song:

I uka kaua i Moe-awakea,(a)
I ka nahele o Ka-li'u, la.
Auwé ho'i, e-e!

TRANSLATION

You shall bed with me in open day
In the twilight groves of Ka-li'u —
Woe is me! I've uttered it now!

Hiiaka's play this time as before was a marvellous show of

(a) *Moe-awakea,* a hill in Puna; here used for its etymological sig-
nification—literally, to sleep at noontime—which is brought out in the
translation.

skill. The kilu seemed possessed with an instinct of attraction for the block that stood as her target. Like a bee that has found a rich honey-flower it returned again and yet again, as if to drain the last particle of sweetness.

Before venturing on his last play, Lohiau discarded the kilu he had been using and chose another, thinking thus to change his luck. He also changed the style of his song, adopting the more sensuous form called *ami honua*,(*b*) or *ku'u pau*:

> Ke lei mai la Ka-ula i ke kai, e;
> Ka malamalama o Niihau i ka malie.
> A malama ke kaao o kou aloha —
> Kou aloha ho'i, e-e!

In the first line of this little song, Lohiau, skilfully playing on the name Pele-ula, which he turns into Ka-ula, under the figure of the ocean tossing about that little island, banters the woman for her display of passion. In the second line, using a similar word-play, by which he turns his own name into Nii-hau, he contrasts the calm of the latter island with the agitation of the former.

TRANSLATION

> Ka-ula's enwreathed by the ocean;
> Niihau looms clear in the calm:
> And clear is the tide of your love,
> The marvelous tide of your love!

Pele-ula, in her surprise at the untimeliness of Loahiau's performance, as well as in her deep concern at his continued failure, expostulated with him: "You have but one more play; why then do you anticipate by indulging in the ami? Perhaps if you were to address your song to my father, Ka-manu-wai, who is a skilled performer — who knows but what you might hit the target for once?"

"Is it likely," Lohiau replied, "is it likely that I shall hit this

---

(*b*) The *ami* was a vigorous action of the body, often employed by dancers. Its chief feature was a rotation of the pelvis in circles of elipses. Though sometimes used with amorous intent, it was not necessarily an attempt to portray sexual attitudes. The *ami honua*, or *ami ku'u pau*, was an exaggerated action of the same description.

time, having missed so many shots before?" Thereupon the
man completed his song:

> O Puna, nahele ulu hala o Kalukalu,(c)
> Wawalu ili a mohole(d) na'ena'e.
> Pehi ala laua'e(e) o Na-pali,(f)
> Ho'olu'e iho la i ke kai;
> Kina'i aku la ka eha, e.

TRANSLATION

> In Puna's famed thickets of hala
> One's body is torn — a network of marks.
> Climbing the walls of Na-pali, the scent
> Of lau-a'e pelts the sense; then fall
> The petals sweet, to drown their pain
> In the ocean that rages below.

The kilu spins on its way — it must hit — no, fate is too
strong for it and turns it from the mark. Lohiau's song is an
admission of painful discomfiture:

> O ka eha a ke aloha ke lalawe nei,
> Eia la iloko, i ku'u manawa.
> Ka eha e! auwe ho'i e!

TRANSLATION

> The smart of love o'erwhelms me;
> It rages in heart and mind —
> This hurt, ah, this hurt!

That Lohiau of all men standing on Hawaiian soil should fail
utterly in a game of kilu was incredible — the man whose art
availed to hit a grass-top teetering in the breeze, to crush the

---

(c) *Kalukalu*, a place in Puna which supported extensive forests of hala
(pandanus), a tree whose sword-shaped leaves were edged with fierce
thorns. In contrast with the smart they produced the poet adduces the
delights of the wilds in his own island of Kauai, instancing the *laua'e* a
fragrant vine that abounds in its mountains.

(d) *Mohole*, an unusual form for *pohole*, to be lacerated, but not quite
so strong.

(f) *Na-pali* (the cliffs), a name given to the precipitous side of Kauai,
where is the wild valley of Ka-lalau.

nimble ant speeding on his way, to swat the buzzing fly flitting through the air! The audience was dumbfounded. In the failure to find excuse sufficient for the occasion, it took refuge in silence.

It only remains for Hiiaka to pluck the fruit which her skill has put within reach of her hand. Her complete victory has become a foregone conclusion. Of that there can be no question. It is, however, a question of great interest to the spectator how she will use her victory, in what terms she will celebrate her triumph over the woman and the recreant man who have combined their wits against hers. The answer to this question is to be found in the song with which she preludes her last play:

> Mehameha, kanaka-ole, ka ho'i
> O Pu'u o Moe-awa,(a) e-e!
> Ko ke auhe'e i ka aina kanaka-ole!

TRANSLATION

> Aye, lonely, man-empty, indeed;
> Cold the couch and bitter the dreams
> From which has been exiled the man!

This ironical thrust is pointed at Pele-ula, who is to see her fond hopes of a renewed liaison with her old paramour blasted by this plucking of the fruit under her very eyes.

And yet again, when Hiiaka has made the final shot that fulfills the promise of victory to her, still relentlessly wielding the sharp blade of irony, she gives it an extra twist in the wound that must have made Pele-ula wince:

> A kulou anei, e uwé ana —
> E uwé no anei, he keiki makua-ole?
> Aohe makua; uwé ho'i e!

TRANSLATION

> Will the orphan now hang his head
> And weep like a motherless child?
> His mother is dead; let him weep!

(a) *Pu'u o Moe-awa.* The full form is *Moe-awakea* (noonday sleep), the name of a hill in Puna. By omitting *kea,* the word awakea (noon) comes to mean bitter, thus imparting to the meaning a cutting irony. Cf. note (a), page 176.

This two-edged blade cuts both lovers at one stroke — the youth in its ironical allusion to tears, the woman in the sly suggestion of motherhood, she being in fact old enough to hold that relation to the young man.

The forfeit paid by Lohiau after his defeat was a dance, which he did with inimitable grace and aplomb to the accompaniment of a spirited song, his costume being the customary paü of the hula:

> Ku'u hoa i ka ili hau o Maná,
> I kula'i 'na e ka wai o Hina;
> Hina ke oho o ka hala,
> Ka oka'i pua o ka hinalo i ka wai, e.
> Eia oe; he waiwai nui kau,
> Ka ke aloha, ina i ona
> Ka mana'o mai e: eia oe e.

TRANSLATION

> Yoke-fellow in toil at Maná,
> I'm swept off my feet in this flood:
> The leaves of the twisted hala,
> The sheath of its perfumy bloom —
> All torn by the rage of the stream:
> You alone remain to me now —
> Your love, if that is yet mine,
> If your heart remains with me still.

Warming to his work, Lohiau continued:

> Ku'u hoa i ke kawelu oho o Malai-lua,
> I ho'o-holu ia, ho'opi'o ia e ka makani,
> Naue ke oho o ka hala,
> Maewa i ke kai o Po'o-ku e, eia oe;
> He ku oe na'u, e ke aloha:
> Ina oe mawaho e, eia oe.

TRANSLATION

> Mate mine through grassy meads, awave,
> Wind-swept and tossed by breeze or storm,

Or when the leaves of screwy palm
Are smitten with brine from the sea,
Thou idol enshrined in my heart,
Though apart, thou art empress within.

Still protesting his love for Hiiaka and deploring his separation from her, Lohiau continues:

A ka lihi au i ka hala o Hanalei;(*a*)
Lei au i ka hala(*b*) o Po'oku e, eia oe.
He ku oe na'u, e ke aloha;
Ina oe maloko e, eia oe.

TRANSLATION

I neighbor the land of the wreath,
My luck, to pine for a palm-crown.
Oh, wouldst thou but twine the wreath, love,
Admit to the shrine of thy heart.

Lohiau, warming to his work, strutted and capered about like a capercailzie cock before his mistresses, lashing his passion — after the manner of a flagellant — with words of wild hyperbole; but ever approaching nearer and nearer to where sat the two women about whom revolved his thoughts. As to which one of them it was that he singled out as the center of his orbit for the time, that is to be deduced from a study of his song:

Aloha wale ka nikiniki,
Ke kanaenae pua o Maile-huna;
E a'e ia ana ia Kapa'a,
I ke kahuli a ke kalukalu:
Honi u i ke ala o ka hinalo, e:
Pe wale ia uä —uä, e!
E lei au —
Lei ho'i au i ke kanáka, i ka mea aloha,
I ka mea i ho'opulapula hou
O ka moe, e: eia au.

(*a*) *Hana-lei*, literally, to make a wreath; a valley on Kauai.
(*b*) *Hala*. It was ill luck to wear a wreath of the hala drupe.

How precious the fillet that binds
Love's token of bloom with maile;
Climbing the wilds above Ka-pa'a,
To watch the surge of waving grass,
Make deep inspire of hala bloom
Beat down by pelting rain, — pour on!
I'd wreath my life with human love,
Plant once again the tender flower
That blooms in the kingdom of dreams.
That is my dream, and here am I.

The audience, moved by Lohiau's ardor, went into riotous applause. Hiiaka could not but admire the pathetic artistry of Lohiau, yet she remained the mistress of her emotions. Pele-ula, in contrast, became visibly more excited at Lohiau's close approach. Turning to the younger woman, she said, "do you respond to this man's appeals?"

"What is it you mean?" quietly asked Hiiaka.

"Can it be that you are not stirred by his protestations?" Put your hand on my bosom," said Pele-ula, "and feel the throbbing of my heart."

Hiiaka convinced herself of the truth of the assertion and, in turn, said, "Do you also lay your hand here and judge of my temper."

"You are as cool as a ti leaf," exclaimed Pele-ula, "while I am as hot as a bundle of luau."

This interchange of attentions between the two women did not escape Lohiau. It inflamed him to another passage of song:

Moe e no Wai-alua ke Koolau,
Ka hikina mai a Ka-lawa-kua;
Lele aoa i ka Mikioi;
Uwé aloha i ka Pu'u-kolu.
Aloha Wai-olohia ke Kohóla-lele, e
He lele pa-iki kau, kau ka manao —
Ka ke aloha kamali'i —
He lalau, e; eia oe!

TRANSLATION

Two rivers that chafe their banks —
A mad rush to enter the sea —
By the tempest whipped into foam;
They roar and bark like hounds:
Two souls that pine with love, —
A yearning for passion's plunge —
Their touch child's play, as they kiss: —
Ah, mine the master's lunge!

From his very nature Lohiau was not qualified to reckon with the supernatural side of Hiiaka. His appeals had been on the plain of human passion — such appeals as would have subdued and won the heart of an ordinary woman. Still acting under these limitations, Lohiau aimed and shot the arrow that emptied his quiver of song:

O Haupu, mauna kilohana,
I ko'e ia e Hula-ia a oki:
Oki laula ka uka o Puna,
Lulumi i ka pua hau o Malu-aka,
Ho'i kao'o i ka wai olohia;
Kinakina'i e eha ka pua o ka hala, la.
Hala ke aloha, hoomanao iaia i akea,
I ka'awale ho'i kau oni'na —
Oni'na mau ho'i, e: eia oe.

TRANSLATION

Thou mount of enchantment, Haupu,
By the dancers greatly beset, —
The whole face of Puna o'errun,
Where clusters the bloom of the hau —
I, back-lame and sore in defeat,
Shall master the smart of my wrong.
The love-bird has flown into space,
Away from this wriggle and squirm.
You may twist, you may turn, you are here!

Lohiau had broken with Pele-ula; his last hope and appeal was

to Hiiaka. He stood before her waiting her fateful decision.
Will she consent to turn the canoe-prow and fly back to Kaua'i
with him? He had won the woman's heart in her, but not the
deity that controlled her nature. The chain that bound her to
the Woman of the Pit was too strong to be broken by any mere
human appeal. Lohiau had failed in his play with the kilu; he
now saw that he had also failed in his attempt to play with this
human heart. The game was up; he sat down.

When Lohiau had retired in defeat, it became the turn of
Wahine-oma'o to entertain the company — Wahine-oma'o, faithful, rustic soul, that she was, whose only acquaintance with this
fine art was what she had picked up from seeing the performances
of her mistress and master. Her wits did not desert her and
were equal to the occasion: best of all, she had the wit to recognize her own limitations. Instead of pitching her song to some
far-fetched hyperbole, she travestied the whole performance in
a wholesome bit of nonsense that drifts down to us across the
centuries as a most delicious take-off:

> O ku, o ka o Wahine-oma'o,
> Wahine ia Lohiau-ipo!

TRANSLATION

> The flim and the flam
> Of the Woman-in-green,
> Handmaid to the man
> Who loveth the Queen.

If Wahine-oma'o had, of set purpose, planned an ironical take
off of the hula kilu, or rather of Lohiau's manner of acting, she
could hardly have bettered her performance. Her dancing was
a grotesque ambling and mincing from one side of the theater
to the other. The unaffected good humor of the girl robbed
the arrow of her wit of all venom while detracting not one whit
from its effectiveness.

Towards morning the audience made clamorous demands that
Hiiaka, the woman whom their suffrage had declared to be the
most beautiful that had ever stood before them, should present
herself before them once again. Hiiaka willingly responded to
this encore:

Ku'u kane i ka makani hau alia
O Maka-huna i Hua-wá, e:
Wa iho la; ke wa wale mai la no
Kaua hilahila moe awa-kea
Iluna o ka laau.
Ho'olaau mai ana ke ki'i,
Kaunu mai ana ia'u ka moe —
E moe ho'i, e!

TRANSLATION

Hot breath from the sea-sand waste —
Love hid from day in a thicket of hau —
For shame, my man, such clamor and haste!
The eye of day is open just now.
Make love, aperch, a bird in a tree!
You clamor for bed in the open:
To bed with yourself! — to bed!

CHAPTER XXXII

HIIAKA EXTRICATES HER CHARGE FROM THE DANGEROUS FASCINATIONS OF THE KILU

Hiiaka, having — by her marvellous skill — extricated her charge from the toils of the enchantress, turned a deaf ear to Pele-ula's urgent persuasions to abide yet longer and taste more deeply the sweets of her hospitaliay. Her determination arrived at, she wasted no time in leave-taking but made all haste to put a safe distance between the poor moth and the flame that was the focus of his enchantment. Their route lay eastward across

According to one version of this story, Hiiaka made free use of her powers of enchantment in withdrawing from the presence of Pele-ula. At the proper psychological moment, with the wreath of victory crowning her brow, while Pele-ula was vainly intent on an effort to turn the tide of her own defeat and gain the shadow of a recognition as mistress of the game of Kilu, Hiiaka, with a significant gesture to her companions, spat upon the ground and, her example having been imitated by Wahine-oma'o and Lohiau, their physical bodies were at once transported to a distance while their places continued to be occupied by unsubstantial forms that had all the semblance of reality.

the dusty, wind-swept, plain of Kula-o-kahu'a — destined in the coming years to be the field of many a daring feat of arms; — then through the wild region of Ka-imu-ki, thickset with bowlders — a region at one time chosen by the dwarf Menehune as a sort of stronghold where they could safely plant their famous *ti* ovens and be unmolested by the nocturnal depredations of the swinish Kama-pua'a. Hiiaka saw nothing or took no notice of these little rock-dwellers. Her gaze was fixed upon the ocean beyond, whose waves and tides they must stem before they reached and passed Moloka'i and Maui, shadowy forms that loomed in the horizon between her and her goal.

Hiiaka, standing on the flank of Leahi and exercising a power of vision more wonderful than that granted by the telescope, had sight of a wild commotion on her beloved Hawaii. In the cloud-films that embroidered the horizon she saw fresh proof of her sister's unmindfulness of the most solemn pledges. It was not her fashion to smother her emotions with silence:

Ke ahi maka-pa(*a*) i ka la, e;
O-wela kai ho'i o Puna;
Malamalama kai o Kuki'i la.
Ku ki'i a ka po i Ha'eha'e,
Ka ulu ohi'a i Nana-wale.
A nana aku nei, he mea aha ia?
A nana aku nei, he mea lilo ia.

TRANSLATION

The fire-split rocks bombard the sun;
The fires roll on to the Puna sea;
There's brightness like day at Kuki'i;
Ghosts of night at the eastern gate,
And gaunt the forms that jag the sky —
The skeleton woods that loom on high.
The meaning of this wild vision?
The meaning is desolation.

At Kuliouou, which they reached after passing through Wai-alae, Wai-lupe and Niu, they came upon some women who were

---

(*a*) *Maka-pa,* an expression used of stones that burst when placed in the fire.

catching small fish and crabs in the pools and shallow water along
the shore and, to satisfy their hunger or, perhaps, to test their
disposition, Hiiaka begged the women to grant her a portion of
their catch to satisfy their need. The answer was a surly refusal, coupled with the remark that Hiiaka would better do her
own fishing. As the sister and representative of the proud god
Pele, Hiiaka could not permit the insult to go unpunished. Her
reply was the utterance of this fateful incantation:

> He makani holo uhá(a)
> Ko Ka-ele-kei a Pau-kua.(b)
> Pau wale ke aho i ka noi ana,
> O ka loa ho'i, e!

TRANSLATION

> Here's a blast shall posset the blood,
> As the chant of kahuna the back.
> Our patience exhausts with delay;
> We're famished from the length of the way.

The magic words operated quickly. As Hiiaka turned to depart, the unfortunate fishing women fainted and died.

After this outburst of retribution, Hiiaka turned aside to address in words of consolation and compliment two forlorn
mythical creatures whom she recognized as kindred. They were
creations of Pele, Ihihi-lau-akea, manifest to us to-day as a
lifeless cinder-cone, and Nono-ula, as a clear spring of water
welling out of the mountain. It was a nice point in Hiiaka's
character that she was always ready, with punctilious etiquette,
to show courtesy to whom courtesy was due.

Fortunately for Hiiaka, her lofty perch afforded a wide-em-
bracing view that included the shadowy forms of Maui and the
lesser islands that nested with it. Not the smallest pirogue could
steal away from the strip of rocky beach at her feet without
her observation. At this moment she caught sight of two sailor-
men in the act of launching a trim canoe into the troubled waters

---

(a) *Makani holo-uha.* The allusion is to a cold wind that chills the
naked legs of the fisher-folk.

(b) *Pau-kua,* a place-name, meaning consumed in the back—a clear
reference to the fact that the kahuna's black art very frequently made its
fatal ravages by attacking first the back.

of the Hanauma cove, and she made haste, accordingly, to come
to them, on the chance of securing a passage, if so be that they
were voyaging in the desired direction. Their destination proving to be Moloka'i, Hiiaka begged the men to receive herself
and party as passengers. Nothing loath, they gave their consent.

"But," said one of them, "your party by itself is quite large
enough to fill the canoe."

His companion, with better show of cheer in his speech, spoke
up and said, "It's but common luck to be swamped in this rough
channel. To avoid it needs only skill. Even if the craft swamps,
these people need not drown; we can swim for it, and we shall
all fare alike. We'll take you with us. Come aboard." Aboard
they went.

The voyage to Moloka'i proved uneventful. They landed at
Iloli, a barren place that offered no provision to stay their hunger. When Hiiaka, therefore, learned that these same canoe-
men were bound for the neighboring island of Maui, she wisely
concluded to continue the voyage with them.

On landing in Kohala, Hiiaka took the road that led up through
the thickly wooded wilderness of Mahiki, the region that had been
the scene, now some months gone, of the most strenuous chapter
in her warfare to rid Hawaii of the mo'o — that pestilent brood of
winged and crawling monsters great and small that once infested
her wilds and that have continued almost to the present day to
infest the imagination of the Hawaiian people. On coming to the
eminence called Pu'u O'ioina,— a name signifying a resting place
— being now in the heart of the damp forest of Moe-awa, they
found the trail so deep with mire that the two women drew up
their paü and tucked them about their waists. At sight of this
action, Lohiau indulged himself in some frivolous jesting remarks
which called out a sharp rebuke from Hiiaka.

As they cleared the deep woods, there burst upon them a
view of the Hamakua coast-wall here and there dotted with
clumps of puhala and fern, at intervals hung with the white ribbons of waterfalls hastening to join the great ocean. As Hiiaka
gazed upon the scene, she uttered her thoughts in song:

(In literature, as in other matters, the missing sheep always
makes a strong appeal to the imagination. Urged by this motive,
I have searched high and low for this mele, the utterance of
Hiiaka under unique conditions; but all my efforts have been
unavailing.)

When they had passed through the lands of Kukia-lau-ania

and Maka-hana-loa and were overlooking the town of Hilo,
Hiiaka was better able to judge of the havoc which the fires of
Pele had wrought in her Puna domains. The land was deso-
lated, but, worst of all, the life of her dearest friend Hopoe had
been sacrificed on the altar of jealousy. In her indignation,
Hiiaka swore vengeance on her sister Pele. "I have scrupu-
lously observed the compact solemnly entered into between us,
and this is the way she repays me for all my labor! Our
agreement is off: I am free to treat him — as my lover, if I
so please. But it shall not be here and now. I will wait till
the right occasion offers, till her own eyes shall witness her
discomfiture."

After this outburst, her thoughts fashioned themselves in song:

> Aia la, lele-iwi(*a*) o Maka-hana-loa!(*b*)
> Oni ana ka lae Ohi'a,(*c*)
> Ka lae apane,(*d*) mauka o ka lae Manienie,(*e*)
> I uka o Ke-ahi-a-Laka:(*f*)
> Oni ana ka lae, a me he kanaka la
> Ka leo o ka pohaku i Kilauea.
> Ha'i Kilauea, pau kekahi aoao o ka mahu nui,
> Mahu-nui-akea.
> E li'u mai ana ke ahi a ka pohaku.
> No Puna au, no ka hikina a ka la i Ha'eha'e.(*g*)

(*a*) *Lele-iwi*, the name of a cape that marked the coast of Puna. The
word also has a meaning of its own, to express which seems to be the purpose of its use here. It connotes a grave-yard, a scaffold, one, perhaps, on
which the body (literally the bones) of a human sacrifice are left exposed.

(*b*) *Maka-hana-loa*, the name of another cape, also on the Hilo-Puna
coast.

(*c*) *Lae Ohi'a*, literally, ohi'a cape, meaning a forest growth that
stretched out like a tongue.

(*d*) *Apane*, a species of lehua that has red flowers, much fed upon by
the birds. (In the original newspaper-text the word was *pane*, evidently
a mistake. There are, regretably, many such mistakes in the original text.

(*e*) *Manienie*, smooth, meadow-like, a name given in modern times to
the Bermuda grass—"fine grass"—said to have been imported by Vancouver,
now extensively seen in Hawaiian lawns.

(*f*) *Ke-ahi-a-Laka*, literally, the fire of Laka, the name of a land.

(*g*) *Ha'eha'e*, the eastern Sun-gate, applicable to Puna as the easternmost district of Hawaii and of the whole group. In claiming Puna as hers—
i.e., as her home-land—Hiiaka seems to have set up a claim to be the
guardian of the Sun's rising, and therefore, by implication of Pele.

See the cape that's a funeral pyre;
The tongue of ohi'a's grief-smitten.
Beyond, at peace, lies Manië;
Above rage the fires of Laka.
The cape is passion-moved; how human
The groan of rocks in the fire-pit !
That cauldron of vapor and smoke —
One side-wall has broken away —
That covers the earth and the sky:
Out pours a deluge of rock a-flame.
My home-land is Puna, sworn guard
At the eastern gate of the Sun.

Hiiaka now entered the woodlands of Pana-ewa, a region greatly celebrated in song, which must have brought home to her mind vivid memories of that first sharp encounter with her dragon foe. From there on the way led through Ola'a; and when they reached Ka-ho'o-kú Hiiaka bade the women, Wahine-oma'o and Paü-o-pala'e, go on ahead.

(A mystery hangs about this woman Paü-o-pala'e which I have not been able to clear up. She withdrew from the expedition, for reasons of her own, before Hiiaka took canoe for Maui; yet here we find her, without explanation, resuming her old place as attendant on the young woman who had been committed to her charge. The effort, which has been made, to associate her in some mystical fashion with the paü, short skirt, worn by Hiiaka, only deepens the mystery, so far as my understanding of the affair is concerned.)

Obedient to the instructions of their mistress, the faithful women, Wahine-oma'o and Pau-o-pala'e, presented themselves before Pele at the crater of Kilauea. "Where is my sister? where is Hiiaka?" demanded the jealous goddess. No explanation would suffice. Pele persisted in regarding them as deserters and, at her command, they were put to death.

CHAPTER XXXIII

HIIAKA ALONE WITH LOHIAU

It has come at last, the situation to which the logic of events has for many days pointed the finger of a relentless fate. For the first time Hiiaka finds herself alone with Lohiau. The history of her life during the past two months seems but a prologue to the drama, the opening scene of which is about to be enacted in the dressing room, as we must call it. For Hiiaka, having gathered a lapful of that passion-bloom, the scarlet lehua, and having plaited three wreaths, with a smile on her face, hangs two of the wreaths about the neck of Lohiau, using the third for her own adornment.

They are sitting on the sacred terrace of Ka-hoa-lii, at the very brink of the caldera, in full view of the whole court, including the sisters of Hiiaka who gather with Pele in the Pit. "Draw nearer," she says to Lohiau, "that I may tie the knot and make the fillet fast about your neck." And while her fingers work with pliant art, her lips quiver with emotion in song:

> O Hiiaka ka wahine,
> Ke apo la i ka pua;
> Ke kui la, ke uö la i ka manai.
> Ehá ka lei, ka apana lehua lei
> A ka wahine la, ku'u wahine,
> Ku'u wahine o ka ehu makani o lalo.
> Lulumi aku la ka i kai o Hilo-one:
> No Hilo ke aloha — aloha wale ka lei, e !

TRANSLATION

> 'Twas maid Hiiaka plucked the bloom;
> This wreath her very hands did weave;
> Her needle 'twas that pierced each flower;
> Her's the fillet that bound them in one.
> Four strands of lehua make the lei —
> The wreath bound on by this maid —
> Maid who once basked in the calm down there:
> Her heart harks back to Hilo-one;
> Wreath and heart are for Hilo-one.

The wreath is placed, the song is sung, yet Hiiaka's arm still clasps Lohiau's neck. Her lithesome form inclines to him. With a sudden motion, Hiiaka throws her arms about Lohiau and draws him to herself. Face to face, lip touches lip, nose presses nose.

The women of Pele's court, chokefull of curiosity and spilling over with suspicion, watchful as a cat of every move, on the instant raise their voices in one Mother-Grundy chorus: "Oh, look ! Hiiaka kisses Lohiau ! She kisses your lover, Lohiau !"

The excitement rises to fever heat. Pele is the coolest of the lot. At the first outcry — "they kiss" — Pele remarks with seeming indifference, "The nose was made for kissing."(a) (The Hawaiian kiss was a flattening of nose against nose). But when Hiiaka and Lohiau sink to the earth wrapped in each other's arms, and the women of Pele's court raise the cry, "For shame! they kiss; they embrace !" At this announcement, the face of Pele hardens and her voice rings out with the command: "Ply him with fire."

From Pele's viewpoint, the man, her lover, Lohiau was the sinner. The role played by the woman, her sister, Hiiaka — the one who had, in fact, deliberately planned this offensive exhibition of insubordination and rebellion — was either not recognized by Pele or passed by as a matter of temporary indifference. Hiiaka's justification in motives of revenge found no place in her reasoning.

When the servants of Pele — among them the sisters of Hiiaka — found themselves under the cruel necessity of executing the edict, they put on their robes of fire and went forth, but reluctantly. In their hearts they rebelled, and, one and all, they agreed that, if, at close view, they found him to be the supremely handsome mortal that fame had reported him to be, they would use every effort to spare him. On coming to the place, their admiration passed all bounds. They could not believe their eyes. They had never seen a manly form of such beauty and grace. With one voice they exclaimed:

> Mahina ke alo,
> Pali ke kua.
> Ke ku a ke kanáka maikai,
> E ku nei i ke ahu' a Ka-hoa-lii.

TRANSLATION

> Front, bright as the moon,
> Back, straight as a mountain wall:
> So stands the handsome man,
> This man on thy terrace, Hoa-lii.

(a) "I hana ia ka ihu i mea honi."

Hale-o-Keawe on lava at Honaunau, Hawaiʻi.

Pele's fire-brigade went through the form of obeying their orders. They dared not do otherwise. Acting, however, on their preconcerted plan, they contented themselves with casting a few cinders on the reclining form of Lohiau and, then, shamefaced, they ran away — an action that had the appearance of reproof rather than of punishment.

The effect on the mind of Hiiaka, whose insight into the character of Pele was deeper than that of Lohiau, was far different from that of mere admonition or reproof. She recognized in the falling cinders a threat of the direst import and at once braced herself to the task of averting the coming storm and of disarming the thundercloud that was threatening her lover. "Have you not some prayer to offer?" she said to Lohiau.

"Yes," he answered, and at her request he uttered the following:

> Ua wela Pu'u-lena i ke ahi;
> Ua wela ka mauna ou, e Kahuna.
> Uwé au, puni 'a i ke awa;
> Kilohi aku au o ka mauna o ka Lua,
> E haoa mai ana ke a;
> Ka laau e ho'o-laau —
> Ho'o-laau mai ana ke ki'i,
> Ke moe, i o'u nei.
>
> Ia loaa ka hala, ka lili, kaua, paio;
> Paio olua, e.

TRANSLATION

> Pu'u-lena breathes a furnace blast;
> Your mount, Kahuna, is a-blaze;
> I choke in its sulphurous reek.
> I see the mountain belching flame —
> A fiery tree to heaven upspringing;
> Its deadly shade invades my stony couch.
>
> Is there fault, blame, strife, or reproach;
> Let the strife be between you two.

To this proposal of her chivalric companion, who would throw upon the woman the whole burden of fault, punishment, and strife, Hiiaka made answer in this address to Pele:

Puka mai ka Wahine mai loko mai o ka Lua,
Mai loko mai o Muliwai o ka Lena,(*a*)
Mai ka moku(*b*) po'o a Kane.
E noho ana o Kane-lau-apua(*c*) i ke one lau a Kane;
Ninau mai uka, "Nowai he wa'a?"(*d*)

(*a*)   *Muliwai o Lena.*   There is a stream of this name in Waianae, it is said.   Lena is also said to be the name of a place in Kahiki.   The word *lena*, yellow, strongly suggests the thought of sulphur.

(*b*)   *Moku po'o a Kane*, literally, the fissured head of Kane.   The first land formed by Kane.

(*c*)   *Kane-lau-apua*, the same as Kane-apua.   One of the numerous avatars or characters of Kane.   He appeared in Kahiki—Kukulu o Kahiki— and gained a reputation as a benevolent deity, whose benign function— shared by Kane-milo-hai—was to pluck from the jaws of death those who lay at the last gasp (*mauli-awa*), or whose vital spark was at the last flicker (*pua-aneane*).   He healed the palsied, the helpless and hopeless, those who were beyond the reach of human aid.   On one occasion he restored himself to perfect health and soundness by the exercise of his own will; hence his name, Kane-apua.   On another occasion he illustrated his power by restoring to life some okuhekuhe which the fisherman had already scaled and laid upon the fire.   The motive for this act seems to have been that this fish was a form in which he sometimes appeared.   The story of his adventure with Kane-lelei-aka is worthy of mention.   At one time while standing on a headland that reached out into the ocean like the prow of a ship, his eye caught a gleam from something moving swiftly through the water.   He saw it repeatedly passing and repassing and wondered what it was.   It was the shadowy form of Kane-lelei-aka, but he knew it not.   He scanned the surrounding mountains and cliffs, if perchance he might get sight of the body, bird, or spirit that produced this reflection.   He discovered nothing.   In pursuit of his quest, he started to go to Kukulu-o-Kahiki.   On the way he met his relative Kane-milo-hai, out in mid ocean.

"Are you from Kanaloa?" asked Kane-milo-hai.   That meant are you from Lana'i, Kanaloa being the name formerly given to that little island.

"Aye, I am from Kanaloa and in pursuit of a strange shadowy thing that flits through the ocean and evades me."

"You don't seem to recognize that it is only a shadow, a reflection.   The real body is in the heavens.   What you are pursuing is but the other intangible body, which is represented by the body of Kane-mano.   He is speeding to reach his home in *Ohe-ana*" (a cave in the deep sea, in the Kaipopolohua-a-Kane).

"How then shall I overtake him?" asked Kane-pua.

"You will never succeed this way.   You are no better off than a kolea (plover) that nods, moving its head up and down (*kunou*).   Your only way is to return with me and start from the bread-fruit tree of Lei-walo (*Ka ulu o Lei-walo*).   You must make your start with a flying leap from the topmost branch of that tree.   In that way you can come up to him and catch him."

The rest of the story: how he followed the advice given him by Kane-milo-hai and succeeded is too long for insertion here.

(*d*)   *Nowai he wa'a?*   To speak of a lava flow as a *wa'a*, a canoe, is a familiar trope in Hawaiian mele.   (See U. L. of H., p. 194).   The canoe in this case is the eruption of fire sent against Lohiau, the *hoapaio*, against whom it is launched, Lohiau and Hiiaka.

No ka hoa-paio o Ai-moku(*e*) wahine:
Ninau a'e i kona mau kaikaina;
A lele e na hoali'i —
Ka owaka o ka lani,
Ka uwila nui, maka ehá i ka lani.
Lele mai a huli, popo'i i ka honua;
O ke kai uli, o ke kai kea;
O ke ala-kai a Pele i hele ai.
E hele ana e kini(*f*) maka o ka La o Hu'e-ehu'e,
E nana ana ia luna o Hualalai;
Aloha mai ka makani o Kaú.
Heaha la ka paú(*g*) o ka wahine?
He palai, he lau-i, ka paú hoohepa o ka wahine, e Kini, e.
Ha'aha'a iluna ke kihi(*h*) o ka Mahina;
Pau wale ke aho i ke Akua lehe-oi;(*i*)
Maka'u wale au i ke Akua lehe-ama.(*j*)
    Eli-eli kapu, eli-eli noa!
Ua noa ka aina i ka puké(*k*) iki, i ka puké nui,

(*e*) *Aimoku wahine.* An *aimoku* is one who eats up the land, a conqueror, a literal description of Pele.

(*f*) *Kini maka o ka la.* In the original text from which this is taken the form is Kini-maka, offering the presumption that it is intended as a proper name. Kini-maka was a malevolent *kupua, demigod,* against whom, it is charged that she was given to scooping out and eating the eyes of men and her fellow gods. Her name was then called Walewale-was-Ku. Kane, it is said, took her in hand and weaned her from her bad practice; after which she was called Kini-maka, Forty-thousand-eyes. The phrase *o ka la* affixed to her name discountenances the idea that she is the one here intended. It becomes evident that the whole expression means rather the many eyes of the Sun, i. e., the many rays that dart from the Sun; and this is the way I construe it.

(*g*) *Pau o ka wahine?* The question as to the kind of pau, skirt, worn by the women—those of Pele's fire-brigade, as I have termed them—is pertinent, from the fact that the answer will throw light on their mood and the character of their errand, whether peaceful, warlike, etc. The answer given in the text (line 20 of the translation) is *Their skirts were fern and leaf of the ti.* A pau of fern was said to be hanohano, dignified. *Ua kapa ia ka palai he palai alii; o ka la-i, ua kapa ia he mea kala* the (pau of fern was worn by chiefs; the pau of ti leaf was a sign of propitiation.) A woman wore a ti leaf during her period of monthly infirmity. The whole subject will bear further investigation.

(*h*) *Kihi o ka Mahina,* the horn of the Moon. The manner of fastening the pau, knotting or tucking it in at each hip, gave it a crescent shape, with an angle at each hip. This seems to have suggested to the poet a comparison with the horns of the young Moon.

(*i*) *Akua lehe-oi,* an undoubted reference to Pele,—the sharp devouring edge, lip, of her lava-flow.

(*j*) *Akua lehe-ama.* This also must refer to Pele—her gaping lips.

(*k*) *Puke,* the archaic form of *pu'e,* a hill of potatoes, yams and the like.

I ka hakina ai, i ka hakina i'a, —
I kou hakina ai ia Kuli-pe'e i ka Lua, la.
   Eli-eli, kau mai!
Ma ka holo uka, ma ka holo kai.
   Eli-eli kapu, eli-eli noa!
Ua noa ka aina a ke Akua!

TRANSLATION

The Woman comes forth from the Pit,
Forth from the river with yellow tide,
From the fissured head of Kane,
Kane-apua, the cheater of death,
Presides o'er his much-thronged sandy plain:
The mountains re-echo the question,
"Gainst whom do they launch the canoe?"
Against her foes, the land-grabber's.
To her sisters she puts a question,
Up spring the high-born, the princes —
What splendor flashes in heaven!
The fourth eye of heaven, its flaming bolt.
With swell of wave and break of surf a-land
Was her flight o'er the blue sea, the gray sea —
The voyage Pele made from Kahiki.
From his western gate fly the Sun-darts,
Their points trained up at Hualalai —
The wind from Kaú breathes a blessing.
Pray tell me, what skirts wear the women?
Their skirts are fern and leaf of the ti
Bound bias about the hips, O Kini;
One horn of the sickle moon hangs low;
My patience faints at her knife-like lips
And I fear the Goddess's yawning mouth.
Deep, deep is the tabu, deep be the peace!
The land is fed by each hill, small or big,
By each scrap of bread(a) and of meat —
Food that is ravaged by Kuli-pe'e.
Plant deep the foundations of peace,

(a) The Hawaiians had no such thing as bread. The Hawaiian word *ai*, in line 20 of the original, means vegetable food. The necessities of the case seem to justify the use of the word bread in the translation. The reader will pardon the anachronism.

A peace that runs through upland and lowland.
Deep, deep the tabu, deep be the peace!
Peace fall on the land of the Goddess!

CHAPTER XXXIV

PELE'S BRIGADE IS SENT TO THE ATTACK
OF LOHIAU

Pele broke forth in great rage when her people slunk back, their errand not half accomplished. "Ingrates, I know you. Out of pity for that handsome fellow, you have just made a pretense and thrown a few cinders at his feet. Go back and finish your work. Go!"

Hiiaka, on witnessing the second charge of the fire-brigade, again broke forth in song:

Hulihia Kilauea, po i ka uahi;
Nalowale i ke awa(a) ka uka o ka Lua.
Moana Heëia — la kapu i ke Akua!
Haki palala-hiwa ke alo o ka pohaku;
Ai'na makai a'ahu, koe ka oka —
Koe mauka o ka Lae Ohi'a.
Haki'na ka hala, apana ka pohaku;
Kiké ka alá; uwé ka mamane —
Ka leo o ka laau waimaka nui,
O ka wai o ia kino á pohaku,
Kanaka like Kau-huhu ke oko o ke ahi;
Ho'onu'u Puna(x) i ka mahu o ka Wahine.
Kahá ka lehua i ka uka o Ka-li'u;
Makua ke ahi i ka nahelehele —
Ke á li'u-la o Apua.
E ha'a mai ana i ku'u maka
Ka ponaha lehua mauka o Ka-ho'i-kú;
Puni'a i ke awa ka uka o Nahunahu:
Kiná Puna, e poá i ke Akua.
Ua kaulu-wela ka uka o Olueä;

(a) *Awa.* The full expression would probably be *ua awa,* bitter rain, i.e., bad weather.

Ua haohia e ke ahi, ku ka halelo.(b)
Moku kahawai, niho'a ka pali;
Ua umu pa-enaena ke alo o ka pohaku.
O Ihi-lani,(c) o Ihi-awaawa,(d)
Hekili ke'eke'e, ka uila pohaku;
Puoho, lele i-luna, ka alá kani oleolé,
Kani au-moe, kani ku-wá, kani helele'i;
Owé, nakeke i ka lani, nehe i ka honua;
Ku'u pali kuhoho holo walawala i-luna, i-lalo;
Ka iho'na o ka pali uhi'a e ka noe;
Pa'a i ka ohu na kikepa lehua a ka Wahine;
Ho'o-maka'u ka uka — he ahi ko ka Lua.
Ke ho'o-malana a'e la e ua na opua;
Ne'ene'e i kai o Papa-lau-ahi.
Lapalapa ka waha o ke Akua lapu;
Hukihuki(e) ka lae ohi'a o Kai-mú,
E hahai aku ana i-mua, i-hope.
Hopo aku, hopo mai;
Hopo aku au o ka ua liilii noe lehua i ka papa.
O Pua'a-kanu(f) oheohe, me he kanáka oa(g) la i ka La;
Ke'a ka maha lehua i kai o Ka-pili nei:

(b) *Halelo,* rough, jagged like aa. The following quotation is given:

Ku ke a, ka halelo o Kaupo,
I ho'okipa i ka hale o ka lauwili:
E-lau-wili. He lau-wili ka makani, he Kaua-ula.

TRANSLATION

How jagged stand the rocks of Kaupo,
That once held the house of the shiftless!

(c) *Ihi-lani,* literally, the splendor of heaven; said to be a god of lightning, also the name of a hill.

(d) *Ihi-awaawa,* said to be the name of a god of lightning, as well as the name of a hill.

(e) *Huki-huki,* literally, to pull, to haul with a succession of jerks. The action here figured is eminently descriptive of the manner of advance of a lava-flow. It is not with the uniform movement of a body of water. It shoots out a tongue of molten stuff here and there; and as this cools, or is for cause arrested, a similar process takes place at some other point. This movement bears a striking resemblance to the action of a body of skirmishers advancing under fire. Its progress is by fits and starts.

(f) *Pua'a-kanu.* In spite of the fact that this is claimed by Hawaiians to be a place-name, I must see in it an allusion to a swine, devoted to sacrifice, connoting Lohiau himself.

(g) *Oa,* a poetical contraction for loa, long.

I pili aku ho'i maua o haele,(*h*)
E pi'i i ka uka, e kui, e lei i ka lei,
Ka lehua o ka ua nahuhu — (nahunahu)
Nahu'a e ke ahi — uli ke a —
Mahole ka papa, manihole i ka ai ia e ke Akua:
Ai kolohe ka Wahine ia Puna,
Ho'o-pohaku i ka Lae Ohi'a.
Ka uahi o ka mahu ha'a-lele'a i uka;
Ka hala, ka lehua, lu ia i kai.
Ha'aha'a Puna, ki'eki'e Kilauea:
Ko Puna kuahiwi mau no ke ahi.
O Puna, aina aloha!
Aloha-ino Puna, e moe'a nei,
Ka aina i ka ulu o ka makani!

The language of this mele is marked by a certain mannerism
that can hardly be described as either parallelism or as antithesis,
though it approaches now one and now the other. It is as if each
picture could not be accomplished save by representing its group-
ing from more than one point of view.

TRANSLATION

Kilauea breaks forth: smoke blurs the day;
A bitter rain blots out one half the Pit;
Heëia is whelmed by a tidal wave; —
Dread day of the fiery Goddess!
The face of the cliff is splintered away;
The lowlands are littered with fragments
Her besom spares other land, not the park.
The screw-palms are rent, the rock-plates shattered;
The bowlders grind, the mamanes groan:
I hear the pitiful sob of the trees.
The tree-gods weep at their change into stone.
Man, like the roof-pole, strangles in smoke;
Puna chokes with the steam of the Woman;
How groan the lehuas of Ka-li'u!
A quivering flame enwraps Apua.
Mine eyes are blinded at the sight
Of the forest-circle of Ho'o-kú;

(*h*) *Haele.* By a figure of speech—metonymy—the word *haele*, meaning to travel, is used to signify a fellow traveler, the companion, of course,
is Hiiaka herself.

Nahunahu is swallowed up in the rack.
Puna, how scarred! by the Goddess ravaged!
Olueä's uplands quiver with heat —
What ravage! its rocky strata uptorn;
Deep-gullied the canyons, toothed are the cliffs;
Like an oven glows the face of the rocks.
Now Heaven hurls her forked bolts
And bitter thunder-bombs; rocks burst and fly.
A crash of splintered echoes breaks the night,
Shatters the heavens and rends the earth.
My towering cliff is shook like a reed;
The trail adown the cliff is wreathed in steam;
Mist veils the ragged spurs of lehua —
A reign of terror! flames leap from the Pit;
The storm-clouds spread their wings for rain;
They rush in column over the plain.
The mouth of the demon vomits flame —
A besom-stroke to wooded Kai-mú.
Destruction follows before and behind;
What terror smites a-far and a-near!
A brooding horror wraps my soul
As the fine rain covers the plain.
A spectacle this for the eye of Day!
An offering 's laid — a pig? a man!
Deem'st it a crime to snuggle close in travel?
That we gathered flowers in the woods?
That we strung them and plaited wreaths?
That we hung them about our necks? —
Red blossoms that sting us like fire —
A fire that burns with a devilish flame,
Till the blistered skin hangs in rags:
And this — is the work of the God!
The faithless Woman! Puna sacked!
The Park of Lehua all turned to rock!
The column of rock moves ever on;
Lehuas and palms melt away,
As the fire sweeps down to the sea.
For Puna's below and Pele above,
And Puna's mountain is ever aflame.
Oh Puna, land close to my heart!
Land ever fore-front to the storm!
I weep for thy sorrowful plight!

"Cowed, and by a boy!" said Pele as her servants, with shame in their faces, slunk away from their unfinished task. "This is no job for women," she continued. "These girls can't stand up before a man — not if he has a smooth face and a shapely leg."

As she spoke the fire-lake in Hale-ma'u-ma'u took on a ruddier hue, lifted in its cauldron and began to boil furiously, spouting up a score of red fountains.

"Men, gods, take these fires and pour them upon the man," said Pele, addressing Lono-makua, Ku-pulupulu, Ku-moku-halii, Ku-ala-na-wao, Kupa-ai-ke'e, Ka-poha-kau, Ka-moho-alii, Kane-milo-hai and many others.

The gods well knew on what perilous ground they stood, with whom they had to deal, the fierceness of Pele's wrath when it was stirred; yet, in their hatred of a great wrong, they moved with one purpose to push back the fires that were threatening Lohiau. With their immortal hands they flung away the embers and masses of flame until the heavens were filled with meteor-fragments.

Pele's wrath rose to a mighty heat at this act of mutiny and disloyalty and she cursed the whole assembly. "Go," said she, "back to Huli-nu'u whence you came. Let the land on which you stand remain barren and yield no harvest nor any food for mortal or for immortal."

Now Pele was one of the chief gods on earth. The land was hers. Did she not make it? Her authority extended also to heaven. Did not her flames mount to the zenith? All the gods, even the great gods Ku, Kane, Kanaloa and Lono, depended on her for certain things. When she voyaged from Kahiki to the new land of Hawaii they were constrained to follow her. Not because of any command she laid upon them did they do this, but because such was their inclination. Where Pele was there was food, wealth, the things they had need of. They followed as a dog tags after its master.

The threat made by Pele was, then, no idle breath. It was a thing of terrible moment — to be stripped of their fat offices and banished to a far-off barren land, a terrible sentence. Some of the gods gave in at once and made their peace with the terrible goddess. Of those who stood firm in their opposition were Ku-moku-hali'i, Ku pulu-pulu, Ku-ala-na-wao, Kupa-ai-ke'e and Ku-mauna.(x) Condemned to banishment, they were indeed in a

(x)   See note at the end of the chapter.

sorry plight. They found themselves on the instant deprived of
their jobs and of their power. Food they had not, nor the means
of obtaining it; these were in the possession of Kane and Kanaloa. The ocean was not free to them; it was controlled by Ka-
moho-alii. In their extremity they became vagabonds and took
to the art of canoe-making. Thus were they enabled to fly to
other lands.

New dispositions having been made and fresh stratagems set
on foot, Pele turned loose another deluge of fire, Lono-makua
consenting to manage the operation. The fire burst into view at
Keaau, from which place it backed up into the region of Ola'a
and there divided into two streams, one of which continued on the
Hilo side, while the other followed a course farther towards
Kau. Lohiau, thus surrounded, would find himself obliged to
face Pele's wrath without the possibility of retreat.

Hiiaka, not fearing for herself but seeing the danger in which
her lover was placed, bade him pray; and this was the prayer he
offered:

> Popo'i, haki kaiko'o ka lua;
> Haki ku, Haki kakala, ka ino,
> Popo'i aku i o'ü o lehua,
> I Kani-a-hiku;(a) wahine(b) ai lehua,
> A ka unu(c) kupukupu, a eha ka pohaku
> I ka uwalu a ke ahi,
> I ke kaunu a ka Pu'u-lena:(d)
> Huli ka moku, nakeke ka aina;

(a) *Kani-a-hiku,* a place-name—that of a village in the remote valley
of Wai-manu—here used, apparently, for its meaning. To analyze its
meaning, *Kani* = a sound, a voice, probably a bird-song; *Hiku,* a celebrated
kupua, the mother of the famous mythical hero *Mawi.* It is said that when
the wind, locally known as the *Kapae,* but more commonly named the
Ho'olua—the same as our trade-wind—blew gently from the ocean, the
listening ears of Kani-a-hiku heard, in the distance, the sound of hula
drums and other rude instruments mingling with the voices of men chanting
the songs of the hula. This seems to be the kani referred to.

(b) *Wahine ai lehua,* Pele. Who else would it be?

(c) *Unu kupukupu* (also written, it is said, haunu kupukupu), a hum-
mock or natural rock-pile, such as would be selected by fishermen, with
the addition, perhaps, of a few stones, as an altar on which to lay their
offering and before which to utter their prayers. *Kupukupu* indicates the
efficacy of such an altar as a luck-bringer.

(d) *Pu'u-lena,* a wind felt at Kilauea that blew from Puna. The word
lena, yellow, suggests the sulphurous fumes that must have added to it their
taint at such time as the wind passed over the volcanic pit.

Kuhala-kai,(e) kuhulukú(f) ka mauna;
Pehu ka leo i Pu'ukú-akahi;(g)
Hano ka leo i Pu'ukú-alua;(h)
Aheahe ana i Mauna Kua-loi(i) —
I kauhale a ke Akua.
I ke ahu a Ka-hoa-lii.(j)
Kahá ka leo o ka ohi'a;
Uwé ka leo o ke kai;
Huli ke alo o Papa-lau-ahi.
Kai ho'onaue hala ko Keaäu;
Kai lu lehua ko Panaewa;
Ke popo'i a'e la i ke ahu a Lono, e.
E lono ana no anei? He ho'okuli;
He kuli ia nei, he lono ole.

TRANSLATION

A storm and wild surf in the Pit,
The fire-waves dashing and breaking;
Spume splashes the buds of lehua —
The bird-choir — O consumer of trees,
O'erthrowing the fishermen's altar;
The rocks melt away in thy flame;
Fierce rages the Pu'u-lena;
The island quakes with thy tremor;
A flood of rain on the lowland,
A wintry chill on the highland.
A boom, as of thunder, from this cliff;
A faint distant moaning from that cliff;
A whispered sigh from yonder hill, —
Home of the gods, inviolate,

(e) *Ku-hala-kai,* a plentiful fall of rain.

(f) *Ku-hulu-ku,* a chilling of the atmosphere.

(g) *Pu'uku-akahi,* (h) *Pu'uku-alua,* names applied to hills on one or the other side of the fire-pit, whence seem to come those sonorous puffing or blowing sounds that accompany the surging of the fires.

(i) *Kua-loi.* This is probably shortened from the full form *Kua-loiloi,* The reference is to a law, or custom, which forbade any one to approach Pele from behind, or to stand behind her. *He kua loiloi ko Pele,* the meaning of which is, Pele has a fastidious back.

(j) *Ka-hoa-lii,* literally, companion of kings; the shark-god, a relation of Pele, who occupied a section of the plateau on the northwestern side of the caldera, a place so sacred that the smoke and flames of the volcano were not permitted to trespass there.

Shrine of the God Hoalii.
Now groans the soul of the tree a-flame;
Now moans the heart of the restless sea.
Uptorn are the ancient fire-plates.
The Kea-au sea uproots the palms;
Pana-ewa's sea scatters the bloom;
It beats at the altar of Lono.
Does she lend her heart to my cry?
Deaf — her ears are deaf to my prayer.

Let us picture to ourselves the scene of the story that now has
the stage — a waterless, wind-swept, plain of volcanic slag and
sand, sparsely clad with a hardy growth whose foliage betrays
the influence of an environment that is at times almost Alpine
in its austerity. Above the horizon-line swell the broad-based
shapes of Mauna-kea, Mauna-loa and Hualalai. In the immediate foreground, overlooking the caldera — where are Pele's
headquarters — we see two figures, standing, crouching, or reclining, the lovers whose stolen bliss has furnished Pele with the
pretext for her fiery discipline. Measured by the forces in opposition to them, their human forms shrink into insignificance.
Measured by the boldness of their words and actions, one has
to admit the power of the human will to meet the hardest shocks
of fortune. Listen to the swelling words of Lohiau as Pele's
encircling fires draw nearer:

Hulihia ka mauna, wela i ke ahi;
Wela nopu i ka uka o Kui-hana-lei;
Ke á pohaku; pu'u lele mai i uka o Ke-ka-ko'i —
Ke-ka-ko'i ka ho'okela mai ka Lua.
O ka maiau(a) pololei kani le'ale'a;
O ka hinihini kani kua mauna;
O ka mapu leo nui, kani kóhakohá;
O kanáka loloa(b) o ka mauna,
O Ku-pulupulu i ka nahele;
O na 'kua mai ka wao kele;

(a) *Maiau pololei,* land shells found on trees, generally called pupu-
kanioi.

(b) *Kanaka loloa,* Ku-pulupulu, one of the gods of the canoe-makers;
here spoken of as a tall man in contradistinction, perhaps, to the dwarfish
Kini-akua, who were his followers.

O Kuli-pe'e-nui(c) ai-ahua;
O Kiké alawa o Pi'i-kea;(d)
O ka uahi Pohina i uka;
O ka uahi mapu-kea i kai;
O ka uahi noe lehua, e;
O ke awa nui, i ka mauna;
O ke po'o o ke ahi, i ka nahele;
O ka ai'na a Pele ma, i uka;
Ua ku ke oka, aia i kai.
Pau a'e la ka maha laau —
Ka maha ohi'a loloa o Kali'u,
A ka luna i Pohaku-o-kapu.
Kapu mai la Puna, ua kulepe i ke ahi;
Ua puni haiki Kilauea.
Ua ha ka lama i ka luna i Moku-aweoweo;
Ua ha ka uka i Ke-ahi-a-Laka;
Ai'na a'e la o Moe-awakea i Ku-ka-la-ula,
A ka luna, i Pohaku-holo-na'e.
Ku au, kilohi, nana ilaila e maliu mai:
O ku'u ike wale aku ia Maukele,
I ka papa lohi o Apua —
He la lili'u, e nopu, e wela ka wawae.
Pau ke a, kahuli ha'a ka pahoehoe,
A pau na niu o kula i Kapoho.
Holo ke ahi mahao'o(x) o Kua-uli;
Pau Oma'o-lala i ke ahi:
I hi'a no a á pulupulu i ka lau laau.
Kuni'a ka lani, haule ka ua loku;
Ka'a mai ka pouli, wili ka puahiohio;
Ka ua koko, ke owé la i ka lani.
Eia Pele mai ka Mauna, mai ka luna i Kilauea,
Mai O'oluea, mai Papa-lau-ahi a hiki Maláma.
Mahina ka uka o Ka-li'u;
Enaena Puna i ka ai'na e ke 'Kua wahine.

(c) *Kuli-pe'e-nui,* a deity, or an idealization, of a lava flow. The feature that seems to be emphasized is the stumbling, crawling, motion, which as seen in a flow, may be compared to the awkward ataxic, movement of one whose knees are dislocated and leg-bones broken.

(d) *Pi'i-kea,* the god of the roaches, who is described as given to making certain tapping motions with his head which, I believe, are practiced by the roach at the present time.

(x) *Mahao'o,* an epithet applied to a dog that shows a patch of yellow hairs on each side of his face. It has somewhat the force of our expression, breathing out flames.

Kahuli Kilauea me he ama(e) wa'a la;
Pouli, kikaha ke Akua o ka Po;
Liolio i Wawau ke Akua o ka uka;
Niho'a ka pali, kala-lua i uka;
Koeä a mania, kikaha koa'e;
Lele pauma ka hulu maewaewa.
A'ea'e na akua i ka uka;
Noho Pele i ke ahiü;
Kani-ké ilalo o ka Lua.
Kahuli Kilauea, lana me he wa'a(f) la;
Kuni'a a'e la Puna, mo'a wela ke one —
Mo'a wela paha Puna, e!
Wela i ke ahi au, a ka Wahine.

TRANSLATION

The Mount is convulsed; the surging fire
Sweeps o'er the height of Kui-hana-lei;
The rocks ablaze; the hillocks explode
Far out by Ax-quarry, aye, and beyond,
Where gleefully chirped the pololei,
And the grasshopper trilled on the mountain
A resonant intermittent cry.
Now comes the tall man of the mount,
Ku-pulupulu, the Lord of the Woods.
In his train swarm the pigmy gods of the wilds,
The knock-kneed monster Kuli-pe'e —
That subterraneous eater of towns —
And watchful Pi'i-kea, the Roach god.
A blinding smoke blurs the hinter-land;
A milk-white cloud obscures the lowland,
Enshrouding the groves of lehua.
The smoke-rack bulks huge in the upland; —
The fire has its head in the Mount,
And thence the Pele gang start on a raid.
The ash of their ravage reaches the sea:

(e) **Ama wa'a.** The commotion in Kilauea is here compared to the up-setting of the canoe's outrigger (ama). When an outriggered canoe capsizes the outrigger, ama, as a rule, lifts out of the water.

(f) **Wa'a.** The reference seems to be to the masses of solid lava that, not infrequently may be seen to break off from the wall of the fire-pit and float away on the surface of the molten lake, even as an iceberg floats in the ocean.

She's made a fell sweep of forest and grove
Clean down to Pohaku-o-kapu.
Now, tabu is Puna, forbidden to man:
The fire-tongues dart and hedge it about.
A torch buds out from Moku-aweö,
To answer the beacon flung by Laka.
Now she's eaten her way from sleepy noon
Till when the windy mountain ridge
Buds with the rosy petals of dawn.
Here stand I to wait her relenting:
I see naught but desolate Puna
And the quivering plain of Apua:
All about is flame — the rock-plain rent;
The coco-palms that tufted the plain
Are gone, all gone, clean down to Ka-poho.
On rushes the dragon with flaming mouth,
Eating its way to Oma'o-lala.
For tinder it has the hair of the fern.
A ghastly rain blots out the sky;
The sooty birds of storm whirl through the vault;
Heaven groans, adrip, as with dragon-blood.
Here Pele comes from her fortress, her Mount,
Deserting her resting place, her hearth —
A wild raid down to Malama.
Kali'u's highlands shine like the moon;
All Puna glows at the Goddess' coming.
The crater's upset; the ama flies up;
The God of night plods about in the dark;
The Upland God makes a dash for Vavau.
The pali are notched like teeth, dissevered,
Their front clean shaven, where sailed the bosen, —
White breast of down — on outstretched wings.
The gods ascend to the highlands;
The goddess Pele tears in a frenzy;
She raves and beats about in the Pit:
Its crumbled walls float like boats in the gulf:
An ash-heap is Puna, melted its sand —
Crisp-done by thy fire, Thine, O Woman!

When Hiiaka recognized the desperate strait of her friend and lover she urged him to betake himself again to prayer.

"Prayer may serve in time of health; it's of no avail in the day of death," was his answer.

It was not now a band of women with firebrands, but a phalanx of fire that closed in upon Lohiau. The whole land seemed to him to be a-flame. The pictures that flit through his disturbed mind are hinted at in the song he utters. The pangs of dissolution seem to have stirred his deeper nature and to have given him a thoughtfulness and power of expression that were lacking in the heyday of his lifetime. Hiiaka called on him for prayer and this was his response:

> Pau Puna, ua koele ka papa;
> Ua noe ke kuahiwi, ka mauna o ka Lua;
> Ua awa mai ka luna o Uwe-kahuna —
> Ka ohu kolo mai i uka,
> Ka ohu kolo mai i kai.
> Ke aá la Puna i ka uka o Na'ena'e;(a)
> O ka lama kau oni'oni'o,(b)
> O na wahine i ke anaina,
> I ka piha a ka naoa(c) o mua nei.
> Oia ho'i ke kukulu(d) a mua;
> Oia ho'i ke kukulu awa;
> O kai awa i ka haki pali,
> O kai a Pele i popo'i i Kahiki —
> Popo'i i ke alo o Kilauea;
> O kai a Ka-hulu-manu:(e)
> Opiopi(f) kai a ka Makali'i;
> Ku'uku'u kai a ka pohaku,

(a) *Na'ena'e*, said of an object that looks small from a distance. The use of the particle emphatic *o*, placed before this word, implies that it performs the office of a proper name, here a place-name. Such a use of the particle emphatic before a noun not a proper name indicates that the word is used as an abstract term.

(b) *Lama kau oni'oni'o.* When two strings of kukui nuts are bound together to form one torch, the light given by it is said to be of varying colors. The word oni'oni'o alludes to this fact.

(d) *Kukulu a awa,* said of those in the rear of the company that came against Lohiau. I cannot learn that this is a military term.

(e) *Kai-a-ka-hulu-manu,* literally, the sea of the bird feathers. Some claim this as being the same as the Kai-a-ka-hinali'i; others, and I think rightly, claim that it was a distinct flood that occurred at a later period and that destroyed all birds and flying things.

(f) *Opiopi.* The waves of the sea in the season of Makali'i are compared to the wrinkles in a mat, the contrast with those of the Kai-a-ka-hulu-manu, and the *kai a ka pohaku.*

Male hula dancer, by John Webber (artist with Captain Cook, Hawaii, 1778–79).

Ke ahi a ka noho(*g*) uka,
Kukuni i ke kua(*h*) o ka makani.
Wela ka ulu(*i*) o ka La i Puna, e;
Kiná Puna i ka ai'na e ke Akua, e.
He akua(*j*) ke hoa, e;
Ke kuhi la iaia he kanáka —
He akua ke hoa, e!

TRANSLATION

Puna is ravaged, its levels fire-baked;
Fog blots out the forest-heights of the Pit;
Uwé-kahuna's plain is bitter cold —
A mist that creeps up from the sea,
A mist that creeps down from the mount;
Puna's dim distant hills are burning —
A glancing of torches — rainbow colors —
The whole assembly of women.
In pity and love they stand before us;
They form the first line of battle
And they make up the second line.
The raging waves engulf the steep coast —
The sea Pele turmoiled at Kahiki,
That surged at the base of Kilauea —
The bird-killing flood Ka-hulu-manu.
Makali'i's waves were like folds in a mat;
A smiting of rock against rock
Is the awful surge of the Pele folk.
The wind-blast enflames their dry tinder.
The face of the Sun is hot in Puna.
I companioned, it seems, with a god;
I had thought her to be very woman.
Lo and behold, she's a devil!

(*g*) *Noho,* a seat, or to sit. Here used for the people there living.
(*h*) *Kua o ka makani* (literally, at the back of the wind). Koolau, the windward side of an island, was its kua, back. The whole line contains an ingenious reference to the manner of fire-lighting. When the smouldering spark from the fire-sticks has been received on a bunch of dry grass, it is waved to and fro to make it ignite. To the old-fashioned Hawaiian familiar with this manner of fire-making this figure is full of meaning.
(*i*) *Ulu o ka La,* the figure of the Sun as it touched the horizon, or its glare.
(*j*) *Akua,* literally, a god. This is a generic term and includes beings that we would call heroes, as well as devils and demons.

Apropos of the meaning of *na'ena'e* I will quote the words of a Hawaiian song by way of illustration:

Makalii lua ka La ia Ka-wai-hoa,(*a*)
Anoano i ka luna o Hoaka-lei:(*b*)
Lei manu i ka hana a ke kiü;(*c*)
Luli ke po'o, éha i ka La o Maka-lii,
Hoiloli lua i na ulu hua i ka hapapa.

TRANSLATION

Wondrous small looks the Sun o'er Waihoa,
How lonesome above Hoaka-lei!
Birds crown the hill to escape from the Kiü;
Men turn the head from the Sun's winter heat
And scorn the loaves of the bread-fruit tree.

In answer to these words of Lohiau Pele muttered gruffly, "God! Did you take me to be a human being? That's what is the matter with you, and your clatter is merely a wail at the prospect of death."

Under the torture of the encircling fires Lohiau again babbles forth an utterance in which the hallucinations of delirium seem to be floating before him:

Wela ka hoku, ka Maláma;
Ua wela Makali'i, Kaelo ia Ka-ulua;(*d*)
Kai ehu ka moku, papápa ka aina;
Ha'aha'a(*e*) ka lani; kaiko'o ka Mauna,
Ha ka moana; popo'i Kilauea.
Ale noho ana Papa-lau-ahi;
O mai Pele i ona kino —
Hekikili ka ua mai ka lani;
Nei ke ola'i; ha ka pohakahi a ka Ikuwá;

(*a*) *Ka-wai-hoa,* the southern point of Niihau.

(*b*) *Hoaka-lei,* a hill on Niihau.

(*c*) *Kiu,* the name of a wind.

(*d*) *Makalii, Kaelo* and *Ka-ulua* are cold months. Lohiau found them hot enough.

(*e*) *Ha'aha'a,* literally, hanging low. I am reminded of an old song uttered, it is said, by a hero from the top of Kauwiki hill, in Hana, Maui: "Aina ua, lani ha'aha'a." Land of rain, where the heavens hang (ever) low.

Ku˙mai Puna ki'eki'e;
Ha'aha'a ka ulu a ka opua,
Pua ehu mai la uka o Ke-ahi-a-Laka;
Pau mahana i kahi Wai-welawela(c) o ka Lua, e;
Iki'ki i ka uwahi lehua;
Paku'i ka uwahi Kanáka.
Pua'i hanu, eä ole i ke po'i a ke ahi.
E Hiiaka e, i wai maka e uwe mai!

TRANSLATION

The stars are on fire, and the moon;
Cold winter is turned to hot summer;
The island is girdled with storm;
The land is scoured and swept barren;
The heavens sag low — high surf in the Pit —
There's toss of a stormy ocean,
Wild surging in Kilaueä;
Fire-billows cover the rocky plain,
For Pele erupts her very self.
A flood of rain follows lightning-bolt;
Earth quakes with groaning and tossing,
Answered with shouts from the Echo god.
Once Puna was lifted to heaven;
Now the cloud of dark omen hangs low.
White bellies the cloud over Laka's hearth;
Wai-wela-wela supplies a warm skirt.
I choke in this smoke of lehua —
How pungent the smell of burnt man!
I strangle, my breath is cut off —
Ugh! what a stifling blanket of fire!
Your tears, Hiiaka, your tears!

(c) *Wai-wela-wela,* a hot lake in lower Puna.

(x) Note on *Ku-mauna.* See page 201.

(d) *Ku-mauna,* a rain-god of great local fame and power; now represented by a monolithic bowlder about thirty feet high, partly overgrown with ferns and moss, situated in the lower edge of the forest-belt, that lies to the south and Kau of Mauna-loa, deserves more than passing mention. The region in which this rock is situated is declared by vulcanologists to have been one vast caldera and must have been the scene of tremendous disturbances.

Up to the present time the Hawaiians have continued to hold Ku-mauna in great reverence mingled with fear. The following modern instance is not only a true story, and interesting, but also furnishes an illustration of the attitude of mind of the Hawaiian people generally,—or many of them—towards their old gods.

During a period of severe drought in the district of Kau, Hawaii, a gentleman named S———, while hunting in the neighborhood of the rock that bears the name Ku-mauna, took occasion to go out of his way and visit the rock. Standing before the rocky mass and calling it by name, he used towards it insulting and taunting epithets, professing to hold it responsible for the drought that was distressing the land. He concluded his tirade by discharging his rifle point blank against the face of the rock, resulting in the detachment of a considerable fragment.

The vaqueros in the employ of Mr. S.———, who were assisting in the hunt, horrified at the sacreligious act, at once put spurs to their horses and made off, predicting the direst consequences from the rash act of Mr. S———.

Now for the denouement: Within about ten days of this occurrence, the valley, on one side of which Mr. S——— had his residence, was visited by a violent rain-storm—such as would in popular speech be termed a cloudburst. There was a mighty freshet, the waters of which reached so high as to flood his garden and threaten the safety of his house, which he saved only by the most strenuous exertions. The land which had been his garden was almost entirely washed away and in its place was deposited a pell-mell of stones.

Needless to say, that, by the natives, this incident was and is regarded to this day as conclusive evidence of the divine power of Ku-mauna and of his wrath at the audacious person who insulted him. Special significance is attached to the fact that as part of Ku-mauna's reprisal the place that had been a garden was turned into a field of rocks. The only wonder is that Mr. S——— got off with so light a punishment.

CHAPTER XXXV

THE DEATH OF LOHIAU

Lohiau, in his last agony, wandered in mind and babbled of many things. To his credit, be it said that his thoughts were not wholly centered on himself. There was a margin of regard for others, as when he sang in these words:

> Aloha na hale o makou i makamaka ole,
> Ke ala hele mauka o Huli-wale la, e.
> Huli wale; ke huli wale a'e nei no,
> I ka makana ole, i ka mohai ole e ike aku ai,
> E kanaenae aku ai la ho'i, ia oe, ia oe!

TRANSLATION

My love to the homes made desolate,

On the road which makes this turning.
I turn away with an empty hand,
Lacking an offering fit to make peace,
To soften thy heart and appease thee —
To soften thy heart and content thee.

At the last flicker of life, when the rocky encasement had well nigh completed the envelopment of his body, Hiiaka, daring the barrier of fire that had come between them, sprang to his side and, with the last kiss, whispered into his ear, "Go not on the side whence the wind blows; pass to leeward, on the day of our meeting." (*Mai hele i ka makani; hele i ka pohu, ma ka la a kaua e halawai ai.*) By this cryptic expression, Hiiaka meant to put Lohiau on his guard against enemies that lay in wait for him. If he went to the windward he might reveal himself to them by his flair. She also embodied her warning in song:

Aloha ko'u hoa i ka ua pua-kukui,
Kui lehua o Moe-awakea,
Lei pua o Ka-la-hui-pua,
Kae'e lehua o Pu'u-lena, la, mauka:
Mauka oe e hele ai,
Ma ka ulu o ka makani;
O moe'a oe e ka á Pu'u-lena la —
Make, make loa o oe!

TRANSLATION

My love to thee, mate of the sifting rain,
Such time as we strung the lehua,
In the snatches of noonday rest,
On the days when we dreamed of reunion;
And this was done in the uplands.
In the uplands you shall safely journey;
Safe in the hush and lee of the wind;
Lest the blasts of Pu'u-lena shall smite
And sweep you away to an endless doom.

A swarm of emotions buzzed in the chambers of Hiiaka's mind, of love, of self-destruction, of revenge. In an agony of indecision she strode this way and that, wringing her hands and wailing in a strictly human fashion. The master passion came

to the front and had sway: she would find Lohiau, and with him
renew the bond of friendliness which had grown up in the midst
of the innocent joys and toils of travel shared by them in common.   An access of divine power came to her.   She immediately
began to tear up the strata of the earth.   As she broke through
the first stratum and the second, she saw nothing.   She tore her
way with renewed energy: rock smote against rock and the air
was full of flying debris.

After passing the third stratum, she came upon a ghastly
sight — the god of suicide, suspended by the neck, his tongue
protruding from his mouth.   It was a solemn lesson.   After
passing the fourth stratum she came upon the stratum of Wakea,
and here she found the inanimate bodies of her former companions of travel, the faithful Wahine-oma'o and Paú-o-pala'e.
She restored them to life and animation, bidding them return
to the beautiful world of sunshine and fresh air.

She came at last to the tenth stratum with full purpose to
break up this also and thus open the flood-gates of the great deep
and submerge Pele and her whole domain in a flood of waters.
That, indeed, would have been the ruin of all things.   At this
moment there came to Hiaaka the clear penetrating tone of a
familiar voice.   It was the voice of her fast friend and traveling
companion, Wahine-oma'o, who had but recently left her and
who, now, under the inspiration of the great god Kane, had come
to dissuade Hiiaka from her purpose.   For the execution of that
purpose meant a universe in confusion.   It was time, then, for
Kane to interfere.   He did this by putting into the mouth of
of her dearest friend on earth an appeal to which Hiiaka could
not but listen and, listening, heed:

> A po Kaena i ka ehu o ke kai;
> Ki-pú iho la i ka lau o ke ahi;
> Pala e'ehu i ka La ka ulu o Poloa, e!
> Po wale, ho'i; e ho'o-po mai ana ka oe ia'u,
> I ka hoa o ka ua, o ke anu, o ke ko'eko'e!
> Auhea anei oe?   Ho'i mai kaua;
> He au Ko'olau(a) aku ia.

(a)   Ko'olau, a term applied generally to the windward side of an island,
which was, of course, the stormy side.   The expression au Ko'olau, or
Ko'olau weather, is one of great significance.

Kaena is darkened with sea-mist;
Eruptions burst up mid lakes of flame;
Scorched and gray are Po-loa's bread-fruits.
Now, as a climax, down shuts the night.
You purpose to blind with darkness
The woman who went as your fellow
Through rain and storm and piercing cold.
List now, my friend: return with me —
We've had a spell of nasty weather!

For Hiiaka to give ear to the pleading voice of her friend, the woman who had shared with her the shock of battle and the hardships of travel from Hawaii to Kaua'i and back again, was to run the risk of being persuaded.

"Come with me," said Wahine-oma'o; "let us return to our mistress."

"I must first seek and find Lohiau," answered Hiiaka.

"Better for us first to go before Pele. She will send and bring Lohiau." Thus pleaded the woman Wahine-oma'o.

Hiiaka turned from the work of destruction and, hand in hand, they made their way back into the light and wholesome air of the upper world.

The sisters — those who bore the name Hiiaka — received her cordially enough. They prattled of many things; buzzed her with questions about her travels of long ago — as it now seemed to Hiiaka. It was not in their heart to stir the embers of painful issues. No more was it in their heart to fathom the little Hiiaka of yesterday, the full-statured woman of to-day. Beyond the exchange of becoming salutations, Hiiaka's mouth was sealed. Until Pele should see fit to lend ear and heart to her speech not a word would she utter regarding her journey.

But Pele lay on her hearth silent, sullen — no gesture, no look of recognition.

The kino wailua, or spirit from Lohiau, in the meantime, after having in vain tried to solace itself with the companionship of the forest song-birds and having found that resource empty of human comfort, fluttered across the desolate waste of ocean like a tired sea-bird back to his old home and there appeared to his aikane Paoa in a vision at night.

"Come and fetch me," he said (meaning, of course, his body). "You will find me lying asleep at Kilauea."

Paoa started up in a fright. "What does this mean?" he said to himself. "That Lohiau is in trouble?"

When he had lain down again the same vision repeated itself. This time the command was imperative: "Come and rescue me; here I am in the land of non-recognition." (a)

Now Paoa roused himself, assured that Lohiau's sleep was that of death, but not knowing that he was, for the second time, the victim of Pele's wrath. He said nothing to anyone but made all his preparations for departure in secret, reasoning that Kahua-nui, the sister of Lohiau, would not credit his story and would consequently interfere with his plans.

He entered his canoe and, pressing the water with his paddle, his craft made a wonderful run towards Hawaii. It was necessary for him only to dip his paddle in the brine at intervals and to direct the course. The canoe seemed almost to move of itself That same morning he arrived at Waipio. To his astonishment, there, in a boat-shed on the beach lay the canoe which he recognized as that of his friend Lohiau. The people of the district had been wondering whose it was and how it had come there.

Paoa found many things that were new and strange to him in this big raw island of Hawaii. Not the least of these was the land on which he trod, in places a rocky shell covering the earth like the plates on the back of the turtle, or, it might be, a tumble of jagged rocks — the so-called aä — a terrain quite new to his experience. It seemed as if the world-maker had not completed his work.

Of the route to Kilauea he was quite ignorant, but he was led. There flitted before him a shadow, a wraith, a shape and he followed it. At times he thought he could recognize the form of Lohiau and, at night or in the deep shadows of the forest, he seemed to be looking into the face of his friend.

When night came he lay down in a sheltered place and slept. In the early morning, while darkness yet brooded over the land, he was roused by the appearance of a light. His first thought was that day had stolen upon him; but no, it was the kino wailua of his friend that had come to awaken him and lead him on the last stage of his journey.

(a)   *E ki'i mai oe ia'u; eia au la i ke au a ka hewahewa.*

CHAPTER XXXVI

PAOA SEEKS OUT THE BODY OF HIS DEAD FRIEND LOHIAU

Under the lead of his spiritual guide, Paoa arrived that day at Kilauea and, standing at the brink of the great caldera, he saw the figure of Lohiau beckoning to him as it stood on a heap of volcanic debris. The wraith dissolved into nothingness as he approached the spot; but there lay a figure in stone having the semblance of a man. It was more an act of divination than the exercise of ordinary judgment that told him this was the body of Lohiau. "I thought you had summoned me to take home your living body, my friend!" was his exclamation. His voice was broken with emotion as he poured out his lament:

Mau a'alina oe mauka o Ka-la-ke-ahi;
Ma Puna ka huli mai ana;
Ka ua a Makali'i,
Ke ua la i Laau,
I Kaú, i Ka-hihi, i Ka-pe'a,
I ke wao a ke akua.
Eia ho'i au la, o ka Maka-o-ke-ahi;
Aole ho'i na la o ka Lawa-kua,
Ke Koolau la, e, aloha!
Aloha ku'u hoa i ka ua anu lipoa,
Hu'ihu'i, ko'eko'e, kaoü:
He ahi ke kapa o kaua e mehana ai,
E lala ai kaua i Oma'o-lala;
I pili wale, i ha'alele la, e.
Ha'alele i Wailua na hoa aloha —
O Puna, aina aloha,
O Puna, i Kaua'i.

TRANSLATION

Thou bundle of scars from a fiery day,
'Twas at Puna our journey began,
With a dash of rain in the summer;
Rain again when we entered the woods,
Rain, too, in Kaú, in the jungle,
In the forest-haunts of the gods,

Rain at each crossing of road and path: —
Here stand I, with fire in my eye:
Our days of communion are gone;
You've bidden adieu to Ko'olau:
Hail now to my mate of the gloomy rain —
When wet and cold and chilled to the bone,
Our garment of warmth the blazing hearth;
Then basked we at Oma'o-lala,
Haunting the place, then tearing away.
E'en so you tore away from your friends,
Those friends of Wailua, of Puna —
That dear land of Puna, Kaua'i!

(Here is another version of the eloquent prayer of Paoa;
furnished by Poepoe, who obtained it from Rev. Pa'aluhi):

O mau a'alina oe,
O mau kakala ke ahi.
Ma Puna ka hiki'na mai
A ka ua makali'i,
Ka ua a'ala ai laau,
I ka hiki, i ka pa'a,
I ke ahu a ke Akua.
Eia ho'i au, la.
O ka maka o ke ahi;
Aole ho'i na la,
O ka lawakua(a) a ke Koolau.
E, aloha o'u hoa,
I ka ua a ka lipoa,(b)
Lihau anu, ko'eko'e, ka-o-ú —
He ahi ke kapa e mehana ai,
E lála(c) ai kaua i Oma'o-lala.(d)
I pili wale, i ha'alele la, e.
Ha'alele i Puna na hoaloha, e,
Ka aina i ka houpu a Kane(e)
He aikane ka mea aloha, e
He-e!

(a) *Lawakua,* an intimate companion, a friend.
(b) *Ua a ka lipoa,* a fine, cold rain; a Scotch mist.
(c) *Lala,* to bask in the sunlight.
(d) *Oma'o-lala,* a place in upper Ola'a, named from the bird *oma'o.*
(e) *Aina i ka houpu a Kane,* a proverbial expression applied to **Puna,**
signifying the affection in which Puna was held.

TRANSLATION

You've encased him tight in a lava shell,
Scorched him with tongues of flame.
Puna, the place of thy landing,
First impact of winter rain —
Sweet rain, feeding the perfume,
Drunk by vine and firm-rooted tree —
The wilderness-robe of the gods.
Here am I, too, eye-flash of flame;
As for them, no friends they of mine:
Companions mine of the stormy coast,
My love goes forth to my toil-mate
Of the mist, cold rain and driving storm;
A blazing hearth our garment then,
And to bask in the sun at Oma'o-lála.
Those seeming friends, they went with us,
And then, they left us in Puna —
Land dear to the heart of Kane:
Who eats of your soul is your true friend.
Woe is me, woe is me!

Hiiaka, not yet come back from her adventures in the under-world, heard this lament of Paoa and wondered at his performance — that he, a handsome man, should be standing out in the open with not even a malo about his loins to hide his nakedness, "I wonder what is his name," she said aloud.

Paoa, intent on supersensual things, heard the wondering words of Hiiaka and responded to them:

Hulihia ke au, pe'a ilalo i Akea;
Hulihia ka mole o ka honua;
Hulihia ka ale ula, ka ale lani,
I ka puko'a, ka a'aka,(a) ke ahua,
Ka ale po'i, e, i ka moku.
Nawele ke ahi, e, a i Kahiki;

(a) A'aka, an ocean cave (definition not given in the dictionary.)

Nawele ka maka o Hina-ulu-ohi'a.(*b*)
Wela ka lani, kau kahaeä;(*c*)
Wahi'a ka lani, uli-pa'a ka lani;
Eleele ka lau o Ka-hoa-li'i;
Ka pohaku kuku'i o ka Ho'oilo;
Nahá mai Ku-lani-ha-ko'i;(*d*)
Ke ha'a-lokuloku nei ka ua;
Ke nei nei ke ola'i;
Ke ikuwá mai la i uka.
Ke o'oki la i ka piko o ka hale,
A mo' ka piko i Eleuä,(*e*) i Eleaö:
Ka wai e ha'a Kula-manu,(*f*)
Ka nahele o Ke-hua,
I loa i ke kula o Ho'o-kula-manu.
E Pele, e wahi'a(*g*) ka lani;
E Pele e, ka wahine ai laau o Puna,
Ke ai holoholo la i ka papa o Hopoe;
Pau a'e la Ku-lili-ka-ua(*h*)

(*b*) *Nawele ka maka o Hina-ulu-ohi'a.* By metonymy, a figure of speech for which the Hawaiian poets showed great fondness, the name of the goddess, or superior being, Hina-ulu-ohi'a, is here used instead of the fruit which seems to have been her emblem. This fruit, the *ohi'a puakea,* is a variety of the *ohi'a ai,* or mountain apple, as it is commonly called. The common variety is of a deep red color shading into purple; but this variety, departing from the usual rule, is of a pale lemon color. This pale variety shows a faint pink or reddish ring about the *maka,* or eye where the flower was implanted. The poet's fancy evidently makes a comparison between this delicate aureole and the dim glow by which the volcanic fire made itself perceived in its periphery at Kahiki.

(*c*) *Kahaea,* a pile of white cumulus clouds, or a single large cloud, which was regarded by weather prophets, soothsayers and diviners as a significant portent.

(*d*) *Ku-lani-ha-ko'i.* The old Hawaiians imagined that somewhere in the heavens was an immense reservoir of water, and that a heavy down-pour of rain was due to the breaking of its banks. When the clouds of storm and rain gathered thick and black, they saw in this phenomenon a confirmation of their belief, which gained double assurance when the clouds discharged their watery contents.

(*e*) *Eleua....Eleao.* When a Hawaiian house had a door at each end, the door at one end was named *Ele-ua,* that at the other end *Ele-ao.*

(*f*) *Kula-manu.* A plain or tract of land that was flooded in wet weather and thus converted for a time into a resort for water-fowl, was termed a kula-manu or bird plain.

(*g*) *Wahi'a ka lani.* This passive form of the verb has here the force of entreaty almost equivalent to the imperative. The opening here spoken of was the parting and drawing aside of the dark clouds that shut in the heavens, an opening that would be equivalent to the restoration of peace and good will.

(*h*) *Ku-lili-ka-ua,* the name applied to a grove of pandanus in Puna.

Ka nahele makai o Keäau,
A ka mahu a ka Wahine,
Ka uahi keä i uka,
Ke ai la i Pohaku-loa,(*i*)
I ke ala a Lau-ahea;(*j*)
He wawaka ka huila o ka lani.
E Ku-kuena (*k*)e, na'u ho'i e noho
Ka la puka i Ha'eha'e.
O ka luna o Uwé-kahuna;
O ka uwahi hauna-laau;
O ke po'o ku i ka pohaku;
O ka alá kani koele;
A ka nakolo i ka nei.
Ma'alili ole ai ua 'kua ai i ke a;
Nakeke ka niho o Pele i Kilauea;
Pohaku wai ku kihikihi,(*m*)
Ku hiwa ai i ka maka o ka pohaku —
Pohaku ai-wawae o Malama;
Hopo aku ka haka'i hele i ka la.
Pi'i a ka wai i uka,
Moana ai wai a ka Olohe;(*n*)
Kawa lele ai Kilauea;
Hohonu ai ka lua i uka,
Kapuahi ku-ku-ku.
Nau ke ku'i o ke Akua;
Holo ka paku'i, lahe'a i na moku.
Nou ka lili, no ke Akua:

(*i*)   *Pohaku-loa*, the name of a rocky ledge or cliff in Puna.

(*j*)   *Lau-ahea*. This was a deceitful voice, a vocal Will-o'-the-wisp, that was sometimes heard by travelers and that enticed them into the wilderness or thicket there to be entrapped in some *lua meke* or fathomless pit.

(*k*)   *Kuku-ena*, a sister of Pele who, like Kahili-opua, was a physician and of a benevolent disposition. She was wont to act as the guide to travelers who had their way in the mazes of a wilderness. So soon, however, as the traveler had come clear into a clear place and was able to orient himself, she modestly disappeared.

(*m*)   *Ku kihikihi*, to stand cornerwise or edgewise. In the ebullition that stirs the mass of a lava lake at seemingly rhythmical intervals the congealed crust that has formed on the surface is seen to break up, become tilted on edge, and then be sucked down into the depths by the vortex of the lava-pit. The allusion here is to the tilting of the plate on edge in this wonderful phenomenon.

(*n*)   *Olohe*. This is explained and described as meaning a spectral appearance of human figures and of objects animate and inanimate moving about in the firmament. The description given of it almost leads one to think it a mirage or *fata morgana*.

Lili'a i uka, lili'a i kai —
O ka lili kepa i o kipi-kipi.
O haele a Mauna Pu'u-kuolo(o)
A ka ehu o lalo
Paú mahana ai ka Wai-welawela.
E Ku e, ke'ehia, ke'ehia ka pae opua;
Hina ololo i Ulu-nui:
Hina aku la, palala ke ao —
He ao omea a Ulu-lani.
Ke wela nei ka La;
Ke kau nei ka malu hekili iluna:
Ku'i, naue ka leo o ka opua, e —
Opua ai laau la;
A ka luna i Moku-aweo-weo
Hua'i Pele i ona kino;
Lawe ka ua la, lawe ke kaupu e;
Opiopi kai a ke Akua;
Kuahiwi haoä(p) i Kaú i waena.
Ho'po mai la Puna i ka uwahi a ke Akua;
Poá ino no ka pua e lu ia nei.
Pau ku'u kino lehua a i kai o Puna:
Hao'e Puna, koele ka papa;
O ka uwahi na'e ke ike'a nei.
Kai-ko'o ka lua, kahuli ko'o ka lani
Ke Akua ai lehua o Puna,
Nana i ai iho la Hawaii kua uli:
Wahi'a ka lani; ne'e Hiiaka-i-ka-ale-i;(q)
Ne'e Hiiaka-i-ka-ale-moe;
O Hiiaka-pa'i-kauhale;
Hiiaka-i-ka-pua-enaena;(r)
Hiiaka-i-ka-pua-lau-i;
O Hiiaka-noho-lae;(s)

(p) *Kuahiwi haoa,* a term applied in Kau) to a forest-clump which a devastating lava flow has spared, after having laid waste the country on all sides of it.

(q) *Hiiaka-i-ka-ale-i,* Hiiaka of the bounding billow. The number of the sisters in whose names that of Hiiaka formed a part was considerable, as may be inferred from the fact that the names here mentioned do not include the whole list of them.

(r) *Hiiaka-i-ka-pua-enaena,* Hiiaka of the burning flower. Her emblem was the little budlike pea-blossom flame. This name is sometimes given as Hiiaka-i-ka-pua-aneane, a more delicate but less striking epithet.

(s) *Hiiaka-noho-lae,* Hiiaka who dwells on the cape. She was recognized by a trickle of blood on the forehead.

Hiiaka-wawahi-lani;
Hiiaka-i-ka-poli-o-Pele,
Halanalana waimaka e hanini nei;
Wela mai ka maka o ka ulu o Ho'olono, e.
Ho'olono au o Ho'olei'a.
O Ho'olei'a au; o Kalei (au) a Paoa;
O Paoa au la, i lono oe.

TRANSLATION

The world is convulsed; the earth-plates sink
To the nether domain of Wakea;
Earth's rooted foundations are broken;
Flame-billows lift their heads to the sky;
The ocean-caves and reefs, the peopled land
And the circle of island coast
Are whelmed in one common disaster:
The gleam of it reaches Kahiki:—
Such blush encircles the pale apple's eye.
Heaven 's blotted out, the whole sky darkened;
Hoali'i's cliffs are shadowed with gloom.
Now bellows the thunder of Winter;
Ku-lani-ha-ko'i's banks are broken;
Down pours a pitiless deluge of rain;
There's rumble and groan of the earthquake,
The reverberant roar of thunder,
The roof-stripping swoop of the tempest,
Tearing the thatch over Ele-uä,
Tearing the thatch over Ele-ao.
The freshet makes home for the water-fowl,
Flooding the thickets at Kehau,
The wide-spread waters of Kula-manu.
O Pele, fold back the curtains of heaven;
Thou Woman, consumer of Puna woods,
Swift thy foray in Hopoe's fields:
The land of contending rains is wiped out,
And the lands that border Keäau.
Up springs the steam from her caldron,
A white cloudy mountain of smoke:
She's consuming the bowlders of Long-rock,
The treacherous paths of Lau-ahea.
A flash of lightning rends the sky!

O Ku-kuena, 'tis for you to dwell
In the flaming Eastern Gate of the Sun.
The plateau of Uwé-kahuna
Breathes the reek of burning woods;
There's pelting of heads with falling stones
And loud the clang of the smitten plain,
Confused with the groan of the earthquake.
Yet this cools not the rock-eater's rage:
The Goddess grinds her teeth in the Pit.
Lo, tilted rock-plates melt like snow —
Black faces that shine like a mirror —
Sharp edges that bite the foot of a man,
The traveler's dread in the glare of the sun.(t)
The fire-flood swells in the upland —
A robber-flood — it dries up the streams.
Here's cliff for god's jumping, when wild their sport;
Deep the basin below, and boiling hot.
The Goddess gnashes her teeth and the reek
Of her breath flies to the farthest shore.
Thine was the fault, O Goddess, thine, a
Jealous passion at all times and places —
The snap and spring of a surly dog.
Let your gnashing range to its limit,
Till it reaches the fringe of your skirt,
Your hot paü at Wai-welawela.
Trample down, O Ku, these ominous clouds;
Let them sag and fall at Ulu-nui.
They flatten, they break; look, they spread.
White loom, now, the clouds of Ulu-lani;
Fierce blazes the Sun, and Thunder
Unrolls his black curtains on high.
Then bellows his voice from the cloud —
The ominous cloud that swallows the trees.
From the crest of Moku-aweö
Pele pours out her body, her self —
A turmoil of rain and of sea-fowl.
Now boils the lake of the Goddess:
In Ka-ú an oasis-park remains;
Her smoke covers Puna with night.
What a robbery this, to crush the flowers!

(t) *O ka la ko luna. O ka pahoehoe ko lalo.* The sun overhead. The lava below.

My bodily self, my lehuas, gone!
My precious lehuas, clean down to Puna!
And Puna — the land is trenched and seared!
The smoke that o'erhangs it, that I can see.
High surf in the Pit, turmoiling the sky —
The god who ate Puna's Lehuas,
She 'twas laid waste green-robed Hawaii.
The heavens — let them rend, Hiiaka!
Plunge you in the wild tossing sea;
And you, who delight in the calm sea;
Hiiaka, thou thatcher of towns,
Hiiaka, soul of the flame-bud;
Hiiaka, emblemed in ti-bud;
Hiiaka, who dwells on the headland;
Hiiaka, who parts heaven's curtains;
Hiiaka — of Pele's own heart!
These tears well from eyes hot with weeping,
The eyes of this scion, this herald:
I proclaim that he's outcast and exiled.
'Tis I, Paoä announce this:
He speaks what is meet for your ear!

CHAPTER XXXVII

PAOA COMES BEFORE PELE

The eminence of Akani-kolea stood near at hand and offered
Paoa a vantage ground for better contemplation of the mysterious earth-pit, and when the first tide of emotion had swept by
thither he repaired. Looking down into the desolate abyss, his
gaze centered on a group of human figures, beautiful women,
seated on the vast plates of pahoehoe that made the floor of the
caldera. He saw but four of them, Pele herself not being visible.
He had no clue as to their identity and was only impressed as
by the sight of beautiful women who were to him as goddesses.
The grandeur and strangeness of the scene moved him to song:

> Hulihia ka Mauna,
> Wela i ke ahi a ka Wahine;
> Wela na ohi'a o Kulili i ka ua;
> Wela, a nopu ke ahi o ka Lua.

Ai kamumu, nakeke ka pahoehoe;
Wela, a iluna o Hale-ma'uma'u;
Malu ka pali o Ka-au-eä.
Auwe, e Hiiaka-i-ka-poli-o-Pele, e,
E ola, e, e ola Lohiau-ipo,
I ka pali o Keé, i Haena, e!

TRANSLATION

Destruction and turmoil in the Pit:
The fires of the Woman have done it —
Consuming the forests of Ku-lili —
Fires that boil from the depths of the Pit,
Shaking the stone-plates till they rattle.
It's furnace-hot in that House-of-fern,
But there's shelter at Ka-au-eä.
Oh Hiiaka of Pele's heart,
Life to thee, and life to dear Lohiau —
Soul plucked by thee from death at Keé,
Death in the cliff Keé, at Haena.

Pele, in the retirement of her gloomy cavern, was quite out of the range of Paoa's eye-shot, but his voice rang in her ears distinctly. "What a handsome man is that standing on the edge of the cliff at Akani-kolea!" exclaimed Pele's women, unable to repress their admiration.

"Call to him and invite him to come down here where we can talk together," said Pele. "Way up there on the pali wall — that's no place for us to talk and become acquainted with each other. Tell him to come down here and we'll discuss matters great and small, look upon the large stem and the small stem; see one another face to face; learn each other's heart's desire."(a)

For all her fine words, Pele did not at once come forward and meet her visitor face to face. She lay unrecognized in her stygian boudoir, to all appearance a withered hag.

Paoa, well versed in the wiles of Woman, adept in the logomachies and etiquettes of court-life, was quite put to his trumps and found it necessary to summon all his diplomacy and exer-

---

(a) Aohe o kahi nana oluna o ka pali. Iho mai a lalo nei; ike i ke au nui me ke au iki, he alo a he alo; nana i ka makemake. The exact meaning of *ke au iki* and *ke au nui* is not clear.

cise all his power of self-command in dealing with the shrewd
and attractive women that surrounded him.   It was evident to
the watchful eye of our heroine — Hiiaka — that he was danger-
ously attracted by the voluptuous beauty of her sister, Hiiaka-
of-the-waves.   In the persistent silence of Pele, upon her fell
the leading part of the conversation with Paoa:

"What might be the purpose of your pilgrimage?" she asked.

"I come in answer to the call of my friend, Lohiau."

"But Lohiau is dead," chorused the women.

"Yes, dead! And what was the cause of his death?"

"He kissed Hiiaka," the woman answered.

"Ah! but who killed him?"

"Pele." Her voice sank to a whisper, and the name she uttered was to be made out, or guessed at, rather by a study of
the protruding lips and the sympathetic arching of the brow than
by any sound emitted.   Her eyes also made a half-turn in the
direction of Pele's cave.

"He came to Hawaii in the expectation that Pele would be
his life." Paoa spoke with thoughtful deliberation. "How came
it about that she should cause his death?" . . . After a moment's
pause, he continued: "He tasted death once at Haena and, now,
again, here, on this barren . . . a second death, and through
the wrath of Pele!"

Pele roused herself at this and spoke up: "What is that you
say? that Lohiau died at Haena?"

"Yes, he tasted of death there," Paoa answered firmly.

"How, then, did he become alive again?" asked Pele sharply.

"Hiiaka, she treated him, and by her gracious skill and power
brought his soul and body together again.   That done, they
sailed away for Hawaii."

The eyes of Pele were literally, as well as metaphorically,
opened. She turned herself about and, in a lowered voice, with
a show of astonishment, for the first time, addressed Hiiaka:
"Is this true, that you worked over Lohiau and restored him to
life?"

"It is true, and it is also true that, not until you had put to
death Hopoe, did I bestow any dalliance or caress of love upon
Lohiau."

Hiiaka's expression as she faced Pele was such as might have
sat upon the countenance of a judge passing sentence on a con-
fessed criminal at the bar.

Pele sat impenetrable, sphinxlike, deep in her own labyrinthine philosophy of the obligations due to a social autocrat and a goddess.

Paoa broke the silence: "Shall not Lohiau, then, live again?"

"Go back to Haena," said Pele, "and when you hear that Lohiau lives again, then will be the time for you to come and take him home."

"That would be well, then," said Paoa.

A spell of confusion, of enchantment, seemed now to fall upon the man whilom so boastful. "But where is Pele?" he asked, looking from face to face.

"That is Pele," said the goddess, pointing to her sister Wave (Hiiaka-i-ka-ale-i).

"I have a sign by which I may know Pele; let me apply the test to these women," said Paoa.

The company could but agree to this; whereupon, beginning with Wave, he took each one of them in turn by the hand, carrying it to his cheek, the better to test its warmth, holding the hollow to his ear to catch any murmur that might reverberate from it. Each hand he found to be only of natural heat. Turning, then, to Pele herself, he proposed to inspect her hand. At this the goddess drew back.

"If none of these beautiful women is Pele, how can you think that a wrinkled old woman like me is the divine and beautiful Pele?"

Paoa insisted and Pele had to consent. He reached out and took her hand and, on the instant, dropped it; it was burning hot.

"This is Pele!" he exclaimed.

Paoa stood in awed silence before the goddess. Resentment and thoughts of revenge, like evil birds, had taken flight.

At Pele's command, the women led him away to take refreshment in the sacred dining hall of Mauli-ola. Before seating himself, Paoa uttered this memorable pule, a mele that has drifted down to us from the *wa po*

> Hulihia ke au, ka papa honua o kona moku;
> Hulihia, kulia mai ka moku o Kahiki —
> Aina no Kahiki i ka la kahi,
> Aina ho'owali'a e Haumea:
> Ho-omoe aku la Kahiki-ku,
> Kulapa mai ka ulu wela, o mai ke ahi.

Keehi aku la no e nalo(a) kapua'i, e —
Kapua'i akua no Pele.
Ke ke'ekeehi wale la no i ka lani;
Haule, u'ina i Polapola;
Noho i ka lau ha'a o ka moku.
Hina Kukulu o Kahiki;
Hina ka omuku i ka makani;
Hina ka pae opua ki'i ke ao;
Hina ka onohi ula(b) i ka lani;
Kanewenewe opua i ke kai.
Eä mai ana ma Nihoa,
Ma ka mole mai o Lehua,
Mai Kaua'i nui a Oahu, a Moloka'i,
Lana'i a Kanaloa, mai Maui a Hawaii,
Ka Wahine — o Pele — i hi'a i kana ahi
A á pulupulu, kukuni, wela ka lani:
He uwila ku'i no ka honua;
Hekili pa'apa'ina i ke ao;
Pohaku puoho, lele iluna;
Opa'ipa'i wale ka Mauna;
Pipili ka lani, pa'a iä moku.
Nalo Hawaii i ka uahi a ka Wahine,
I ka lili a ke Akua.
Oliliku ka ua mai ka lani;
Lili ana ho'i i kana ahi;
Lili ana ho'i Pele
Hama-hamau ka leo, mai pane!
Eia Pele, ko'u Akua!
Ke lauwili nei ka makani;
Hoanoano mai ana na eho lapa uwila;
Hekili wawahi ka lani;
Ku loloku ka ua i uka;
Ku'i ka hekili, nei ke ola'i;
Lele kapu i kai.(x)
Hiki lele ai i lalo o Kane-lu-honua.
O Kane-pua-hiöhiö, wili, —
Wili ia i uka, wili ia i kai;

(a) *Keehi . . . . e nalo kapua'i.* I am informed that Hawaiians, in order to conceal their goings, would erase their footprints by blurring them with their feet.

(b) *Onohi ula i ka lani,* a fragment of a rainbow.

(x) *Lele kapu i kai.* This may be put,—the old order has passed.

Wili ia i luna, wili ia i lalo;
Wili ia i ka uä,
I ka hoöle akua, hoöle mana —(c)
Ka ho'o-malau,(d) e, ka ho'o-maloka;(e)
Ke A-papa-nu'u,(f) ke A-papa-lani.(g)
O Mano-ka-lani-po,(h) o ke aka lei-hulu —
Hulu o manu kiü, o manu ahiahi;
O manu aha'i lono:—
Ha'ina a'e ana ka mana o ko'u Akua
Iwaho nei la, e; ha'ina ho'i!
Kukulu ka pahu kapu a ka leo:(i)
He ala(j) hele, he ala muku,
No Kane, laua o Kanaloa;

(c) *Hoole akua, hoole mana.* (To deny God, to deny supernatural power). It thus appears that the old Hawaiians were not unacquainted with those phases of skepticism that have flourished in all philosophic times.

(d) *Ho'o-malau,* to treat one's religious duties, or solemn things, with scorn.

(e) *Ho'o-maloka,* to be neglectful of one's religious duties, or of solemn things. In old times, how often did the writer hear the term *ho'o-maloka* applied as a stigma to those who persistently neglected and showed indifference to the services and ordinances of the church.

(f) *Apapa-nu'u,* the under-world and its spiritual powers.

(g) *Apapa-lani,* the heavens and their spiritual powers.

(h) *Mano-ka-lani-po.* This distinguished name was borne by that one of Kaua'i's kings who preceded its last independent monarch, Ka-umu-alii, by fourteen generations, which would bring his reign in the first half of the fifteenth century. He has the honor, unique among Hawaiian kings, of having his name affixed as a sobriquet to the island that was his kingdom. Whether the use of his name in this connection, apparently as a god, is to be regarded as antedating its occurrence in the Ulu genealogy (given by Fornander. See *The Polynesian Race;* vol. I, p. 195.), or whether, on the other hand, it is to be considered as an apotheosis of a name justly held in veneration, we cannot decide.

(i) *Pahu-kapu a ka leo.* The best-informed and most thoughtful among the Hawaiian authorities have poorly defined and contradictory notions as to the meaning of this term. Its literal meaning may be given as sacred (or tabu pillar. Mr. Tregear, in his incomparable *Maori Comparative Dictionary,* gives one meaning of the word to be sanctuary. One thoughtful Hawaiian defines it as a pillar, such as Pele set up, due regard for which demanded silence. Another, equally well informed, defines it as an edict, de-canon. To the writer it seems more logical and safer to adopt the material view regarding this phrase.

(j) *Ala hele* . . . . *ala muku,* (literally, a short path or road). This *ala hele* . . . *ala muku* was probably the rainbow. It is said in Hawaiian story that when Hiiaka came down from the cave where she found the body of Lohiau she used a rainbow as her way of descent. In an old mele occurs this line: *O ke anuenue ke ala o Kaha'i.* The rainbow was the path of Kaha'i.

He·ki(*k*) ho'iho'i kanawai;
He kai(*l*) oki'a kanawai;
He kua(*m*) a kanawai —
No Pele, no ko'u Akua, la!

TRANSLATION

There's turmoil and heaving of strata
In the land She claimed for her own.
Kahiki was land at the dawn of time,
A land by Haumea mixed and tempered;
Then She spread out Kahiki-ku;
She kindled her fires; the flames leapt high.
The Goddess covers her footprints —
The foot-marks of Goddess Pele —
She treads the path of the heavens;
Swoops down and lands at Polapola.
She dwells in the level island plain.
Down fall the pillars of Kakihi;
The wind topples over the ruins;
Down tumble the sun-kissing clouds;
Down sinks the blood-red eye of Heaven
And big-bellied clouds that loom at sea.
Pele heaves in sight at Nihoa —
That limpet stuck to Lehua's base.
From famed Kaua'i to Oahu;
Thence on to Mother Hina's isle;
To Lana'i of Kanaloa;
To Maui and, last, to Hawaii:
This the route of the Woman — Pele.
Then she rubs her fire-sticks to a blaze:
Up flames her touchwood, kindling the heavens.

(*k*)   *Ki ho'iho'i*. Hawaiian authorities differ as to the meaning of this phrase. After much cogitation and search, I concluded that the word *ki* has the same root-meaning as *i*, to utter. (I find myself supported in such an interpretation by no less an authority than Edward Tregear. Maori Comparative Dictionary.)

..(*l*)   *Kai oki'a*. Hawaiian authorities are quite at sea as to the meaning of these words. I think it means that the ocean is a gulf that swallows up and destroys. A very stringent tabu, says one, that regulated the diet, cutting off bananas and the like.

(*m*)   *Kua a*. Pele is said to have had a back that was so hot that any fabric laid upon it was reduced to ashes. It was also said to be tabu for any one to approach Pele from behind.

Earth sees the flash of lightning, hears the boom
Of thunder echoed by mountain walls —
Rocks flung in space bombard the day,
Shaking the mountain to its base.
The firmament sags, clings to the earth;
Hawaii is lost in Her smoke,
At the passion-heat of the Goddess.
Down clatters the rain from the sky —
A damper this to the Goddess' fires;
It rouses the wrath of Pele.
Keep silence! retort not! never a word!
'Tis the voice of Pele; she's my God.
The wind veers; there's far-off corruscation;
The thunder wrenches heaven's gates;
A sobbing of rain in the mountains,
The crash of thunder and earthquake:
Old tabus take flight to the ocean.
Now starts up the Earth-shaker Kane,
And Kane, the whirl-wind-breeder —
A tempest-whirl, o'er mountain and sea;
A tempest-whirl, in heaven and on earth;
A tempest-whirl, sodden with rain,
The atheist and the skeptic,
The scorner and unbeliever —
Powers of the under-world and the air. —
The hero Mano-ka-lani-pó,
His emblem a feathery wreath —
Plume from the bird that spies and tattles,
From the bird that makes proclamation,
Declaring the might, the power, of my God;
Out here, in the open, declare it.
Proclaim the edict of silence —
A short way, a true way, this way
Of Kane, of Kanaloa —
Compact this and bind in one bundle;
Let Ocean then swallow the rest.
A jealous flame is Pele's back:
That is the law of Pele, of my God!

This *pule,* which I have heard spoken of as *ka pule kanawai* —
from the use of the word kanawai in the last part of the mele,
dates back, it is said, to the time of Paao, the priest and chief who

came to Hawaii from Samoa in the remote ages. Paoa's argument — if he can be said to have had any — seems to be that Pele should cast away, throw into the ocean, the lumber of old laws and tabus and start afresh.

Before leaving the subject — the consideration of the mele — I must mention, apropos of the expression *pahu kapu a ka leo,* in verse 54, an incident related to me by a Hawaiian friend (J. M. P.). He says that when he was a boy, his mother, when a thunder-storm arose, would often say to him, "keep silence! that's Kane-hekili." In Kahuku, island of Oahu, at a place not far from the sugar-mill, is a cave, known as *Keana.* In former times this cave was the home where lived a mother and her two sons. One day, having occasion to journey to a distance, she left them with this injunction, "If during my absence you hear the sound of thunder, keep still, make no disturbance, don't utter a word. If you do it will be your death." During her absence, there sprang up a violent storm of thunder and lightning, and the young lads made an outcry of alarm. Thereupon a thunderbolt struck them dead, turning their bodies into stone. Two pillar-shaped stones standing at the mouth of the cave are to this day pointed out in confirmation of the truth of the legend.

As Paoa concluded his prayer-song the eyes of the whole company were turned upon him, and on the lips of them all was the question, "Was she then your God?"

"She is my God," he answered, "and my ancestors from the earliest times have worshipped her." . . . Then, turning his eyes about him, as if to survey the land, he continued, "If this were my land, as is Kaua'i, there would be no lack of good and wholesome food-provision, and that of all kinds. Things are different here . . . I am a stranger in this land."

On hearing these words, which had in them the sting of truth, for poison had been mixed with some of the food, the women stealthily hid away certain dishes and substituted for them others.

At the conclusion of the repast the women who had been in attendance brought him a girdle delicately embroidered with fibers from the coconut that he might be suitably appareled for his interview with the woman Pele. "You will find," they said, "that Pele is in reality a woman of wonderful beauty. . . . In order to win her, however, you will need to use all your arts of fascination . . . and your caution as well. Make hot love to her, but, look out! don't let your fancy lead you to smile upon any other beauty."

Pele at first kept Paoa at a distance and, with deep subtlety, said to him, "Here are beautiful women — women more beautiful than I — take one of them."

Paoa, well schooled in courtly etiquette and logomachy, was not tripped up by any such snare as Pele laid for him. He stood his ground and faced the god as an equal.

As Pele contemplated Paoa it dawned upon her that here stood a man, a being of gracious power, one who combined in himself qualities – attractions – she had never before seen materially embodied in the human form. The woman in Pele laid aside the god – the akua – and came to the front All thought of bantering talk and word-play slunk away: her whole being was sobered and lifted up. The change in her outward, physical appearance kept pace with the inward: the rough armor that had beset her like the prongs of horned coral, both without and within, melted and dropped away; the haglike wrinkles ceased to furrow her profile. Her whole physical being took on the type of womanly perfection.

And what of Paoa, the man who had come with heart full of bitterness, determined on revenge? He was conquered, overwhelmed.

Their meeting was that of lovers, who stood abashed in each other's presence. Pele's beauty and charm were like that of a young bride coming to the nuptial couch. . . .

The dalliance and love-making of Pele and Paoa was a honeymoon that continued for three days and three nights. By virtue of this mysterious union with the goddess, Paoa acquitted himself of a ceremonial duty, as it were, and thus gained Pele's dispensation from further obligations to her bed and the liberty of exercising free choice among all the beautiful women that thronged Pele's court. It was there he made his abode until the time for his return to his own Kaua'i.

CHAPTER XXXVIII

HIIAKA AND LOHIAU . . . A REUNION

Hiiaka's sense of outrage touched every fiber of her being and stirred such indignation against her sister that she could not again take her former place as a member of Pele's court. Hawaii was the largest island of the group, but it was not large enough to hold herself and Pele. Of all the islands Kaua'i was the one most remote from the scene of her troubles; it was also the land which Lohiau had claimed as his own — and his was a name that called up only the most tender emotions. To Kaua'i would she go.

The company of those who shared her feelings and whose personal attachment to her was sufficient to lead them with herself in a venture of new fortunes was not large. It included, of course, her two staunch attendants, Pau-o-pala'e and Wahine-oma'o and, strangely enough, a considerable quota of the sisters who shared with her the name Hiiaka (qualified though it was in each case by some additional distinguishing epithet). Towards Kaua'i, then, did they set their faces or, more literally, turn the prow of their canoe.

Many unforeseen things, however, were to happen before the God of Destiny would permit her to gain her destination. Other strands stood ready to be interwoven with the purposeful threads Hiiaka was braiding into her life.

In the ancient regime of Hawaii, the halau, as the home and school of the hula, stood for very much and for many things. It served, after a fashion, as a social exchange or clearing house for the whole nation; the resort of every wandering minstrel, bohemian soul or *beau esprit* whose oestrus kept him in travel; the rallying point of souls dislocated from an old and not yet accommodated to a new environment; a place where the anxious and discouraged, despairing of a new outlook, or seeking balm for bruised hearts, might quaff healing nepenthe.

It is not to be wondered at, then, that Hiaaka, not yet healed of her bruises, on reaching Oahu and finding herself in the peaceful haven of Kou, should turn her steps to the home of that hospitable siren and patroness of the hula Pele-ula, as to a sanitarium or hospital whose resources would avail for the assuagement of her troubles. It was almost an article of Pele-ula's creed that in the pleasures and distractions of the hula was to be found a panacea for all the wounds of the spirit; and Pele-ula, as if taking her cue from the lady of the Venusberg, offered her consolations generously to every comfort-needing soul that fared her way.

Hiiaka stepped into the life at Pele-ula's court as if she had been absent from it for only a day. Madame Pele-ula, good sport that she was, bore no grudge against the woman who had outplayed her at every turn, and would do it again. She received Hiiaka with open arms. As to entertainment, the play was the thing thing and that, fortunately, was already appointed for the same evening. It was the same old performance, the hula kilu, with but slight change in the actors and with full opportunity for Hiiaka to display her marvelous skill in hurling the kilu.

It was Hiiaka's play and she, following the custom of the game, was caroling — in sober strain — a song of her own; when, to her astonishment, a voice from the crowd struck in and carried the song to completion in the very words that would have been her's. Hiiaka stood and listened. The voice had a familiar ring; the song was not yet in the possession of the public, being known only to a few of her own household, among whom was to be reckoned Lohiau. There was no avoiding the conclusion: it was Lohiau.

It remains to tell the miracle of Lohiau's reappearance among men in living form and at this time. While the body of Lohiau lay entombed in its stony shroud, his restless spirit fluttered away and sought consolation in the companionship of the song-birds that ranged the forests of Hawaii.

When the magician La'a, who lived in Kahiki, contemplated the degraded condition of Lohiau, alienated from all the springs of human affection, living as a wild thing in the desert, he determined on his rescue and despatched Kolea (plover), one of his ancestral kupuas, to fetch him. The mission of Kolea was not a success. The voice, the manner, the arguments of the bird made no appeal to Lohiau; they were, in fact, distasteful to him and rather increased his devotion to his other bird-friends.

"Well, Kolea, what sort of a place is Kahiki?" asked Lohiau.

"A most charming place," he answered, nodding his head and uttering his call, "Ko-lé-a, Ko-lé-a."

Lohiau was disgusted with his performances and would have nothing more to do with Kolea.

When Kolea returned and reported his failure to La'a, that magician sent another bird on the same errand, one of more seductive ways, Ulili. There was something in the voice and manner of Ulili that touched the fancy and won the heart of Lohiau at once and he began to follow him. Ulili skilfully lured him on and at last brought him to Kahiki and delivered him over to his master. La'a ministered to the soul of Lohiau with such tenderness and skill that he became reconciled once more to human ways. But the soul of Lohiau still remained an unhoused ghost, and at times ranged afar in its restless excursions.

Now it happened that at the very time when these events were taking place Kane-milo-hai, an elder brother of Pele, was voyaging from Kahiki to Hawaii. His canoe was of that mystical pattern, the leho (cowry) in which Mawi had sailed. While in the middle of the Ïëïë-waho channel he caught sight of the distracted spirit of Lohiau fluttering like a Mother Carey's chicken over the expanse of waters. The poor ghost, as if desirous of companionship, drew nigh and presently came so near that Kane-milo-hai captured it and, having ensconced it in his ipu-holoho-lona,(a) he sailed on his way.

Reaching Hawaii and coming to the desolate scene of Lohiau's tragedy, he recognized a charred heap as the former bodily residence of the shivering ghost in his keeping. He broke the stony form into many pieces and then, by the magical power that was his, out of these fragments he reconstructed the body of Lohiau, imparting to it its original form and lineaments. Into this body Kane-milo-hai now introduced the soul and Lohiau lived again.

The tide of new life surging in the veins of Lohiau stirred in him emotions that found utterance in song:

> I ola no au i ku'u kino wailua,
> I a'e'a mai e ke 'lii o Kahiki,
> Ke 'lii nana i a'e ke kai uli,
> Kai eleele, kai melemele,
> Kai popolo-hua mea a Kane;
> I ka wa i po'i ai ke Kai-a-ka-hina-lii —
> Kai mu, kai lewa. Ho'opua ke ao ia Lohiau;
> O Lohiau — i lono oukou.
> Ola e; ola la: ua ola Lohiau, e!
> O Lohiau, ho'i, e!

(a) A calabash, often covered with a net, used by a fisherman to hold his spare hooks and lines and, by the traveler, his belongings.

> I lived, but 'twas only my soul;
> Then came Kahiki's King and took me —
> The King who sails this purple and blue,
> An ocean, now black, now amber,
> The dark mottled sea of Kane,
> The sea that 'whelmed those monarchs of old,
> A sea that is ghostly, foreign, strange.
> Lohiau flowers anew in the sunlight;
> It is I, Lohiau! Do you hear it?
> New life has come to Lohiau!
> To Lohiau, aye, to Lohiau!

Having come to himself, Lohiau sought his own. His chancing at Kou and his appearance at the halau in which Pele-ula was holding her kilu performance, and on the very evening of Hiiaka's arrival, was an arrangement of converging lines that reflected great credit on the god of Destiny.

Lohiau arrived at the kilu hall just in time to witness the opening of the game. Having seated himself quietly in the outskirts of the assembly, he begged a neighbor to permit him, as a favor, to conceal himself under the ample width of his kihei, exacting of him also the promise not to betray his retreat. Thus hidden, he could see without being seen. The sight of Hiiaka, the words of her song — he had heard them a score of times before — stirred within him a thousand memories. Without conscious effort of will, the words of his response sprang from his heart almost with the spontaneity of an antiphonal echo. Let us bring together the two cotyledons of this song:

> O ka wai mukiki a'ala lehua o ka manu,
> O ka awa ili lena i ka uka o Ka-li'u,
> O ka manu aha'i kau-laau o Puna: —
> Aia i ka laau ka awa o Puna.
> Mapu wale mai ana no ia'u kona aloha,
> Hoolana mai ana ia'u, e moe, e;
> A e moe no, e-e-e.

And now comes the unexpected antiphone by Lohiau:

O Puna, lehua ula i ka papa;
I ula i ka papa ka lehua o Puna:
Ke kui ia mai la e na wahine o ka Lua:
Mai ka Lua a'u i hele mai nei, mai Kilauea.
Aloha Kilauea, ka aina a ke aloha.

TRANSLATION

Nectar for gods, honeyed lehua;
Food for the birds, bloom of lehua;
Pang of love, the yellow-barked awa,
Quaffed by the dryads in Puna's wilds;
Bitter the sweet of Puna's tree-awa.
His love wafts hither to me from dreamland —
The cry of the soul for love's fond touch;
And who would forbid the soul's demand !

ANTIPHONE

Puna's plain takes the color of scarlet —
Red as heart's blood the bloom of lehua.
The nymphs of the Pit string hearts in a wreath:
Oh the pangs of the Pit, Kilauea !
Still turns my heart to Kilauea.

We must leave to the imagination of the reader the scene that occurred when Lohiau, the man twice called back from the dead, leaves his hiding place and comes into Hiiaka's encircling arms lovingly extended to him.

Thus was accomplished the reunion of Hiiaka and Lohiau, and thus it came to pass that these two human streams of characters so different, in defiance of powerful influences that had long held them apart, were, at length, turned into one channel — that of the man, not wholly earthly, but leavened with the possibility of vast spiritual attainment under the tonic discipline of affliction; that of the woman, self-reliant, resourceful, yet acutely in need of affection; human and practical, yet feeling after the divine, conscious of daily commerce with the skies; and, yet, in spite of all, in bondage to that universal law which gives to the smaller and weaker body the power to introduce a perturbation into the orbit of the greater and to pull it away from its proper trajectory.

The old order has passed away, the order in which the will of

Pele has ruled almost supreme, regardless of the younger, the human, race which is fast peopling the land that was hers in the making. Hitherto, surrounded by a cohort of willing servants ready at all times to sacrifice themselves to her caprice, — behold, a new spirit has leavened the whole mass, a spirit of dissent from the supreme selfishness of the Vulcan goddess, and the foremost dissident of them all is the obedient little sister who was first in her devotion to Pele, the warm-hearted girl whom we still love to call Hiiaka-i-ka-poli-o-Pele.

INDEX OF FIRST LINES